D0559679

WITHDRAWN

NADER

The
People's
Lawyer

NADER

The People's Lawyer

By

Robert F. Buckhorn

PRENTICE-HALL, INC.
Englewood Cliffs, New Jersey

2-13-74

Printed in the United States of America 3

Prentice-Hall International, Inc., London
Prentice-Hall of Australia, Pty. Ltd. North Sydney
Prentice-Hall of Canada, Ltd., Toronto
Prentice-Hall of India Private Ltd., New Delhi
Prentice-Hall of Japan, Inc., Tokyo

Library of Congress Cataloging in Publication Data

Buckhorn, Robert F., date
    Nader: the people's lawyer.

    Bibliography: p.
    1.   Nader, Ralph.   I.   Title.
KF373.N3B8   340'.0924 [B]   76-38579
ISB 0-13-609222-5

To Rita
For all the love she has given

AUTHOR'S NOTE

I became a Nader-watcher early on. First, because I was a reporter for United Press International, I had no choice; covering Nader was part of my job. Later he became a fascination. Here was "a different kind of guy" in the Washington arena, which is known more for its ego-heavy politicians, cautious bureaucrats, and wooden diplomats than it is for reformers.

Others began to watch Nader too, but because I had access to him, I became a target for some of those who wanted to know "What's Ralph Nader really like?" and they never let up trying to find out. Over the last five years, I have been asked by a Nixon cabinet officer if a "quiet meeting" with Nader could be worked out (it couldn't); husband-hunting secretaries, lured by GM's barren report on his sex life, wanted introductions to Nader in order to try their luck; lawyers and public-relations men wanted to discuss his tactics in boring detail; congressmen and senators wanted "briefings"; "investment counselors" wanted his address. But most of the questions I received came from persons who wanted nothing from Nader—they felt a rapport with him, and simply wanted to know more about him. This book is for them.

Nader cooperated fully for which I am deeply grateful. The only door he failed to open was the one that led to his room in a rooming house, which was, he said, "my last private place." But even here, I entered the foyer and sat in a red velvet chair surrounded by rubber plants and a Gibson girl bust while the landlady, a retired opera teacher, clopped up the staircase of what had been the residence of the pre-World War II Japanese ambassador, crying, "Mr. Nader! Mr. Nader! A visitor, Mr. Nader!"

The main material for this book comes from a series of intensive interviews with Nader conducted between October 1, 1970, and September 25, 1971. Nader also allowed me to travel around the country with him, and supplied me with leads and materials pertaining to his work, his friends, and even his enemies. Over two hundred interviews were conducted with persons who have associated with Nader at some point in his life—from his charming mother, Mrs. Rose Nader, to James Roche, the chairman of the board of General Motors. Roche deserves a special bow for his willingness to defend his position in a book on Ralph Nader. His stance can be contrasted with that of Henry Ford, who refused a request to be interviewed.

The final sources of information were Nader's own prolific outpouring of articles, the court records of his law suit against GM and his detailed testimony before congressional committees. Added to this were my own files, which included not only my news stories, but many done by fellow newsmen. I want to make special note, too, of the assistance I got from Ted Jacobs, Nader's key aide. Working with a whirlwind like Nader is difficult enough without the added problem of nursemaiding bookwriters. But Jacobs performed with unfailing good humor. In this same category is Donald Baskerville of the Library of Congress whose aid was greatly appreciated.

I also want to thank a trio of top newsmen—Frank Jackman of the New York *Daily News*, and Joe Myler and Louis Cassels of United Press International—for their help in editing the manuscript. To my three young sons—Robert, Dean, and Burke—thanks too for "staying out of the back room" while this book was being written. Finally, a sweeping bow to a Brooklyn rose, my typist and editorial assistant, Rita Therese Murnane.

—Robert F. Buckhorn
Falls Church, Virginia

CONTENTS

NADER

The
People's
Lawyer

1

GM'S HIRED DICKS

The decision that an investigation of Mr. Ralph Nader should be undertaken was made by me in the discharge of my responsibilities as the general counsel of General Motors.

—Aloysius F. Power, March 22, 1966

Corporations cannot commit treason, nor be outlawed, nor excommunicated for they have no souls.

—Sir Edward Coke, 1612

Ernie Barcella heard the insistent ringing of the telephone as he came through the door of his home in a Maryland suburb of Washington. A hard-charging, one-time Washington bureau chief for United Press International, Barcella was now General Motors' public relations strategist in the capital, but at the moment his mind was far from corporate image-making. His son, his pride, was threatened by a possible death sentence from cancer. Stunned, Barcella had turned to his church for strength, and as he reached for the telephone his mind was still fresh from the prayers he had offered at a novena where he implored God's help for his son's fight.

"Ernie," the deep voice on the other end of the line said, "this is Jim Roche." For just a moment there was a flutter of

1

nervousness in Barcella as there was in most GM executives when Jim Roche spoke from the Olympian heights of the GM president's chair. Barcella did not have to be told that something was wrong; calls from "Mr. Roche" (Barcella seldom called him anything else) were not that common. Roche got right to the point. Had Barcella seen the Sunday *New York Times*, he asked. On page 94 of the second section, spread across eight columns, was the headline that triggered Roche's call. CRITIC OF AUTO INDUSTRY'S SAFETY STANDARDS SAYS HE WAS TRAILED AND HARASSED; CHARGE CALLED ABSURD, the headline read. Over reporter Walter Rugaber's byline was a story about how Ralph Nader claimed he was being spied on by someone who was obviously trying to intimidate him because of his testimony before Congress on auto safety. Rugaber quoted Nader as saying he was being harassed by late-night telephone calls, and was even followed into the New Senate Office Building by private investigators. Nowhere in the story was there any charge as to who was responsible, but Nader had left little doubt that the trail led back to the automakers of Detroit. "Industry sources," however, told Rugaber that Nader's charge was "absurd." None of the automakers would try a clumsy trick like shadowing a witness before a congressional hearing, the sources said. But Roche wanted confirmation from Barcella that GM was not involved. "That's not our company they're talking about, is it, Ernie?" he asked. To Barcella, the answer to that question was "No." A short, bullnecked man who came out of Dartmouth thirty years before, Barcella prided himself on knowing the Washington scene, and he knew nothing about any "shadowing of Nader" by GM or anyone else. Conceivably one of the other auto companies could be guilty, or it could be that the conspiracy-conscious Nader was passing off his fantasizing to Rugaber as actual facts. Always sensitive to any corporate quivers that could turn into an avalanche, Roche had been placing telephone calls around the GM system from the auto giant's New York office on that March 6, 1966. The feedback was the same on each of the calls. A check in Detroit produced

2

nothing. Barcella was a blank, and so was GM's Washington legal staff.

Actually, the *Times* story that had upset Roche was not even new. The small liberal *New Republic* magazine had the story first. Nader had given it to reporter James Ridgeway who put it all together in an article that was written on the Friday before under the title of "The Dick." Several days before, the very tip of the iceberg appeared when the Washington *Post* ran a small squib on how one of its reporters, Bryce Nelson, had been followed by private eyes who thought they were shadowing Nader. This story was even clipped by GM's Washington staff and sent to Detroit, but it produced no reaction.

Slowly, Roche pulled in his antennae, and by March 8, Tuesday, still in New York, he was in the process of ordering the GM public relations department to counteract the Nader innuendo with a news release which would deny, as Ford already had done, that GM had any part in the "alleged" surveillance of Nader. That evening Roche was draped with an albatross. He was told that indeed it was GM which had ordered Ralph Nader investigated. That night he boarded a plane for Detroit "to find out specifically what did happen."

When President Johnson picked Hubert Humphrey for his running mate at Atlantic City, N.J., in August, 1964, he set in motion an involved series of disconnected events which climaxed in James Roche's apology to Ralph Nader.

Humphrey's decision to tie his career to Johnson's meant that the Minnesota senator had to give up the congressional spoils he had gathered through the seniority system. One of these plums was the chairmanship of a harmless-sounding subcommittee of the Senate Government Operations Committee called the Subcommittee on Reorganization and International Organizations. Under the seniority system, the next in line for Humphrey's chairmanship was Senator Ernest Gruening, the Alaska Democrat. After Gruening came Connecticut's Senator Abraham Ribicoff. But Ribicoff felt that he had established poacher's rights to Humphrey's subcommittee chairmanship because Humphrey, who was busy in late 1963 and 1964 with his job as Senate whip and with helping the Democratic party get ready for the election campaign, had had no time for the tedious work of planning and conducting committee hearings, and in effect, had said to Ribicoff, "Here, I don't have time for this subcommittee, you use it." But with Humphrey quitting the Senate to take over the Vice Presidency, Gruening could exert his rights. Ribicoff, however, hatched a scheme that allowed Gruening to get what the seniority rules promised him, but which also gave Ribicoff a subcommittee of his own. Ribicoff convinced Gruening, and more importantly, Senator John L. McClellan of Arkansas, the chairman of the parent Government Operations Committee, who had the power to approve the plan, that the subcommittee should be split up into two committees—a subcommittee on executive reorganization run by Ribicoff, and a subcommittee on international organizations headed by Gruening, who fancied himself a foreign affairs expert. Ribicoff's argument was hard to deny. Gruening would get what he could do best, and Ribicoff, a former governor and Health, Education, and Welfare Secretary, was ideally suited to handle a subcommittee on Executive Reorganization. McClellan agreed, and by November, 1964, Ribicoff had his committee chairmanship and began to cast around for ways to use it. The job of finding areas that might warrant investigation fell to Committee Counsel Jerry Sonosky, a brassy, shrewd young lawyer from Minnesota who came of age on the Hill and was as crafty in the ways of congressional politics as any of the old pols. Short, and beefy, with a flare for creating good news copy, Sonosky liked the idea of staging, producing, and if possible, acting in committee hearings. Certainly no shrinking violet, Sonosky was the first to admit that he was "a PR flack, but watch the LLB after my name when the hearing opens." But even for Sonosky, finding the right vehicle for Ribicoff's subcommittee was not all that easy. Ribicoff told Sonosky to make a list of possible targets—problem areas on the domestic-social front where more than one federal agency was involved. This was a necessity since the subcommittee needed to raise the question of interagency coordination to get a jurisdictional peg for an investigation. One of the items on the list that Sonosky turned over to Ribicoff was highway traffic safety, an area that involved no less than sixteen federal agencies, but traffic safety spurred no special interest in either Sonosky or Ribicoff; it was just another category of possibilities. But on Sunday, December 20, the combination of *The New York Times* and a telephone call played another role in the Nader story. This time the call was made to Sonosky, and the caller was Ribicoff who had an idea he wanted to try out on Sonosky. Had he seen the front page of the *Times*, Ribicoff asked. More interested in coaxing breakfast out of his Catholic wife before she went off to Mass, Sonosky admitted he hadn't. "Get it," exclaimed Ribicoff, "and read it." What had excited Ribicoff was a *Times* story on a newly published book called *Accident Research: Methods and Approaches*, by Dr. William Haddon and two co-authors, E. A. Suchman, and D. Klein. Haddon was a young but recognized expert in the auto safety field. A medical man, he was pushing the idea that not enough attention was being paid to what causes the deaths and injuries in automobile accidents because too much emphasis was being placed on what caused the accident itself. Continue to seek ways to prevent automobile collisions, Haddon and his associates argued, but remember the collision was basically inevitable because of the number of cars on the highway, so prevention of death and injury in the accident was equally as important. This approach fascinated Ribicoff. Before he landed in national politics, he had made a national reputation as the tough Connecticut governor who had launched highly publicized campaigns to keep drunks and speeders off the state highways through stiff fines and driver license revocations. "I think the article challenged him," Sonosky said. "What Haddon was saying in effect was, 'Hey, Governor, you might not have been doing the right thing!' " The more Ribicoff talked about the concept, the more convinced he was that this was a legitimate area for his new committee even though it meant exploring the question of

5

how the Detroit auto companies make decisions on safety priorities and who makes them, a touchy subject given Detroit's power. However, the subject was not new to Congress. Congressman Kenneth Roberts of Alabama had conducted hearings in July, 1956, which must be credited with laying the groundwork for federal intervention in the area of auto safety. But Ribicoff felt that he could pick up and expand on Robert's work which had eventually culminated in a bill allowing the General Services Administration to set some safety standards for the fleets of cars the government—the auto industry's single biggest customer—bought each year.

With the Roberts hearing having established a precedent, Ribicoff thought the time might be right for a breakthrough. The tide was running with Ribicoff. For years, there had been a slow, but steadily growing revulsion over the highway slaughter. In 1964, the death toll stood at 48,000, a ten percent jump over 1963. Since the first traffic death was recorded in 1899, over 1,500,000 Americans had been killed in highway accidents. Not surprisingly, private polls showed that traffic safety was one of six things that worried Americans most. Despite this gory story, there was no public policy on traffic safety. "To say that our national policy is to leave traffic safety to the states and the private sector is to have no national policy," Ribicoff was to say when the hearings got underway. With his mind made up, Ribicoff told Sonosky to put together a committee staff. In Washington, where job-hopping is a way of life, the notice brought a rash of telephone calls to the subcommittee office in Room 162 of the Old Senate Office Building, and one of them came from a friend of Sonosky's named Ralph Mueller, who was then working for the Bureau of the Budget. When Sonosky explained to Mueller what the committee planned to investigate, Mueller's reaction was immediate. "You've got to meet a friend of mine," he told Sonosky. But at this point, Sonosky was only interested in collecting a few resumés and tried to put off Mueller and his "friend." But Mueller was insistent that if Sonosky really wanted a fresh viewpoint on auto safety he should see his friend who worked for Pat

6

Moynihan, assistant secretary of labor. Sonosky still held out. It wouldn't help him to talk to "an expert" if he didn't know, even generally, what was being done in the field of auto safety, he said. But Sonosky was a political animal first and a subcommittee counsel second. When Mueller mentioned that his friend was from Connecticut, and therefore a constituent of Ribicoff's, Sonosky bit. "Okay, okay, I'll see him! What's his name?" "Ralph Nader," said Mueller.

After his conversation with Sonosky, Mueller called Nader, and Nader called Sonosky and made an appointment. "I was going to give him twenty minutes of my valuable time," Sonosky said. But when Nader sat down, he didn't leave for three hours. Sonosky claimed Nader was "sniffing" him out in their first meeting. "He wasn't going to waste his time if he thought the committee was not going to conduct a serious investigation," Sonosky claimed. But Sonosky did a little "sniffing" of his own. He called Ribicoff's state office in Connecticut to ask if the office staff knew anything about "a guy named Nader." The only information he got was that Nader was indeed from Winsted, and a lawyer. But Sonosky claimed his real "security clearance" on Nader was Nader's job as a traffic safety consultant for Moynihan. "If he was good enough for Moynihan, he was good enough for Sonosky," Sonosky said. "I didn't need a CIA check on him."

From the moment Nader made his commitment to Sonosky, he began emptying his great horde of auto safety knowledge into Sonosky's mind and into the subcommittee's files. He haunted the subcommittee office, a typical tatty series of partitioned cubicles overflowing with files and reports on present, past, and never-born investigations.

The first subcommittee hearing on traffic safety was scheduled for March 22, 25, 26, a "quick kickoff" that was possible only because of Nader's expertise. The hearings centered on federal officials concerned with auto safety, and showed, as Ribicoff put it, "that the federal government's efforts in the traffic safety field were pitifully small and disorganized and uncoordinated." A second set of hearings

7

followed on July 13, 14, 15 and 21, when the subcommittee switched its attention from what Washington was doing to what Detroit was doing, bringing in the auto moguls to testify, led by Frederic Donner, then chairman of the board of GM. By the July hearings, Nader was so deeply a part of the hearings that he sat behind a door in the back of the committee rostrum and passed questions out to Sonosky who fed them to the committee members as if they were his own. In between his work for the committee, Nader was holed up in his room on Nineteenth Street putting the final touches on his manuscript for *Unsafe At Any Speed*, and because of its damning indictment of the Corvair car, making sure it was "lawyer-proof" against court suits. On November 30, Grossman Publishers brought out Nader's book which was launched with a flood of flattering reviews. A gratified Nader was to say, "It speaks well for the country when GM, which grosses $20 billion, came up against a $5.95 book and had to give it attention."

"Attention" was too weak a word. Both Nader and his book were being intensely scrutinized by what was later shown to be a very unlovable group known collectively as GM's legal staff, headed by 38-year veteran Aloysius F. Power, GM's general counsel, and his assistant Louis Bridenstine. Lawyers who work on the staffs of giant corporations are by the nature of their jobs a suspecting lot. Their guiding principle is that the customer is always lurking outside the corporate headquarters waiting for an opportunity to gouge the company's profits with a lawsuit which claims some kind of damage from, or defect in, the company's product. As the king of kings among the world's corporations, GM's lawyers were more paranoid than most. On paper, the lawyers did have a problem, however. Owners of the 1960-63 Corvair cars had filed 106 lawsuits against GM totaling $40 million in damage claims. There was little doubt among the legal staff, however, that they could "handle" most of the suits, but Nader's timely book laying out the case against the Corvair would bolster the strength and bargaining power of those who had already sued, and undoubtedly would touch off a rash of new lawsuits.

But months before the publication of the book, Nader had already become an annoyingly recurring irritant to Power and Bridenstine. As early as July, 1965, Nader's name appeared in letters written by Thomas F. Lambert, editor-in-chief for the American Trial Lawyers Association's publications. In answering queries from lawyers who were involved in Corvair litigation, Lambert referred them to Nader, who he said had "a substantial amount of information on the Corvair." Power was later to describe GM's reaction to the appearance of Nader's name in the ATLA letters this way: "Who was the 'lawyer' with whom the ATLA editor was on a first-name basis? At that time Mr. Nader was not listed as counsel in any pending Corvair case. Where did he obtain such a 'substantial amount of information on the Corvair,' and how had he 'developed expertise'?" These were the questions GM wanted answered, Power said. But apparently the lawyers already were convinced in their minds that Nader was trying to turn the Corvair into a money-making legal proposition for himself.

GM got its hands on its first copy of a Lambert letter on July 25. Three days later a brief was filed in the U.S. Court of Appeals for the Fifth Circuit in the case of Barbara June Muncy and Charles Muncy vs. General Motors. The suit involved, not the Corvair, but an ignition switch and stuck accelerator problem on a 1960 Chevrolet. The car, running out of control, climbed the curb and struck Mrs. Muncy whose leg was so badly injured it had to be amputated. When a copy of the brief got back to GM's legal office, it sounded an alarm. There was that name again—Nader was listed as a counsel on the appeal brief. (Nader came into the case in an advisory capacity after the first trial was lost. On the second try, and with Nader's advice, the couple got a $225,000 judgment. Nader's reimbursement was $475 to cover expenses. However, on appeal the lower court was reversed and the case dismissed.) Still one more piece of information had been collected on Nader. GM researchers found an article

Nader had written for the January, 1965, issue of ATLA's magazine *Trial*. The article, titled, "Patent Laws Prime Source to Secure Safer Auto Design to Reduce Highway Deaths," attacked the Corvair's design stability. All of these bits and pieces were being put together by a tough-minded woman named Eileen Murphy who ran GM's law library in Detroit. Miss Murphy, a lawyer, did not fit the stereotype of the shy, bookish librarian who took out her aggressions by "shushing" loud talkers. She was a competitor in a man's world, and her experience was varied and included a tour of duty as a law librarian at the Justice Department in Washington.

On October 8, 1965, the San Francisco *Chronicle* ran a preview of Nader's upcoming book in which it was billed as "a searing document that may become the *Silent Spring* of the automotive industry." Then in quick succession came two more Nader articles. One showed up in Miss Murphy's library when the mails delivered the latest volume of *American Jurisprudence Proof of Facts*. This legal reference work had a 153-page article by Nader on "Automobile Design Hazards" in which Nader attacked the industry for "building in" to cars the potential for death and injury. Right behind this detailed indictment came the November 1 issue of *The Nation* with an article titled "Profits vs. Engineering—The Corvair Story," which was a blistering attack on the safety of the compact car adapted from a chapter in Nader's upcoming book. In testimony before Congress, Power was to argue that that chapter in Nader's book was "a matter of great concern to the General Motors lawyers responsible for defending Corvair litigation, and raised a number of questions in their minds." According to Power, Nader was resurrecting the same charges about defects in the design of the Corvair which had been the basis for two lawsuits against GM and had been rejected by the jury in each case. Despite this, Power said Nader made no reference to these cases. "Were the Nader article and his forthcoming book part of an organized nationwide publicity campaign to pre-try the Corvair cases by television, newspaper, and magazine, and to pre-condition prospective jurors in the cases still to be tried throughout the United States?" was the question GM wanted answered, Power claimed. On November 18, Power moved to get the answer. He ordered one of the lawyers on his staff to call the Royal-Globe Insurance Company, a Boston-based GM product liability insurer. The question put to the Royal-Globe office: Could it recommend a private investigator to investigate Ralph Nader?

The man who got the job of probing Nader in his hometown was an investigator from East Hartford, Connecticut, by the name of William F. O'Neill. O'Neill nosed around Winsted checking all the obvious sources for information, and filling a seven-page report with information such as Mary Curtis, the court clerk, reporting that Nader was "a swell kid," or that Nader "carried papers for the Winsted *Evening Citizen* in 1949" and once had spent a summer working as a cashier in Yosemite National Park. O'Neill, to bolster his expertise, also mentioned that "the writer has eaten at the Highland Arms [the restaurant run by Nader's father] occasionally and the food is good and the place seems well run."

He checked with "acting superintendent of police" Irving S. Milano who admitted knowing Nader since "he was a little boy," and he contributed the thought that Nader had "specialized in Maritime Law" at Harvard. O'Neill did find correctly that Nader was a part-time teacher at the University of Hartford and he made a check by telephone at the Harvard University Alumni Association where he was told that Nader indeed was a Princeton-Harvard Law School graduate, and was advised "that someone else had made a similar inquiry the preceding day." "Accordingly, no other inquiry is being made at Harvard unless instructed," O'Neill wrote in his report. As for the rest of O'Neill's report, there were these pieces of information: Nader had appeared before the Connecticut legislature to testify on auto safety; Nader had attended "Sunday school in the Winsted Methodist Church." But O'Neill's report was a bust on the key points—he didn't find anything that would indicate to GM what Nader's "real" motivation was, nor could he pinpoint Nader's present where-

11

abouts, other than to indicate he was in Washington. O'Neill also failed to discover whether Nader owned an automobile, an item GM particularly wanted to know. When this "thin soup" arrived back in Detroit, Power began to look elsewhere for information on Nader, and in a meeting with his legal staff, Eileen Murphy provided the next plan of action.

Three days before Christmas, 1965, a light flickered on the switchboard in the offices of Alvord & Alvord, a law firm in downtown Washington. The caller, a woman, wanted to speak to Richard Danner, an attorney with the firm. Danner, a former FBI agent, took the call and found himself talking to Eileen Murphy, who then began to explain to Danner GM's new plans for Ralph Nader; plans which would eventually climax in what James Roche termed in a massive understatement "an unhappy episode." Miss Murphy gave Danner an outline of what GM wanted. A detective who could do an in-depth investigation on Nader was the prime requisite, and Danner would be the man to hire the kind of investigator who could do the job well. Plans were laid for a face-to-face meeting, and Eileen Murphy agreed to meet with Danner in his office January 11, bringing with her the O'Neill investigation report, and the rest of the Nader file GM had so laboriously collected, including a seven-page memo outlining the areas GM wanted investigated.

In testimony before the Senate Subcommittee on Executive Reorganization, Danner described the meeting in these bland words:

"Miss Murphy furnished me all the information which she had concerning Mr. Nader, including a copy of an investigative report covering some activities in Connecticut and some background data that she had apparently compiled from press, magazines, and other publications. She also related to me other facts and matters for investigation. Miss Murphy stated that it was strongly believed by her and the legal department of GM that Mr. Nader was in some manner connected with or working for the plaintiff's attorneys in the Corvair negligence suits against General Motors, but that no compelling proof of this had been adduced as yet."

The man Danner singled out to do the job was Vincent Gillen, a barrel-chested Irish-American who ran a detective agency in New York, and by his count had done twenty-five previous investigations for GM. A lawyer by virtue of a diploma from a subway school called Brooklyn Law School, Gillen had spent three years in the FBI, and then held a string of jobs ranging from a life insurance investigator to a personnel man with Otis Elevator. In June, 1958, he set up his own business, Vincent Gillen Associates. On the same day Eileen Murphy called Danner about the Nader investigation, Danner called Gillen, and two days after Eileen Murphy met with Danner, Gillen was seated across the same desk. Gillen had a penchant for tape recorders, and was later to claim that he secretly switched on a pocket recorder when Danner gave him his instructions. In documents filed in court when Nader sued General Motors for invasion of his privacy, Gillen said he transcribed from the tape these excerpts of what was said:

Danner: This is a new client . . . could be a very important one. They came to me and I'm anxious to do a good job because they have had trouble getting investigators . . . they want me to work with someone I trust. . . . It concerns this fellow who wrote this book. . . . They have not found out much about him. His stuff there is pretty damaging to the auto industry. . . . What are his motives? . . . Is he really interested in safety? Who are his backers, his supporters? . . . Some left-wing groups try to run down all industry. . . . How does he support himself? . . . Who is paying him, if anyone, for this stuff? . . . Was he put in there deliberately? . . . Is he an engineer? . . . No evidence of it: He went to Harvard Law. . . . They made some half-baked investigation in Connecticut. . . . He is not there and apparently is or has been in Washington. . . . I don't know where he is. . . . Strange, but he doesn't show anywhere in any directory. . . . Here is what they gave me on him. . . . You take this with you and a copy of the book and take over from here.

Gillen: This is dynamite. I remember reading a review of

13

three books on this stuff in *The New York Times* recently. . . . This book got the biggest play.

Danner: Yeah, that's why they are interested. . . . Apparently he's in his early thirties and unmarried. . . . Interesting angle there. . . . They said "Who is he laying? If it's girls, who are they? If not girls, maybe boys, who?" They want to know.

Gillen: Wow, this is dynamite that might blow, Dick, you know that.

Danner: Yeah, he seems to be a bit of a nut or some kind of a screwball. . . . Well, they want to know, no matter what. . . . They want to get something, somewhere, on this guy to get him out of their hair, and to shut him up. I know it is a tricky one . . . that's why I called you. . . . I told them how you handled . . . and thought you could do this. . . . You're a lawyer, as I recall. . . . How do you think you will approach this?

Gillen: I have been trying to figure that out because you know we will have to get close to him to get what they want . . . you know . . . are they prepared for the worst? The subject is certain to learn of the investigation.

Danner: Yes . . . that's why I told them I would know just how you plan to go about it and I want your ideas to see if they fit in with my ideas. . . .

Gillen: I think the answer will be found in a thorough pre-employment investigation. We make hundreds of them every week.

Danner: That's a good idea . . . about the safest . . . I go along with that. . . . Excellent. . . .

Gillen: But Dick, somebody must be in a position to say they authorized you to ask for it. . . . If it blows . . . who will be there to say he is interested in hiring him? . . . a lot of organizations would be glad to have this fellow with his research and writing ability from what I see in the book right now.

Danner: I'll take care of that.

Gillen: You'd better give me an idea of who . . . because I may be forced to identify my client. . . . Suspicion is bound to be on the auto industry. . . . I'm a lawyer. . . .

Danner: Why don't you be co-counsel with me and hire your organization to do the job?

Gillen: I've done that. Good, but I believe as a private investigator in New York I would have to identify my client. . . . I'm not sure as a lawyer I would, but I would just say that I am co-counsel with you. . . . What is it here in D.C.?

Danner: I'm not sure, but I will take care of that and this idea will add an extra lawyer . . . so we'll be much safer. Don't worry about it. . . . Who will you use in Washington?

Gillen: Dave Shatraw, an ex-agent, do you know him? He's retired now.

Danner: . . . Good. If you can't readily determine who his supporters are, who he is dealing with, his sources of income, we may have to put a tail on him. . . . Don't do it without my OK. . . . I think a tail will show who he is contacting. . . . His language in articles and the book is appearing in lawsuits in several parts of the country. . . . I'll tell you in the strictest confidence, to be revealed to no one, even in your own organization. . . . General Motors. . . . If we handle this right, both of us will get a lot of business from them.

On the day Vincent Gillen's pocket tape recorder was slowly turning in Danner's office, Ralph Nader was in Des Moines, Iowa, where he had testified before the State Attorney General's hearing on traffic safety. Despite the sworn testimony of Danner, Gillen, and the GM officials that the investigation of Nader did not start until after the January 13 meeting of Danner and Gillen, Nader claims the entire story still may be untold. Registered at the Kirkwood Hotel in Des Moines from January 7 to 13, Nader was uneasy; he felt he was being watched. He had no evidence he was, but he did have a gut reaction based on his growing controversial role as an auto critic, the publication of his book, and a "kind of uneasy feeling." At the Kirkwood Hotel, he was first touched by the "uneasy feeling" when one man kept reappearing in his view. Once he was on the floor outside Nader's room; then he saw the same man again several times in the lobby of the hotel. Nader is a suspicious man—it seems to be part of his fetish about privacy, but his "suspicions," whether they have to do with double-dealing politicians or shady corporate maneuvers, are based on good intuition and an acute legal mind well-accustomed to drawing proper conclusions from circumstantial evidence. Nevertheless, when Nader began telling his friends that he thought he was being followed, he got the "Yeah, sure," treatment to his face, and snide comments about paranoia behind his back. But on January 14, the day after the Gillen-Danner meeting and the day after he left Des Moines, Nader walked right into the lion's mouth. He went to Detroit on an invitation from General Motors which hoped to convince Nader to tone down his criticism of the Corvair by showing him "the GM side of the story." Nader met with Assistant General Counsel Bridenstine, Vice-President Louis Goad and then Vice-President Edward Cole. Before Nader got the technical briefing GM had planned, Bridenstine asked him the specific question: You do not represent clients in any Corvair cases, do you? Nader's answer was an unequivocal "No."

By mid-February, Nader lost whatever lingering doubts he may have had about being investigated when he placed a telephone call to Harvard Law Professor Harold J. Berman for whom he had worked for six months as a research assistant. Berman was particularly glad to hear from Nader because he wanted to congratulate him on "the new job." Job? Nader said he knew nothing about any job. Well, said Berman, who was the man who had come to his office on February 8 asking about Nader's background and claiming he wanted the information for a client who was considering hiring Nader?

The man "whose client wanted to hire Nader" was actually one of a network of investigators fanning out over Washington, Connecticut, and Boston to check on Nader in an effort to carry out what Gillen said were Danner's instructions to him: "There's something somewhere, find it so they can shut him up."

Gillen had not wasted any time after his session with

Danner. He put together all the information Danner had given him, which in turn had been given to Danner by Eileen Murphy, and out of this hodgepodge, Gillen created a memo for his investigators to work from in tracking Nader. At one point in the memo, Gillen summarized their mission this way: "Our job is to check his life and current activities to determine 'what makes him tick,' such as his real interest in safety, his supporters, if any, his politics, his marital status, his friends, his women, boys, etc., drinking, dope, jobs—in all facets of his life." The rest of the memo, which wandered over six pages, was filled with items like checking to make "sure that Nader was actually admitted to the bar," and to find out why Nader went to Mexico "with a doctor to inoculate people in the country area." [Nader never made any such trip.]

According to a chronology of events made up by General Motors' own lawyers, the private investigators quickly began zeroing in on Nader. On January 25, an investigator checked on teachers at the University of Hartford where Nader had taught on a part-time basis. On the twenty-sixth, George A. Athanson, the lawyer who hired Nader for his firm, was interviewed. On the same day, another investigator checked the publisher of the Winsted *Evening Citizen*, Nader's hometown newspaper. On January 27, the same investigator interviewed Nader's high-school principal, David Nichols, a high-school classmate, Arthur Litin, and two neighbors in Winsted, Marguerite Ryan and Joseph Gabor. On the thirty-first, Gillen called Nader's publisher Richard Grossman at his office in New York City. He also called New York State Senator Edward Speno, another auto safety critic who had worked with Nader. By February 2, two investigators were "casing" the neighborhood around his Washington rooming house, and by February 4, they had the rooming house under surveillance from "8:15 A.M. to 9:00 P.M. but saw no significant activity." On February 5, the investigators were back at the rooming house from 9:00 A.M. to 9:00 P.M., but again "saw no significant activity." On the sixth, the investigators again spent the day watching Nader's rooming house, but still saw "no significant activity." However, on February 7, they watched the rooming house from 7:00 A.M. and caught Nader when he came out. They followed him to places such as the Guardian Federal Savings and Loan, Costin's Sirloin House, and to the Department of Labor, finally breaking off the surveillance at 11 P.M. On February 8, they staked out the rooming house from 5:45 A.M. to 8:20 A.M. but reported no sign of Nader. On the ninth, two investigators "were in the vicinity of Nader's rooming house from 7:30 A.M. for surveillance purposes." This time they followed him to the office of the *New Republic* magazine and then to an office supply store and back again to the *New Republic*, finally ending the surveillance at 4:30 P.M., according to the GM chronology.

To Nader, February 9 was one of the most harassment filled days of all. He had spent the day in his room writing testimony he would give to Ribicoff's subcommittee the next day. All through the day and night he was plagued by a series of telephone calls. First, the callers would say things like "Mr. Nader, this is Pan American," and then hang up. One caller identified himself as a Railway Express clerk, and told Nader to pick up a package. Nader said the calls were designed to find out if he was still at home. But later in the night they turned more vicious, and one caller snarled "Why don't you go back to Connecticut, buddy boy?" Gillen denied all of this. "No harassing phone calls were made to Mr. Nader at his rooming house. The only call made there by our agents was about 11:30 A.M., February 9, to find out if he was there. We had not seen him since 7 P.M. the night before. The landlady answered, said he was there, and went to get him. Our man hung up," Gillen later told Ribicoff's committee.

On the day after his testimony before the Ribicoff committee—February 11—Nader had two appointments on Capitol Hill. In a telephone conversation with Jerry Sonosky, he had agreed to stop by the subcommittee office to pick up a copy of the transcript from the previous day's hearing to go over it for errors, and he also had a television interview

18

scheduled with NBC at a studio in the New Senate Office Building. When Nader stepped out on 19th Street from his rooming house that morning, one of Gillen's waiting detectives spotted him and took up the tail. It was this decision that brought down GM's carefully constructed house of cards.

When Nader got to the New Senate Office Building, the detective lost him, and telephoned another detective to join him. In the confusion over trying to find Nader, the detectives queried a guard near the television studio, asking him if he had seen anyone answering Nader's description. At one point, the detectives also followed Bryce Nelson, a Washington *Post* reporter with a slight resemblance to Nader, who later would be the first newsman to write a story on the Nader-shadowing incident. Nader says the detectives apparently lost him when he punched the "up" button on an elevator, and the detective ran up the staircase to catch the elevator at the next floor. But Nader says he changed his mind, punched the "down" button, and went to the cafeteria. Meanwhile, the guard, noticing that the men continued to lurk around the television studio, reported the incident to a lieutenant of the guards, who told them to leave the building, but not before he took their names.

At this point, Eileen Murphy was unhappy with the results of the investigative reports that Danner was mailing back to Detroit. In a letter to Danner, she said she felt "that everyone is going overboard to impress us with what a great, charming intellectual this human being is—Eagle Scout type. There are too many variances for this to be accurate. . . ."

She told Danner to find out about Nader's Army record: "What did he do for six months in the Army?" She also urged that Nader finances be checked. She asked about his "savings account, stock," and then concluded the letter by telling Danner: "Well friend, have fun." Danner immediately wrote Gillen a letter telling him, "Frankly, I think we are going to have trouble justifying your bills unless information is unearthed that hits a little closer to home where Nader's background is concerned." He then attached a copy of Eileen Murphy's letter for Gillen to see.

But Gillen had been a busy sleuth. On February 21, he had even driven to New Hampshire to interview Frederick Hughes Condon, a classmate of Nader's. Again using the cover name of Mr. Warren, Gillen drew a blank in probing for information on everything from Nader's left-wing politics to questions about why Nader, at thirty-one, was still unmarried. At a later point, after he appeared before Ribicoff's committee to testify on his role in the incident, Gillen said that GM's lawyers advised him to play down the bachelor angle in his testimony, pointing out that President John F. Kennedy "had not been married until he was about thirty-four." But Condon correctly figured "Mr. Warren" for what he was—a private detective—and telephoned Nader.

As for Nader, he was beginning to be more and more apprehensive, particularly after several incidents in late February that Gillen, Danner, and GM deny any knowledge of, but Nader says happened. On February 20, a Sunday, Nader left his rooming house and stopped at a drugstore off Dupont Circle. Flipping through magazines, he was startled by a good-looking young brunette who sidled up next to him with what must be one of the all-time great opening lines. "I know this sounds forward," she said, "but can I talk to you?" With Nader standing there mouth agape, the girl, who was in her mid-twenties, told him that she wanted him to join her group which was discussing "foreign affairs" at a nearby apartment. Even the usually unflappable Nader was taken aback. "I mumbled something about being from out of town," and couldn't go, he said. Without searching for any other "foreign affairs" experts, the girl turned and left. The next day, the same day that Gillen showed up at Condon's office, Nader boarded a plane at Washington's National Airport for a flight to Philadelphia for a taping session with television interviewer Mike Douglas. As usual, Nader hung around too long after the show was over, and was late getting back to the airport to catch his 3:30 P.M. flight to Washington. Loping down to the airline boarding gate with just five minutes to spare before departure time, Nader was handing his ticket to the airline agent when he caught sight of two men who had been seated on a nearby bench. The men quickly boarded the plane and sat close to Nader, who by this time, on the basis of earlier harassments, was convinced he was being followed. Once the plane landed, Nader ran down the ramp, and set off in a crazy quilt pattern of going in and out of doors to throw off his "tails." Finally, he grabbed a cab, and as in a bad movie, watched through the back window for the detectives who apparently were still wandering around the airport lobby hoping to find him again.

While Nader was covering his trail, another investigator was trying to open a new lead. One of Gillen's agents telephoned Dexter Masters who had given Nader's book a favorable review in the widely circulated *Book Week* which was published by the no-longer existent New York *Herald Tribune*. Masters apparently was "suspect" because he was a former director of Consumers Union, but he had never even met Nader. About the time Nader was on his way to the airport in Philadelphia, Masters' phone rang and a man who said he worked for Vincent Gillen proceeded to unleash a barrage of questions about Nader. What did Masters know about him? Did he have a driver's license? Where did he live? Masters told the caller that the only thing he knew about Nader was written on the jacket of his book, "which I urged the caller to read." When the call was over, Masters, who did not like the sound of the questioning, telephoned Richard Grossman, Nader's publisher, to tell him about the caller. Grossman, in turn, called Nader with another piece of information for his now voluminous file of incidents.

But there was still one more major incident to come. On Wednesday, two days after Nader returned from Philadelphia, he was in a Safeway store near his boardinghouse practicing one of his favorite vices—buying cookies. It was evening, the aisles were filled with shoppers, and Nader was puzzling over his choice when a good-looking blonde in slacks headed straight for him. "I need some help," she said. "I've got to move something heavy into my apartment. There's no one to help me. I wonder if I can get you to give me a hand. It won't take much time. Will you help?" Nader turned the girl down flat. She persisted, but when Nader was adamant, she did not try any of the other men in the store, but simply turned and left. To Nader, the girls were sex lures, and he is not sure what specifically they had planned to do if he had followed them. "It might have been the old gimmick of getting you into a compromising situation and then taking a picture for blackmail. It could have been a pot party; again, it would be for blackmail. They simply wanted to discredit me," he says. But Nader says that although he felt queasy about what he termed this "invasion of the self," he did not feel he was in danger of physical harm from the snoopers.

On March 10, James Roche felt the frustration of any man who has let himself be overtaken by events. In his hand was a telegram that read:

Am announcing on Senate floor today that Subcommittee on Executive Reorganization will hold hearings March 22 on Nader-GM matter. Respectfully invite your attendance as a witness.

Abraham Ribicoff
U.S. Senate

Ribicoff's telegram was a result of a statement released late on the night of March 9 that began:

"General Motors said today that following the publication of Mr. Ralph Nader's criticisms of the Corvair in writings and public appearances in support of his book *Unsafe At Any Speed*, the office of its general counsel initiated a routine investigation through a reputable law firm to determine whether Ralph Nader was acting on behalf of litigants or their attorneys in Corvair design cases pending against General Motors. The investigation was prompted by Mr. Nader's

22

extreme criticism of the Corvair in his writings, press conferences, TV, and other public appearances. Mr. Nader's statements coincided with similar publicity by some attorneys handling such litigation.

"It is a well-known and accepted practice in the legal profession to investigate claims and persons making claims in the product liability field, such as in the pending Corvair design cases.

"The investigation was limited only to Mr. Nader's qualifications, background, expertise, and association with such attorneys. It did not include any of the alleged harassment or intimidation recently reported in the press. If Mr. Nader has been subjected to any of the incidents and harassment mentioned by him in the newspaper stories, such incidents were in no way associated with General Motors' legitimate investigation of his interest in pending litigation.

"At General Motors' invitation, Mr. Nader spent a day at the GM Technical Center, Warren, Michigan, early in January visiting with General Motors' executives and engineers. He was shown a number of engineering and research testing and development programs in the field of automotive safety. A number of the accusations in his book were discussed at length, and a presentation was made of the evidence used in the successful defense of the only two Corvair lawsuits tried.

"Mr. Nader expressed appreciation for the courtesy in providing him with detailed information, but he nevertheless continued the same line of attack on the design of the Corvair in a number of subsequent press conferences, TV, and other appearances. This behavior lends support to General Motors' belief that there is a connection between Mr. Nader and plaintiffs' counsel in pending Corvair design litigation."

With these few paragraphs, GM had admitted its guilt, using as an excuse the argument that the investigation was needed to determine Nader's connection with the Corvair litigation and claiming that the probe was limited only to items directly connected with that problem. As Gillen was to write Roche in a letter dated April 5, 1966, the GM admission was stunning. "My surprise was about equal to yours when you made the March 9 announcement," Gillen told Roche.

The thirteen days between GM's statement admitting the shadowing of Nader and the March 22 Senate hearing scheduled by Ribicoff were filled with planning conferences at GM's corporate headquarters. Gillen claims he made his first trip to Detroit on March 11, at the request of Danner, and the next morning the two of them went to the General Motors building. In a memo dictated eight months after the meeting, Gillen said he met with Eileen Murphy, Power, Bridenstine, and a gaggle of other GM lawyers:

"The first questions directed to me were regarding the use of recorders and the use of girls. I was somewhat surprised to receive the impression that they believed that both had occurred. At one stage I mentioned that my directions had been rather specific and when asked by Durkin [a GM lawyer] if he could look at them, I declined to hand them over, saying I thought it would be better if he didn't look at them. All this time, I was under the assumption that they knew the whole story and that it was up to Danner and me to support their position. However, they continued to put stress on the fact that they were seeking information regarding Nader's association with other lawyers and bringing lawsuits against GM. They did not bring up anything about the personal life at all. I remember on one occasion when we were alone in the room, Danner saying in effect, 'Gee, Vince, I may have goofed here and missed something. But I don't remember any instructions regarding his association with other lawyers.' "

On March 14, Gillen was back in Detroit for more conferences with the GM legal staff on how he conducted his investigation, including "more details about the activity in the Senate Office Building." The same type of questioning went on for two more days, Gillen claimed. On March 18, Gillen met Danner in Washington and the pair went to see Jerry Sonosky, who said the Senate Committee wanted a statement from them by Sunday, March 20. In his memo,

Gillen claimed that Sonosky told him that Ribicoff's subcommittee was not interested in him, or Danner—"They're interested in headlines and the fact that General Motors will be here," Gillen quoted Sonosky as saying.

After the meeting, Gillen and Danner went back to Danner's office, and according to Gillen this is what happened: "I began to type on his typewriter my statement to be presented to the Senate. In the midst of that, Danner received a call from GM and when he hung up said in effect 'GM has changed their mind about supporting the investigation, and they are going to dump the whole thing onto the investigator.' "

When Danner told him this, Gillen claimed "I then told Danner for the first time that I had a complete recording of his instructions to me in Washington on January 13 [the day Gillen says Danner gave him the seven-page memo from Eileen Murphy that outlined what GM wanted to find out about Nader]. He knew what they were. I told him that I was going back to New York to gather some more data and finish preparing my statement and suggested he take an early plane to Detroit and in no uncertain terms to let the officials there know that I was not going to take the rap for the investigation."

Inside GM, fierce jockeying was going on in an effort to save the company image. Power was in the most untenable position of all. He had ordered the investigation, and Bridenstine had helped carry out the scheme. Roche, however, was responsible only in that he was the president of GM. Into this morass stepped one more figure whose role is murky today. General Motors, in the week before the Senate hearing was to begin, hired Theodore C. Sorensen as a lawyer for James Roche. Sorensen was the coolly brilliant advisor to President John F. Kennedy, who only six weeks before joined the New York law firm of Paul Weiss, Rifkind, Wharton & Garrison, which was influential in the liberal wing of the New York Democratic party. One of the partners, former Federal Judge Simon H. Rifkind, was a long-time friend and political backer of Ribicoff. Sorensen's appearance, of course, put Senator

Robert Kennedy in an awkward position. But Sorensen had still another link with the subcommittee. He had a long-time acquaintance with Jerry Sonosky, who had worked with Sorensen when Sorensen was President Kennedy's aide, and Sonosky was an aide to Ribicoff who was then Health, Education, and Welfare Secretary. It was Sorensen who apparently devised the Roche strategy on the witness stand; that is to apologize, humbly admit a mistake, and by intimation blame the entire mess on his underlings and through them on a bumbling detective who exceeded his authority. All during the week before March 22, there was a parade of principals to the subcommittee office: Sorensen was one, Power and Bridenstine both met with Sonosky, and, of course, Gillen and Danner also met with Sonosky.

But on the weekend before the hearing was to open, Gillen claims he was in Detroit fighting to prevent GM from "dumping" the blame on him. On Saturday, he and his wife, Irene, were in GM's headquarters building in Detroit, and according to the documents he turned over to the court, "we sat down and Mr. Bridenstine read a draft of Mr. Roche's proposed statement [to be delivered before the Senate Committee] in which he said 'the information in the [detective] report was of no value to General Motors.'" According to Gillen, he claimed "I immediately pointed out to him that I would not permit Mr. Roche to make such a statement and it contradicted their whole statement that the investigation was made to show Nader's connection with attorneys." Gillen said Bridenstine then took the statement and one half hour later returned with a different version of the role of the detectives and showed it to Gillen. Again, Gillen said he rejected the phrasing on the role of the detectives. At this point, Gillen claims he left, saying he would be back the next day, and if the statement didn't suit him, he would, in an allusion to his tape recording of his instructions Danner gave him on the investigation, "take whatever action I considered appropriate."

Gillen returned to GM's headquarters at about 2:15 P.M., he claimed, and again Bridenstine read a new version of Mr.

Roche's prepared statement. Again, Gillen said he rejected it. In his court documents he said he told Danner "privately that if the wording was not changed to my satisfaction that I was going to go to Washington and play the record of instructions and Danner's voice came through loud and clear." Finally, at 4:00 P.M., Bridenstine came to Gillen and read the final version. "I took exception to the sentence in which he stated: 'I deplore the kind of harassment to which Mr. Nader has apparently been subjected.' " Gillen said he told Bridenstine the press would jump on the sentence and would completely ignore the word "apparently." Gillen said he urged Bridenstine to have it changed to something such as "I deplore the alleged harassment to which Nader claims he has been subjected." Gillen said Bridenstine pleaded with him to accept and he finally did.

On the day before the hearing, the Mayflower Hotel was host to most of the principals in the hearing. Bridenstine and Power were there along with Roche and Sorensen, Eileen Murphy, and Gillen. That night, Gillen said he paid a visit to the Power suite. Bridenstine was there, and Gillen described the scene this way: "Power had a TV set on and he and Bridenstine were sitting near it. They had some typical legal briefcases there and I said I wanted to be sure there was no recorder and Power seemed a little insulted saying that he never used a recorder in his life." Gillen said he told Power he still objected strongly to the wording of Roche's apology, but Power urged him to forget it. According to Gillen, Power said: "Look, Vince, what they had done to me. I threatened to resign, but they are afraid to let me resign. If I can take this, you can take it, too."

The huge Caucus Room of the Senate Office Building was jammed long before the 10:00 A.M. starting time. The press tables were filled; all of the television networks were there, and the public seats were packed with major and minor officials of the auto industry—public relations men, lobbyists, trade association officials. A few GM stockholders, and a sprinkling of the curious public made up the rest of the

27

NADER: THE PEOPLE'S LAWYER

audience. On the rostrum, ranged against a white marble wall, were the inquisitors: Senators Abraham Ribicoff (D-Conn.), Robert F. Kennedy (D-N.Y.), Fred Harris (D-Okla.), Henry Jackson (D-Wash.), and Milward Simpson (R-Wyo.). Facing them was James Roche, with the placid-faced Sorensen next to him. Scattered around him were Power, Bridenstine, Gillen, Danner, and Eileen Murphy. The only person missing when the curtain went up was Ralph Nader; he was still downtown near his rooming house trying to hail a cab, all of which on the most important day of his career were blithely ignoring his frantic hand signals. Ribicoff began the hearing at the moment of ten and said: "I have called this special meeting today to look into the circumstances surrounding what appeared to be an attempt by General Motors Corporation to discredit Mr. Ralph Nader, a recent witness before the subcommittee. This large company whose principal executive officers appeared before this same subcommittee last July, has admitted responsibility for undertaking a determined and exhaustive investigation of a private citizen who has criticized the auto industry verbally and in print.

"There is no law which bars a corporation from hiring detectives to investigate a private citizen, however distasteful the idea may seem to some of us. There is a law, however, which makes it a crime to harass or intimidate a witness before a congressional committee. One of our purposes here today is to inquire into the purposes and effects of the action initiated by General Motors."

By 10:15 A.M., Nader still hadn't arrived even though Ribicoff had called a short recess hoping to let Nader be the first witness. Finally, he gave up and asked Roche to testify. With Sorensen at his elbow, Roche began his statement, speaking in his slow and precise baritone. "As President of General Motors, I hold myself fully responsible for any action authorized or initiated by any officer of the corporation which may have had any bearing on the incidents related to our investigation of Mr. Nader. I did not know of the investigation when it was initiated and I did not approve it." Roche also went on to deny that GM employed detectives to

28

follow Nader in Des Moines, Iowa, or Philadelphia, nor did it hire detectives to "constantly ring his private telephone number late at night with false statements or anonymous warnings." He also said that the decision to probe into facets of Nader's life not connected with the Corvair litigation were made "by the people conducting the investigation."

Roche's sharpest questioning came from Senator Kennedy who jabbed continually at Roche, getting him to admit that the original statement put out by GM on March 9 acknowledging it had investigated Nader, but only in a routine manner, was not accurate. Here is an excerpt from the transcript of the hearing in which Kennedy tries to pin down Roche:

Kennedy: Let me ask you now based on the facts that you know at the present moment—the investigation was really much more, far beyond what the original statement of General Motors indicated on March 9?

Roche: I would say that is true; yes sir.

Despite some of Kennedy's incisive questioning, Roche was not really grilled by the subcommittee members. Roche made his formal mea culpas, saying he deplored the type of harassment Nader had been subjected to, and did not condone it. He finally wound up with the announcement "I want to apologize here and now."

But Power was not let off so lightly. Power opposed Roche's humble stance to the end. If he had his way, Roche would not have backed off so far, but would have put up a stronger defense of the investigation. Sonosky claims that the statement Power read to the committee "probably was the one prepared for Roche before Sorensen came on the scene." Power argued that the investigation of Nader "was undertaken as a prudent and appropriate measure in the preparation of the defense of a series of major lawsuits then pending against General Motors. It was not undertaken for the purpose of harassing or intimidating a witness before a congressional or legislative committee. In the light of the situation existing at the time, I could not have arrived at any other decision consistent with my responsibilities as the general counsel of General Motors." He admitted ordering the investigation, and said "definite evidence that Mr. Nader was financially interested [in Corvair litigation] could be used to counter his attack." Power also refused to go along with Roche in admitting that the March 9 statement was misleading, insisting it was at worst "unclear."

Watching the cross examination as closely as anyone in the room was Eileen Murphy, a key figure in the entire episode, but one who was never to occupy the witness stand or even to answer a single question in the hearing. Her name was brought up repeatedly by all of the witnesses, she was discussed by the members of the committee, but she herself never uttered a word for the record. Why wasn't Miss Murphy called? This is another of the still unanswered questions. Sonosky claims that the plan was to keep the hearing to one day; that the committee wanted only to hear from the top officials involved and not "a lowly law librarian." None of the Senators made any real effort to explore deeply Miss Murphy's role. At one point Senator Harris asked Roche if he was aware of what Miss Murphy's instructions were on how the investigation of Nader was to be conducted. Roche admitted he was not, but Kennedy at this point told Roche, "Let's not focus on Miss Murphy," and the line of questioning was changed. The other argument offered against calling Miss Murphy, and it is a shallow one, was that the press would have a field day writing stories about the law librarian who manipulated General Motors, and the bigger issue of top-level guilt would be downplayed. Still another argument, never documented, was that a decision not to call Miss Murphy was worked out in meetings between Sonosky and Sorensen. Miss Murphy's role was particularly important when connected to two key documents GM turned over to the subcommittee. One was the 96-page compilation of reports Gillen sent through Danner to GM as the investigation on Nader progressed. A still unresolved controversy centers on the first page of these detective reports. Gillen claimed later that at the request of Danner, he, Gillen, typed a new first page for the report. The substitute page was needed because the original page reflected "the true purposes" of the GM investigation of Nader which was to "discredit him, and shut him up," Gillen claimed. The "new" first page was then attached to the detective report, but the Senate subcommittee was not told about the change when the document was delivered to the subcommittee office before the hearing started, Gillen charged. The other document was the seven-page memorandum Eileen Murphy delivered to Danner outlining the investigation which included in it instructions raising the question of anti-Semitism in hopes of discrediting Nader in the eyes of Ribicoff who is Jewish, Gillen claimed. Although GM delivered the memo to Sonosky, its full contents were never divulged at the hearing. Sonosky acknowledged later that he never passed the memo on to committee members so that when Ribicoff conducted his one-day hearing, he apparently was not aware of the contents of the memo. Sonosky claimed, however, that the memo would not have changed the outcome to any appreciable extent if it had been introduced.

By now Nader had finally gotten a cab, and was seated in the committee room taking notes as the cross-examination droned on. Bridenstine had no prepared statement, but in answer to questions from Senator Kennedy said that Miss Murphy was receiving the detective reports that were being forwarded by Danner. After the lunch break, Nader testified. One by one he answered GM's charges; he was not profiting in any way from Corvair litigation, but was sincerely interested in alerting the public to the Corvair safety problems which he said made it an "inordinately dangerous" car. He raked GM for bringing the anti-Semitism issue into the case which only "came up because my parents happen to have been born in Lebanon," and he made an eloquent plea against what GM had done.

"It is beneficial to explore the workings of such a routine investigation and its framework of operation. People all over should know that things like this go on so that they can, quite apart from laws, apply the customary social sanctions in a community which can operate to discourage or stifle such probings. But unless some definitions and sharpened values appear soon in our nation to limit such inquisitorial excesses, the employment of this essentially arbitrary power will continue its undermining of individual expression." Then Roche, Power, and Bridenstine, with their lush salaries, were handed one more dramatic example of what Nader was really all about—he pledged all of the royalties from the book they had criticized as profit-making sensationalism to the cause of auto safety.

Danner followed Nader to the witness chair, and painted himself as merely a conduit between GM and Gillen. He admitted hiring Gillen and said, as had the General Motors officials, that he considered the investigation proper since it had, he claimed, "for its purpose to determine what connection, if any, Mr. Nader might have with the plaintiffs' attorney in the Corvair suits." Danner also officially pooh-poohed the sex angle. "As to the use of girls to entice or entrap Mr. Nader, I can state that no such instructions were issued to me by General Motors nor by me to Mr. Gillen to resort to such activities. If such incidents actually happened to Mr. Nader, I am certain that no one connected with us had any knowledge nor involvement whatsoever with this," he said.

The last witness of the day was Vincent Gillen who read a long-winded statement designed to show that he was not engaged in what Senator Gaylord Nelson termed "a seamy trade." Gillen started by listing his law degree and ended by pointing out that he was listed in "Who's Who in Commerce & Industry." In between he told the subcommittee that he had taught school, was elected president of the PTA "of my daughter's high school in Brooklyn," and twenty-five years earlier had been foreman of a grand jury. He also claimed the distinction of having been a member of a zoning board in Glen Cove, N.Y., and was a member of the Society of Professional Investigators. With his credentials out of the way, Gillen specifically denied trailing Nader in Des Moines; he also defended the ruse of a pre-employment check as the only way the information GM wanted could have been gotten. He admitted ordering Nader followed, and said that the decision of his detectives to follow Nader into the New Senate Office Building was made on the scene. "That sort of thing can happen in any investigative organization. I am sure Senator Kennedy knows this from his experience as attorney general when he was responsible for all government investigative agencies," Gillen pointedly told Kennedy. Gillen also denied that his detectives had followed reporter Bryce Nelson by mistake. "That is fantastic. These men had followed Nader several days and knew him well," Gillen said. So adamant was Gillen about the correctness of what he did that at one point he even tried to interpret Roche's apology as applying only in a limited sense, but Roche immediately disabused him of the idea. Finally, at 5:15 P.M., the tawdry story ended, when Ribicoff said "the committee will stand adjourned."

The impact of the drama, however, still is felt. His collision with GM made Nader a national figure, and helps keep him on that level even today. For Roche, however, the confrontation with Nader became like an eczema that stayed with him for all of his remaining career years. Power retired, engulfed in bitterness toward his corporate fellows at GM. Bridenstine never moved up to the general counsel's job, however. Ross Malone was brought in to become general counsel. Eileen Murphy is retired and lives quietly in a Detroit high-rise apartment. She has never commented on the incident despite the claims of many that she has the best tale to tell. The two controversial documents—the detective report, and the seven-page Murphy memo—have been locked away in the U.S. Archives. Sonosky put the documents in the Archives, claiming it was the only equitable solution between the demands of GM, which said the documents were its property, and Ralph Nader, who wanted to show them to the public. Sonosky himself quit the subcommittee, and now handles the business of the Mercedes-Benz automobile company for a large Washington law firm. Danner still maintains a Washington law office. As for Gillen, he collected $6,700 from GM for his investigation, and was later paid another $3,225 for his services between March 11 and 20. As he was then, he is today in the private detective business.

Finally, as for the "girls" and Nader's feeling that he was being shadowed as early as November, 1965, when he testified in Des Moines before the state attorney general's auto safety hearing, these two items remain "open." Some observers definitely feel there was another—a third investigation—that was run by Detroit in conjunction with Gillen's investigation and the short-lived O'Neill investigation. Nader says only that he is still seeking answers.

2

WHAT MAKES RALPH RUN?

You should not allow yourself the luxuries of discouragement or despair. Bounce back immediately, and welcome the adversity because it produces harder thinking and harder drive to get to the objective.

—Ralph Nader in a briefing for
a new group of Nader's Raiders

If Hollywood were casting for the role of Ralph Nader, Ralph Nader would never get the job. Six-foot-four, sad-eyed, shy, and slightly stooped, Nader could easily pass for a small-college basketball coach, or an apprentice to the town undertaker—but a flamboyant crusader, a muckraker, a man who could humble the all-powerful General Motors? Never.

According to the standard scenario for most of America's instant heroes, Nader should have been swept into history's dustbin following his famed confrontation with General Motors. Or, more precisely, he should have returned to the obscurity of a Hartford, Connecticut, law firm like the one run by George Athanson. He hired Nader fresh from Harvard Law School for $75 a week to toil over auto accident cases (the biggest settlement he ever got was $10,000), divorce cases, and will drawings, only to find his young associate preferred to spend almost as much time on free legal-aid work as he did in the pursuit of fees. But Nader didn't fade away; he stayed on the national scene.

35

"I taught Ralph to be human . . . to think of others before he thought of himself. This, I think, is the essence of his appeal," says Nader's mother, Rose. There is no doubt that Nader practices what his mother preached. Once, on a vacation in Puerto Rico, he came back to his hotel room not with the usual cheap souvenirs, but with a slum child whose plight so touched him he had to do something for the boy even if it was only to get him scrubbed up, outfitted in a new suit of clothes, and fed in the hotel dining room. This special human quality, exhibited by Nader with quiet constancy, is also apparent in the dedication of his book *Unsafe At Any Speed*. There is no tribute to the usual list of favorites: parents, old professors, or girl friends "without whom this book never would have been written." Rather, *Unsafe At Any Speed* (60,000 hardback copies, 400,000 paperbacks) was dedicated to Frederick Hughes Condon, a Harvard Law School classmate of Nader's, who was put in a wheelchair for life in 1961. When he fell asleep at the steering wheel of his Plymouth station wagon, the car careened off a New Hampshire highway, rolled over, and trapped Condon half in and half out of the car, crushing his spine. The book itself was planted in Nader's mind as early as 1956 when he "saw a little girl almost decapitated in an accident when the glove compartment door flew open and became a guillotine for the child as she was thrown forward in a 15-mile-an-hour collision."

This sensitivity to the fate of others, this honest outrage at preventable wrongs, and an ability to articulate his feelings, has created a Nader legion—a vast army of persons who see him as their spokesman. Every year he gets a total of 90,000 letters from consumers who want him to carry their spears in some conflict with government or big business. But others relate to him in a more personal way. Connie Smith, a Las Vegas nightclub singer, quit her job and camped on Nader's doorstep until he agreed to give her a job in his movement so she could "do something worthwhile." The show girl was told to report to work as a typist at Nader's Center for Study of Responsive Law. A frustrated owner of a "lemon Cadillac" pleaded with Nader to come and watch him set fire to the car in downtown Philadelphia. Nader gets middle-of-the-night telephone calls from consumers in Europe who just want to *talk* about their "lemons," and when tourists spot him in the halls of Congress, he is badgered for autographs while passing congressmen draw little more attention than the Capitol's countless marble statues of dead politicians. Gordon Sherman, the industrialist who covered the United States with Midas Muffler franchises, was so impressed with Nader at a dinner meeting in Chicago's posh Standard Club that he pledged the Midas Foundation to contribute $300,000 for Nader's Center for Study of Responsive Law.

Does this type of hero worship make Nader think he can become a self-appointed arbiter of all marketplace standards? Nader says "No," definitely not. "The important point I have tried to make is only that individuals still count; that they can generate a momentum for change; that they can challenge large and complex institutions; that there still is a very critical role for citizen action and for the development of citizenship that will improve the quality of life in the country."

Nader will not even accept the idea that he is an idealist in search of a perfect marketplace. "I don't think of myself as an idealist. If you define an idealist as someone who recedes from the real world because he wants his own world to be pure, then I'm not an idealist. I think of myself as being very practical because I want to be effective—I want to make changes and to do this I carefully plan my tactics and I try to use what power levers I can to get the job done. I am a worker; a plodder."

What annoys Nader most is to be questioned about his motivation. According to his critics, he is either a fanatic, a puritan prig, a publicity seeker, or an arrogant moralist. Carl T. Curtis, the Nebraska senator, gave the world his interpretation of Nader's motive when the crusader appeared before the Senate's Subcommittee on Executive Reorganization in 1966 to testify on auto safety. "He is using this forum to sell books," said Curtis. Senator Robert F. Kennedy put the question directly to Nader: "Why are you doing all of this?"

he asked. If he were trying to prevent cruelty to animals, no one would question his motives, was Nader's answer. But "because I happen to have a scale of priorities which leads me to engage in the prevention of cruelty to humans, my motivations are constantly inquired into.

"Basically the motivation is simply this. When I see . . . people decapitated, crushed, bloodied, and broken, and that is what we are really talking about in auto safety . . . the fatalities and the horrible carnage involved . . . I ask myself what can the genius of man do to avoid it? And frankly, I think this country and the auto industry are abundantly endowed with the genius of man to provide an engineering environment of both highway and vehicle which will protect the occupants from the consequences of their errors and which will avoid the very perpetuation of these errors in the first place . . ."

Nader went on to tell Kennedy: "As I became more and more aware of the tremendous gap between what was possible and what was actual, I became, in a sense, incensed at the way there can be a tremendous amount of injustice and brutality in an industrialized society without any accountability, without any responsibility. That people sitting in executive suites can make remote decisions which will someday result in tremendous carnage, and because they are remote in time and space from the consequences of that decision, there is no accountability."

But no matter how many times he repeats basically the same answer he gave Kennedy, Nader is asked to re-explain his motives as he enters each new area of the consumer field. Almost plaintively Nader asks: "Is it wrong to talk about defective cars, diseased meats, corporate cheating? Is it really distasteful that a person cares enough about issues like these to dedicate his life to changing them?" Rose Nader, the one-time Lebanese high-school French teacher, puts the problem into perspective. Asked what makes Ralph Nader tick, she said: "What's more important is why do some other people not tick."

Nader got a running start on his philosophy—not at Princeton, where he was elected to Phi Beta Kappa, and graduated magna cum laude in 1955, nor at Harvard Law School, which was to him a "high-priced tool factory," but in a ten-room white clapboard house at 53 Hillsdale Avenue, Winsted, Connecticut, which was ruled over by Nadra Nader, an energetic, issue-oriented Lebanese from the village of Arsoun, who claimed he "never thought of working for anyone but myself." Nadra, with his bride Rose Bouziane from the neighboring town of Zahle, immigrated to the United States in 1925 and settled in Danbury, Connecticut, where Nadra ran a produce store for two years. But then the family moved to Winsted where Ralph, the youngest in the family, his brother Shafeek, and his two sisters, Claire and Laura, were born. Nadra sunk his savings into two small apartment buildings, opened the Highland Sweet Shop in downtown Winsted, and began selling food to the town's ten thousand residents. Later, he branched out and added baked goods. Then Nadra made the jump to what was to become his life's work—he opened a restaurant called the Highland Arms, a name Nadra devised from Winsted's location in the "highlands" of northeastern Connecticut and the word "arms" to symbolize the idea of "reaching out" to the community.

Nadra wanted his restaurant to be the social focus for Winsted, a place "where you feed the body and the mind." It was. Claire Nader, a Smith College graduate, who took her Ph.D. from Columbia University and is now a social scientist at the Oak Ridge National Laboratories in Tennessee, says "you couldn't get out of Father's restaurant without talking to him, and the conversation was never about the weather."

Nadra was passionately committed to issues. With his oldest son Shafeek, he was the scourge of town meetings, battling for everything from tax cuts to a community college. Inevitably, he made enemies, but never when it could be avoided. Rose says, "Like Ralph, Nadra had a knack; he could argue with you, but no one left the restaurant alienated. I remember once how Nadra argued fiercely with a customer. When the man got ready to leave, he stuck his face right up next to Nadra's. 'Nadra, I hate you!' he shouted. But my husband said to him in a soft voice: 'You don't know what you are missing. I love you.' "

At home, Nadra presided over a dinner table that was more like a college seminar. "My father would pose hypothetical social problems for the family to discuss," said Laura Nader Milleron, who is a full professor of anthropology at the University of California, Berkeley, and a part-time crusader for legal reform. The wife of Dr. Norman Milleron, a nuclear physicist, Laura is certain the family "think sessions" started her brother moving in the direction he ultimately chose. Nadra, who never had more than a grade-school education, saw education in the traditional immigrant sense as a key to success. Success, to him, however, did not necessarily mean dollars and cents as much as it meant the ability to serve people. In his eyes, and later in his son Ralph's eyes, the educated man who could serve the most was a lawyer. To Nadra, who is now retired, the law was the way to bring justice to the frustrated citizen. "We made Ralph understand that working for justice in the country is a safeguard of our democracy," Nadra said. At times, the rhetoric over the dinner plates would get heated. "Even if you were hurt, you were not allowed to run under fire; it was not appropriate to quit. You had to argue for the position you had, but the wonderful thing was that nothing said, no matter how heated, was allowed to disturb the family relationship," Claire said, but admitted smilingly that "if you couldn't stand the truth, you didn't ask Dad." One of Nader's teachers in high school, who also taught his brother and sisters, described the family this way: "They dream dreams and have visions."

The result of the dining-room debates plainly shows on Nader. He is intense when he pleads a cause or makes a charge, but he remains quick to smile and possesses a low-keyed wit that keeps his usually serious subjects from becoming so depressing that they turn the audience off. He can cite "fatfurters" as "the most dangerous missile" this country makes, or urge the makers of Wonder Bread, who claim "to build strong bodies 12 ways," to please explain to him just "one way." Talk to Nader about *Unsafe At Any Speed* and he will tell you not only that Truman Capote's *In Cold Blood* and Jessica Mitford's *American Way of Death* sold better, but that he "could have used either title" too. He also likes to recall the time he asked to examine a dusty government file and was told by a clerk "I've never seen a citizen before." Or the used car salesman in a *New Yorker* cartoon who is confidentially telling a prospective customer: "I happen to know Ralph Nader's mother drives this model." Or the Japanese journalist who told him he wanted to write a story about Nader for his magazine which he claimed was "a Japanese *Harper's*." After the interview, Nader was sent a copy of the magazine and found three pages of high quality color pictures of himself. The rest of the magazine was all pornography.

When Nader was born on February 27, 1934, Winsted was far from a storybook New England town. The depression had slowed the mills along the Mad River, and like the rest of the nation's small businessmen, Nadra kept long hours in his restaurant. The family shared the load. Ralph "took cash," a job he liked because it gave him a chance to talk to customers. It was at the cash register that Nader developed his habit of picking people's brains for information. Later, he substituted hitchhiking. "You met all kinds of people," says Nader, who in four years at Princeton never traveled any other way than by thumb power back and forth to Winsted. "Executives would pick me up, tree surgeons, bricklayers, doctors, truckdrivers. Not only did I learn a lot—outside of my father's restaurant it was the greatest education in the world—but you had to adapt to all kinds of personalities and, remember, you were helping people too. Some of the drivers would pick you up because they were sleepy and you would keep them awake just by talking to them."

As a youngster, he was not much different from any other. "I played sandlot baseball incessantly," says Nader, who even today is a baseball fan with encyclopedic knowledge of team rosters. But even here, when offered a ticket to the 1970 World Series, he couldn't see his way to taking a break from his work routine. When he wasn't playing baseball, it was basketball, in which his height made him a natural, and on Saturdays, his idea of excitement would be a ten-mile hike to Norfolk. "Everybody liked Ralph when he was a boy," Rose claims with a mother's understandable bias. Rose, like her husband, emphasized the value of knowledge, and the former school teacher in her never let an opportunity pass. Proud of her ancestral culture, she taught Ralph Arabic as a boy. When he would come home for lunch from public school, his hot soup and sandwich would be spiced with a chapter of Arabic history read aloud by Rose in her native tongue.

"One day Ralph comes home with a big bundle of books from the library," his mother recalled. " 'What's this?' I say. He tells me, 'Momma, that's the Congressional Record. I'm going to read them all.' That," Rose confessed shaking her head, "I can never forget."

The persons closest to Nader do not accept any of the labels attached to him. Reuben Robertson, a young lawyer, and one of the full-time associates at Nader's Center for Study of Responsive Law terms him a man "who really believes the Ten Commandments. He takes them seriously along with all the other clichés we were handed as children—democracy, the free enterprise system; Nader expects these things to be what they are supposed to be. But he is no puritan, he is not austere; he is, in fact, an exciting personality, a man with unlimited vision and unshakeable integrity." Nader expects dedication from his staffers. "We all live somewhat more parsimoniously than we like," says Robertson whose salary is not more than $15,000, considerably less than his Ivy League background could command in the corporate marketplace. Robertson doesn't subscribe to the notion that Nader is nothing more than a drone who gets weird satisfaction from his eighteen-hour day, his monk-like social life, and his disregard for ego-gratification of any kind. "True, he does what he does out of a compulsion. But he just loves it; he is having a ball."

From the female point of view, Joan Claybrook, once an aide to a Nader-target—Dr. William Haddon, Jr., the first head of the National Highway Traffic Safety Administration—and now a member of Public Interest Research Group, a Nader-run law firm, says the crusader is "a shy, sensitive, deep-feeling person." One of Nader's strong points, she says, is Nader's ability to choose people. "He has this knack of picking bright people without ego problems . . . He is as good at sizing up people as he is at everything else." This is important because Nader is now at a point where an error made by one of his staffers could hurt him in the public's eye.

To Lowell Dodge, a one-time Mississippi civil rights campaigner and now head of Nader's Center for Auto Safety, there is a great contrast between the public Nader and the private Nader. "On television or at a congressional hearing Nader appears intense, driving, ill-at-ease, but in person he is an incredibly interesting person. The closer you get to him, the more dedicated, the more real he is," Dodge says.

However, if the public looks to Nader now, it wasn't always so. After law school he put a good deal of time and effort into a proposal for an American ombudsman—an official whose job it would be to represent the individual citizen with a grievance against the government. The concept has been long-established in Scandinavia, and the need for an American ombudsman became clear to Nader when he started to work in George Athanson's law office. "Little people would come to the office asking for help with their $300 or $400 problem with a government agency. No lawyer would help them; the cases were too small. They'd just be pushed around."

Nader reasoned that the only way to help these "little people" was to create an ombudsman system, and in typical Nader style he started out to do just that. At his own expense he went to Europe and interviewed the ombudsmen in Denmark, Sweden, and Finland. "I came back to the United States, drafted a bill, and had it introduced in the Connecticut legislature in 1963," he said. The then 29-year-old lawyer's idea, however, met with massive indifference from Connecticut lawmakers. But to Nader the campaign was not a complete failure. "That was the start of the ombudsman

43

movement in this country," he said. And like most of the seeds Nader plants, the ombudsman idea is winning more support every year from consumers, lawyers, and government officials.

If his ombudsman campaign got off to a slow start, his first campus protest fell flat. At Princeton, in the era before Rachel Carson's *Silent Spring*, Nader was alarmed over the use of pesticides. When he found that DDT was killing the campus bird population, he was outraged. But his fellow students couldn't get all that upset over a few dead birds, and Nader found the editor of the campus newspaper wouldn't even print his letters of protest. Thirteen years after he graduated, however, Princeton gave so much credence to Nader's views that he was invited back to teach a course on the American corporation. Ted Jacobs, Nader's classmate at Princeton, and now his top aide, says it was obvious from the beginning that "Nader was unique, a special package, a man with vision coupled with enormous determination. He is fascinated with people and they respond. Just look at his constituency; it has someone from everywhere. Old ladies, students, the middle class, politicians from the left and right, even a few corporation executives. Here is one guy, they say, who has done something on his own. How else can you explain things like an unsolicited $10,000 check that turns up in the mail with the notation 'Here, spend this for your summer student project,' or the people who simply want to shake his hand on the street."

Nader himself may have come closer to explaining his appeal when he told an interviewer that the consumer rallied to his side in the auto safety controversy because Americans are "starved for acts of the individual in a conflict situation outside the sports arena."

It was at Princeton that Nader developed his penchant for staying up half the night, something he still does regularly. But now rather than pouring over textbooks ("Nader was the kind of guy who would go to the bathroom and come back telling you all about the new book he finished reading while sitting on the john," says Jacobs), Nader spends his nights preparing congressional testimony or plowing through trade magazines, letters, and technical reports. The variety of Nader's interests at Princeton were a preview of things to come. His major was Oriental studies and he mastered Chinese, Russian, and Spanish. In his third year he received a scholarship to study agricultural problems in Europe and on summer vacations he visited Indian reservations in New Mexico, Arizona, and California to collect information for a school paper on the exploitation of the Indian.

When Nader went to Harvard, he was disappointed to an extreme. He described his stay as "a three-year excursion through legal minutiae, typified by wooden logic and an imperviousness to what Oliver Wendell Holmes once called the 'felt necessities of our times.' " Jacobs, who also went to Harvard with Nader, put it more succinctly. "Ralph paid very little attention to the curriculum. He got through because he was smart." Like Princeton, Harvard now takes a special pride in its critic. His old law school paper went so far as to call him "the most outstanding man ever to receive a degree from this institution."

But if Nader did not set any scholastic records in Harvard, he was laying the foundation of what was to become his auto safety campaign. One of the first things that triggered Nader's thinking on the role of the automobile in highway safety was an article that appeared in the Harvard Law *Review* in 1956, written by Harold Katz, who contended that the law should take auto defects into consideration when it allocated liability. At the same time, Nader began reading the research of the Cornell Aeronautical Laboratory on automobile crashes, and this led him to the congressional hearings on traffic safety held in the mid-1950s. By now he had expanded his original idea of just doing an article on auto safety for the Harvard Law School *Record* to devoting his third-year thesis to the subject. Coincidentally, he got rid of the only car he ever owned—a 1949 Studebaker—not for safety's sake, but because he felt the car was simply not worth the trouble to maintain it. Since publishing his book, however, Nader says he would not buy a car because "it might be misconstrued as a product endorsement."

There is another reason for this: "I believe people should limit their car ownership; there are too many cars in the country. But I am not about to tell people that unless I do it myself. You've got to practice what you preach so that you can preach what you practice." This idea is not a meaningless homily for Nader. When he exposed conditions in meat plants, he stopped eating sandwich meats and frankfurters. He will not fly in a prop-driven airplane because he feels they are much more dangerous than jetliners, nor does he smoke since he accepted the correlation between smoking and cancer.

Nader doesn't do these things to be sanctimonious. He simply does what he believes he should, no matter how lonely the way.

And for Nader, the way has often been lonely. From 1958 to the year his book was published, 1965, Nader held crackpot status. He was just another young idealist who knocked on doors of state legislators in Connecticut and Massachusetts and was mostly ignored, patronized, or assumed to be just another ambulance-chasing lawyer whose attacks on the auto industry would in some way help fatten his bank account. But if Nader seemed an unlikely nemesis, he did not let the disdain of political sophisticates turn his course. He lectured to university students, garden clubs, wrote magazine articles, picked the brains of auto engineers and slowly accumulated an impressive store of knowledge about auto safety. He took time out in 1959 to serve a six-month hitch in the Army at Fort Dix, N.J. The Army had its own view of Nader's talent—Infantry Private Ralph Nader spent his tour of duty in the mess hall making things "like banana cake for 40,000 men." Between banana cakes, Nader haunted the motor pool to keep his auto expertise up to date. The Army never saw Nader's future. When he was mustered out, his discharge papers read: "Equivalent civilian occupation—Executive chef."

To Nader's critics, much of what he does is simply theatrics. He deliberately cultivates "an image of himself as a cross between Abraham Lincoln and one of Christ's apostles," says one. This critic cites Nader's tacky apartment as nothing more than "a piece of showmanship."

"Imagine a guy who collected $425,000 in a lawsuit from GM living in a place like that! I'm not saying he should live in a penthouse, but a rooming house with a landlady who takes messages for him smacks of Madison Avenue image-making to me."

One of Nader's most able adversaries is Lloyd Cutler, the Washington lawyer and lobbyist who was hired by the auto industry to ensure that the auto safety legislation passed by Congress was as consistent as possible with the industry's viewpoint. Cutler says that although Nader is a force for good in the political and social arena, he would be even more effective if he were less critical of the motives of the people he attacks. In congressional committee rooms the same type of criticism is heard. "When Nader first came here he was doctrinaire; everything was either this way or that—he would never agree to a middle ground. Well, he is learning to bend now; to understand that compromise is a necessary part of the system in Congress," one staff aide said.

Nader has even been attacked by the far left for his insistence that reform, not revolution, is the way to change the system. The Reverend Douglas Moore, chairman of the Black United Front in Washington, called him "the biggest damn racist in the United States."

According to Moore, Nader's campaign against pollution was an attempt to divert attention from the nation's black problem. Nor is Nader the darling of all consumers. He gets mail branding him a subversive for his attacks on American business and ridiculing him as a know-it-all who is trying to abridge the consumer's freedom to make his own mistakes. Some of Nader's critics attack him simply because they feel he is attacking them. This type of person, for instance, is someone who spent $3,500 on an automobile and will defend it to the death. If Nader denounces the car as defective, the owner interprets this as a reflection on his judgment and intelligence. This reaction was not uncommon among some Corvair owners who never even conceded the possibility that

47

the car might be faulty, basing their argument on the grounds that it had not turned over while they were driving it. There even exists a *Corvair Society of America* which is dedicated to protecting the car from Nader's attacks.

But the most frequently repeated criticism of Nader today is that he is becoming an institution; that he is turning into the same kind of bureaucracy he opposes. This charge is backed up by pointing to his growing staff, his various organizations, and his increasing need for funds.

If Nader divides himself, these critics argue, his mystique will be diluted, and his effectiveness will dwindle. They point to the Nader Raider organization as a source of this tendency. "Every year it gets bigger. How long is he going to be able to control the enterprise? Remember Ralph Nader is on the hook for everything those students do. What happens when one of them makes a gaff? You know a kid can be a lemon, too. They lie, cheat, and take bribes just like the rest of us establishment types," an aide to a consumer-oriented senator said.

The danger that Nader's credibility may be undermined as he expands seems valid to many. "GM can be caught lying and making defective cars, but if Nader is caught just once on something big, he will be destroyed," said a Washington lobbyist.

Others have grown tired of predicting Nader's demise. "Since 1966, I have been saying he is spreading himself too thin, he will make a mistake, the press will get bored with him. But it hasn't happened yet. Nader is here and he is going to stay," said a former member of a regulatory agency.

As for Nader himself, he sees no need to change anything he has done, is doing, or plans to do. If anything, the critics' predictions puzzle him. He doesn't subscribe to the idea that HE is the consumer movement. Nor does he want a consumer movement based on his personality. He is not, as Ted Jacobs said, "building an empire."

What, then, is Nader doing? His awesome goal, stated in his characteristically flamboyant style, "is nothing less than a qualitative reform of the industrial revolution." Quite a job for what one Naderologist termed "a raggedy pants Arab boy." But Nader feels it can be done. "If one way fails, we'll try another, and we'll keep trying until the job is done."

He insists with Zola-like intensity that "the individual can still generate a momentum for change; he can challenge large complex institutions whether governmental or corporate. There still is a very critical role for citizen strategy that will improve life."

Nader knows exactly what his target is. "In Russia the enemy would be the government." In the United States, big corporations which have become "private governments" are the enemy.

"I am trying to tell people that if they can just organize to make the establishment obey its own rules, they will have created a peaceful revolution of tremendous proportions. This is not radicalism. Who are the real radicals in our society? Is it the hippies who burn the flag which is a symbol of the United States or is it those who pollute the air, the land, and the water that make up the reality that is the United States?

"If we are really concerned about violence why don't we talk about really big forms of violence. I don't know of any horde of hippies or yippies who have managed to smog New York City or contaminate the Gulf of Mexico. But I know companies that have done that. Consolidated Edison smogged New York, Chevron Oil dumped hundreds of thousands of barrels of oil in the Gulf of Mexico with impunity until the law finally came down on it, then only with a $1 million fine—the equivalent of about one hour's gross revenue of Chevron's parent company, Standard Oil. What we have done is to allow the term violence to be defined for us by those very people who produce most of it.

"Is the person who wants to stop this a radical? I say the real radical is the head of the giant corporation whose corporate activity does violence to the health, safety, and well being of his fellowman.

" . . . None of these persons are punished. Corporate crime should be punished, but it isn't, because we have not been conditioned to think in terms of curbing corporate power or punishing it for excesses. There is a corporate crime wave in this country of unprecedented proportions, but if you look at the FBI crime statistics, what do you see? Have you ever seen a company on the "Ten Most Wanted" list? Do you ever see statistics as to how much corporations stole from consumers?"

But corporate violence is just one of a chain of problems facing the United States. Poverty, racial injustice, the dehumanizing effects of big government, all of these must be solved, Nader believes.

"My job is to try to bring these issues out in the open where they cannot be ignored. . . . We have got to know what we are doing to ourselves."

The size of his task is herculean, but Nader never considers the possibility of failure. To him, "the only real defeat is giving up, just as the only real aging is the erosion of one's ideals."

3

NADER AND THE PRESS

The power of the media to determine each day what shall seem important and what shall be neglected is a power unlike any that has been exercised since the Pope lost his hold on the secular mind.

—Walter Lippmann

In June, 1961, Ralph Nader, a 27-year-old Connecticut lawyer left the Moscow Hotel off Red Square, Moscow, and melted into the workday crowd on the streets. He made his way past the yellowish-brown cement buildings which give the city its gloomy cast, and finally turned into one, noticed only by an occasional Russian who eyed with envy the western cut of Nader's suit, a rumpled creation picked off a pipe rack in downtown Hartford. Once inside the building, he opened an office door, and in his best Princeton-learned Russian, announced to the first person he met that he wanted to see the man in charge.

"Nader? Ralph Nader? Who is Ralph Nader? What does he want?" came the annoyed query from the Russian bureaucrat when told a skinny "Amerikanski" armed with a pad and pencil had barged, uninvited, into his office. The Russian was an editor of *Krokodil*, a mass-circulation magazine which uses cartoons to lampoon communist bureaucrats who develop capitalist leanings or whose mismanagement of the economy inflicts yet another blow on the consumer-goods starved Russian worker.

What *did* Nader want? His enemies might like to fancy him as an undercover agent for a communist-backed plot to destroy General Motors. Had he come for new instructions to carry out what *Barron's*, the Wall Street financial journal, once described as his campaign of "guerrilla journalism . . . to decrease U.S. consumer consumption as a means of changing the system of capitalism and creating a socialist society"?

The less sensational truth was that Nader was simply hoping to earn $40 to help defray the cost of a two-week vacation in the Soviet Union. Unbeknownst to the editors of *Krokodil*, Nader had singled them out for an interview he planned to sell to the *Christian Science Monitor*, "one of my favorite newspapers," under an agreement worked out with the *Monitor*'s business page editor, George Favre. Well aware of the Soviet's fetish for time-consuming bureaucratic procedures, particularly when western journalists want to see government officials, Nader had merely decided to do the thing he does best—challenge the system directly.

"I just walked in off the street and told them I wanted to talk about how they put their magazine together. They didn't know what to do with me, so I kept talking, and after a while we sat down and I got them to tell me what I wanted to know."

This was Nader the reporter in action. His brashness is invariably tempered with a disarming earnestness that leads even Washington's industry lobbyists—never famed for their graciousness toward critics—to often preface a torrent of abuse with: "Personally, I like Ralph . . . but . . ."

If he had chosen journalism, Nader might have been able to line the shelves of his tacky apartment with a pride of Pulitzer Prizes for his investigations into auto safety, the meat industry, gas pipelines, and coal mine safety. But Nader never seriously considered newspapering because "it was always the law with me."

His preference for the law, however, did not stop him from becoming a journeyman reporter-writer with a waspish style and a range of topics that prompted General Motors Chairman James Roche to brand him as one of the "bitter gypsies of dissent" who plague society. Roche was at least partially right—gypsy-like, Nader honed his writing style by bumming around the world on vacations and turning out articles on what he saw. He sent the *Monitor* stories ranging from agricultural problems in Ethiopia and the economic prospects for Brazil's Altiplano area to the meat industry in Uruguay and the legal system in Scandinavia. But Nader's mother claims his newspaper career started when he began delivering his hometown newspaper, the Winsted *Evening Citizen*, and "built up the largest route in town."

Nader himself says he got his first real journalism experience at Harvard when he was picked as an editor for the Harvard Law School *Record*, the school newspaper. To Nader, even in his student days, the value of a newspaper as a communication tool was clear. "The *Record* was one of the most influential legal publications in the nation since it went to ten thousand Harvard Law School alumni as well as the students," is the way he explained his push to get an editorship.

But it was in magazines that Nader really planted the first seeds of his famous crusades. As early as April 11, 1959—six years before Senator Abraham Ribicoff of Connecticut opened the Senate hearing that led to the auto safety standards—Nader's byline appeared on an article in *The Nation* called "The Safe Car You Can't Buy." In the October 12, 1963, issue, he wrote on "Fashion or Safety" in automobiles and when he published *Unsafe At Any Speed* in November, 1965, *The Nation* ran an article of his called "The Corvair Story." What price success? *The Nation* now advertises itself as the first national magazine to discover Nader.

If *The Nation* was first, however, it was the *New Republic* and its editor Gilbert A. Harrison who gave Nader his most effective forum. He bombarded *New Republic* readers with exposés on "fat dogs" and "shamburgers," X rays, job safety, coalminer's black lung disease, business crimes, filthy fish, and "The Infernal, Eternal, Internal Combustion Engine."

53

Under his *modus operandi*, an article in the *New Republic* was usually timed to coincide with an upcoming congressional hearing or to spark a wave of newspaper stories on an issue Nader felt was being ignored. Nader also was aware that the *New Republic* was read closely by and provided an outlet for some of the capital's best reporters, who use its pages to write about controversial issues in a way their newspapers do not allow. Nader, despite his "star quality," never managed to coax more than $150 an article out of the magazine's business office, but in 1969 the *New Republic* did give him a fringe benefit—its first annual "Public Defender Award" which came complete with an inscribed silver bowl and a slab-of-beef dinner in the Chinese Room of the Mayflower Hotel where Nader harangued the audience over dessert with a speech on how Americans "spend nine times more money on the control of halitosis and B.O. than we do on air pollution."

When Nader wasn't publishing his own articles he was salting the *New Republic* staff with information and story ideas. His key contact in this connection was James Ridgeway who hammered away at consumer issues in the Nader style. It was Ridgeway who also gave *New Republic* readers the first detailed account of GM's investigation of Nader's personal life in a series of hard-hitting articles with such titles as: "GM Hired the Dick," "GM Comes Clean," and "The Nader Affair."

Some magazine editors, however, never even let Nader get his foot in the door. Congressman Benjamin S. Rosenthal (D-N.Y.), a consumer spokesman, says a former assistant editor for *Good Housekeeping* told him Nader's comments were cut out of a story about the dangers children face on school buses.

"First my editor claimed that there would be a space problem. Finally, he said that the advertisers would blow their collective tops if they ever saw Nader's name in a *Good Housekeeping* story," the editor told Rosenthal.

In what is becoming typical of Nader, he has moved on and the *New Republic* is no longer a major forum for him.

The way Nader sees the consumer movement and his role in it, cutting back on his contributions to the pages of the *New Republic*, a magazine with 200,000 readers, is the right thing to do since he can now reach more consumers in other ways, and that is all that counts. He assumes the *New Republic* understands this in the same way he does. "I don't break new crusades any more by writing the kind of articles I did for the *New Republic*. I can't justify it. If it is the difference between writing an article for one magazine and putting out a news release that will be read by millions of newspaper readers, I must choose the newspapers. It is just that simple."

Not every newspaper, of course, is eager to run with Nader. The nation's biggest paper—the two-million-daily circulation New York *Daily News*—rates low on Nader's scale. "It may as well be run by Jay Gould, the robber baron, for all it cares about the consumer. The readers get the horror stories, the bank robberies, the sensational trials, and some international news. When the *News* does print a consumer-oriented story, the next day it is denounced on the editorial page. The *News* has simply failed the people," Nader says.

He gives equally bad marks to the small town newspaper that sleeps with the biggest industry in its area no matter what crimes the industry commits, barring one: pulling advertising from its pages. A North Carolina newspaper, he said, once reported after a speech he had given "that while I was denouncing the tobacco industry, I had a cigarette dangling from my hand. I haven't smoked since 1961. It was a lie, a clear lie. But they figured by putting that in the story it would discredit my attack on tobacco."

The newspaper that gets Nader's blessing as "one of the best in the nation" for consumer news is the *Times Union* of Rochester, New York. "It really tears into local business practices with one full page a week of hard-hitting consumer stories." Allen H. Neuharth, president of the Gannett chain, which owns the *Union*, maintains that newspapers should take the leading role in the consumer movement, even to the point of sponsoring community consumer councils.

Until 1969, when it was bought by the Knight Newspaper

NADER: THE PEOPLE'S LAWYER

chain, "the worst newspaper in the country for consumer news," according to Nader, "was the Philadelphia *Inquirer*." Then owned by millionaire Walter H. Annenberg, President Nixon's ambassador to Great Britain, the 500,000-circulation paper seldom gave Nader's consumer revolt a line of type. When it did mention his name it was usually to denounce him as it did when the University of Pennsylvania Law School gave him an award. Nader, who makes no effort to cultivate editors or publishers—"that's what a corporation lawyer would do"—claims he doesn't know why the *Inquirer* ignored him, but "obviously this whole consumer movement struck someone at the top in the wrong way." Rose De Wolf, a popular columnist for the *Inquirer* who now works for the Philadelphia *Bulletin*, sent Nader a crumpled sheet of paper from an unfinished story. According to the lady newshawk, an *Inquirer* editor told her "Nader is not welcome in our pages."

Syndicated columnist Alice Widener is another member of the "I-Hate-Nader-Club." A column of hers attempting to link him through innuendo to left-wing revolutionaries had the image-conscious Nader looking for a way to sue. The columnist pointed out that Nader was a consulting editor for *Hard Times*, a muckraking newsletter started in 1969 by James Ridgeway and Andrew Kopkind of the *New Republic*, and Robert Sherrill, a correspondent for *The Nation*. According to Alice Widener, *Hard Times*, which has since merged with *Ramparts* magazine, was dedicated to "changing the system" and printed stories written by another consulting editor, Fred Gardner, who "testified in Chicago on behalf of Tom Hayden and Abbie Hoffman, U.S.-indicted defendants in the conspiracy-to-riot trial; by such system changers as Belgian revolutionary Marxist Ernest Mandel, who is banned from France and the U.S.; and by Robin Blackburn, guest of honor at a Socialist Scholars conference held at Hofstra College, N.Y." Miss Widener went on to list other radical contributors to *Hard Times*, including two members of the "revolutionary Students for a Democratic Society." To Nader, "this was guilt by association in the old McCarthy style" and should not go unchallenged. So challenge he did and found that newspaper columnists and their syndicates were as good at blocking redress as any of the nation's big corporations. His attempt to get the list of all the newspapers which published the Widener column in order to write a letter to the editors stating his side of the story was rebuffed with the legal argument that the list was a "trade secret." Widener's lawyers claimed the list of subscribers was privileged because the salability of the column could be affected if it was publicly known how many outlets a columnist had, or perhaps had lost from the year before. "Without the list, anyone maligned in a column can never get his side of the story to the public without the time-consuming and often futile process of tracking down the individual newspapers on his own," Nader said.

The only other recourse is to sue and Ralph de Toledano, the right-wing King Features columnist brought Nader to that point with a column that began: "Ralph Nader, the man for all seasons of the consumer movement, may find himself unseasonable on one account: No return for 1969 can be found by the Internal Revenue Service for the Center for Study of Responsive Law, which Nader heads." De Toledano had hit on the one issue that can fire Nader's Lebanese temper: money. General Motors was the first to impugn Nader's motives by attempting to find out if he was getting a rake-off from law suits filed against GM by Corvair owners. Lobbyists have spent hours over their martinis trying to figure out how Nader siphons money into an imaginary Swiss bank account, and who, in which industries, is paying him not to attack a product. The oldest charge, and apparently one that will never die, is that Nader collects fees for referring cases to other lawyers. He doesn't, but Nader feels the gossip can damage his poor-but-honest image unless it is stifled. However, no matter how many times he proves the stories false, there are some newspapers that will not stop digging for the Nader-and-money angle. One publisher, who syndicated canned editorials to newspapers around the United States, attacked Nader for accepting $425,000 to settle his lawsuit with GM. If Nader was really concerned about auto safety, he would give the award to Corvair owners and let them buy new safe cars, the editorialist wrote. His editorial was sophisticatedly titled: "Nader—Put your Money Where Your Mouth Is."

In the case of the De Toledano article, the columnist was wrong; Nader had filed a return. "The problem here was to get the word out to all those readers who believed De Toledano's column. I sent a lawyer to negotiate with King Features and the firm finally agreed to print a retraction," Nader said. But King Features refused to give him a list of De Toledano's newspapers, citing the same reason that had been given in the Widener case. Nader, however, did not give up. He finally uncovered a list showing every paper that took a King Feature. Each of the newspapers got a letter from Nader explaining how he had filed a tax return and urging them to print his letter even if they had run King Features' retraction.

To guard against similar attacks, Nader is considering becoming a columnist in his own right, writing about consumer affairs on a two- or three-times-a-week basis. In addition to helping him reach new audiences, such a column would give him a platform from which to answer his critics directly and quickly.

Nader does not have problems with all columnists. He worked closely with the late Drew Pearson, and he now feeds information to Jack Anderson who took over Pearson's column. For Nader, Anderson's column, with its high readership among House and Senate members and their key aides, a group Nader cultivates with intensity, is a proper tool for prodding those lawmakers who tend either to waver or, worse in Nader's mind, to compromise when the fight with industry gets rough. Not everyone sees Nader's use of Anderson's column the way he does, however. His critics point out that it is an example of how Nader will turn on his friends if they fail to accept his black-and-white approach to an issue.

Again, unlike many of Anderson's tipsters, Nader collects nothing. Anderson, however, is not Nader's only beneficiary. Nader is a cornucopia of leads for every newsman he deals with. But when he is ready to release a story of his own making, no favorites are played. "A lot of reporters want exclusives, but once you start that game you begin legitimately alienating people. Nor is an exclusive fair to the public. Why should I give an exclusive about an automobile defect to one reporter? That would only get to a certain number of citizens—why shouldn't it get to all the citizens?"

To Nader, reaching as many persons as possible is the key to a successful consumer movement. "The consumer needs the information to make an educated choice in the marketplace, and the press has the job of getting the information to the consumer," he says. To make sure his press "delivery system" does not rust, Nader keeps close ties with an impressive list of Washington newsmen. His success with them is based on two pillars: his credibility, and his almost boyish earnestness in peddling a story, a welcome change from the cloying locker-room affability of some of his public relations counterparts in industry. But if Nader is personally convincing, he is also an expert on the workings of the media, in keeping with his philosophy that "I like to know ten times more than I really need to know about a subject."

Nader is familiar with the deadline times and the office politics of all the major papers he deals with. He understands the wire systems of United Press International and the Associated Press as well as the idiosyncrasies of Washington's deskmen and bureau chiefs. He has sat in the editorial board room of *The New York Times* and explained to those present why consumer news qualifies as a part of "All the News That's Fit to Print," and he has passed tips across the table at meetings of the Gridiron Club, a group which modestly bills itself as fifty of the most influential newsmen in Washington. Unlike most lawyers, Nader has perfected the art of turning his legalistic arguments into readable copy designed to hold the attention of news editors.

"I have enough material to come out with a new statement every day; literally every day. And it is good stuff; not sensational stuff, but good stuff. I don't do it; you've got to have a sense of timing and a sense of limitation."

He cites Wisconsin's Senator William Proxmire, a consumer

advocate in Congress, as an example of how not to publicize consumer news. "Proxmire overdoes it. He comes out every day and he usually has good stories, but he often gets only a few paragraphs in the newspaper. I try not to wear out my welcome." Nevertheless, Nader is seldom out of eyeshot of one of the hundreds of news tickers that chatter away in offices around Washington, and if a consumer story breaks, he starts phones ringing in newsrooms around the city to offer a comment or a related tip.

If it is his own story he is trying to get into print, Nader will try to deliver his statement or a copy of a letter he has written directly to the reporter he hopes will handle the story. If he can't do the job himself, a pleasant, long-haired hippie-type may show up with a plain white envelope on which one word—"Nader"—is scrawled in ink in the upper lefthand corner. The letter is followed by a phone call from Nader who often is in a booth in a congressional office building or at an airport waiting to catch a plane to begin yet another speech-making trip. "Tell him it's urgent! Tell him it's Ralph!" is enough to get even the panic-proof city room switchboard operators to cut in on a caller who may be keeping Nader from reaching a reporter. Normally, however, Nader often follows a pony express-like route through Washington that takes him personally into the newsrooms of all his regulars—United Press International, the Associated Press —together they reach all the nation's 1,754 daily newspapers —the Washington *Post* and the Washington *Evening Star*, the *Wall Street Journal, The New York Times, Time* magazine, *Newsweek*, but not *U.S. News & World Report*, labeled by Nader as "the magazine that asks questions it never answers"; the Chicago *Daily News* and the Chicago *Sun-Times*, but not the Chicago *Tribune* which "is just now beginning to creep out of the hoary past." The Los Angeles *Times*, the Gannett newspaper chain, and the Newhouse chain were also on Nader's list of drops.

Like a wire service, Nader breaks his stories down to enable newspapers to make the most of a local angle. For example, in the meat controversy of 1967, he uncovered a trove of information involving meat inspection violations at plants all over the United States. He released a report in Washington, but he also sent out a state-by-state breakdown on meat plant conditions to newspapers from Hartford to Los Angeles, from Minneapolis to St. Louis. Nader will even try to spot a story in the *Christian Science Monitor*, though the paper may require up to thirty-six hours lead time.

But he tries hardest to hit the *Wall Street Journal* because it is the "only consistently critical publication in the business world." Nader says *The New York Times* is a poor second. "The *Times* business page has not been noted for its crusading zeal. It has been very closely associated with the business institutions it covers. Some of its reporters have come right out of these institutions and they have just never had that investigative instinct." But changes may be in the making. Nader says that *Times* vice-president and columnist James Reston is "very dissatisfied with the business page."

Nader does not rely on television to tell his story. He admits "I am probably wrong," and some of his aides insist he is, but "I am a little old-fashioned when it comes to the print media; I think it has more of an impact. It certainly does with the people who are responsible for making the key decisions in industry and government." Nader admits television can create an issue almost overnight but so far it has led the way in only two consumer causes—the fight for better meat inspection and the story on cyclamates, which Nader says NBC actually broke.

Increasingly conscious of the medium's impact, he makes periodic guest appearances on the late night talk programs to reach their massive audiences. In 1970 he put together an educational television network series called "The Nader Report," a documentary show that focussed on such subjects as the company town of Kannapolis, North Carolina, where Cannon Mills virtually controls the lives of 35,000 inhabitants and on how the $125 billion food industry waters down orange juice and chemically doctors food.

Nevertheless, Nader is under growing pressure from his younger staffers to do more with television. They argue that certain problems such as pollution, with its strikingly visual manifestations, can be dramatized more effectively on television. They also want to expose the public to Nader's charismatic personality, thus attracting increased support for his causes. Ironically, they insist that their chief, the arch nemesis of big business, should be marketed to the American public as efficiently as a dishwasher detergent.

To those who argue that he "uses" the press Nader replies that the consumer movement actually has produced a better press.

"When I came to Washington in 1964, there weren't more than eight full-time investigative reporters in a city that had about one thousand working reporters. The *Wall Street Journal* had only one investigative reporter to cover industry's dealings with the government. *The New York Times*, the most influential newspaper in the nation, did not have even one. But now, because of the stories uncovered by the consumer movement, the press is changing. What I really think has happened is that the consumer movement has matured the press."

One indication of this new maturity is that the practice of hiring consumer reporters has become so widespread that even the Chicago *Tribune*, never known to reject an opportunity to lag behind, now has a full-time consumer reporter. But to Nader, the most important change in newspapers as far as the individual consumer is concerned, is this:

"Newspapers have become far less reluctant to name products by brand name in critical context. This means the newspaper reader, who is a consumer, is getting the information he needs to make an educated decision on which product he will buy. The newspapers are finally telling their readers exactly which automobiles, by make and model, are defective, which drugs, by brand names, are more expensive or harmful, and are even listing the specific names of children's toys labelled harmful by consumer groups or government agencies. To me, this is the news media's biggest advance."

Without the press, Nader admits he would be nothing. But

the press courts him precisely because he is Nader, a man without guile, without ego, a man who is almost hysterically honest—attributes always in short supply in Washington. Every year lobbyist and public relations men for the major corporations spend millions of dollars on "press relations"—a euphemism for propagandizing their point of view among newsmen. The government does the same. Almost every agency is equipped with a public information office, and Xerox machines multiply handouts designed to justify every governmental decision or lack of decision.

The press has long been pampered by government and industry, and though favors are usually small, they are many. There are gifts at Christmas, junkets to warmer climes under the guise of covering newsworthy stories, hard-to-get football tickets, free-lance assignments for industry publications, and the perennial invitation to yet another free lunch. For the newsman who needs a new car, the automakers can produce a discount as high as fifty percent or a leasing arrangement so favorable as to bring a blush to the face of the most hardened freeloader of the Fourth Estate. The promise of a good-paying job is always there to be dangled in front of the reporter, and becomes a type of "deferred bribe" for those who refrain from rocking the government-industry boat with critical news coverage. There are television and radio panel spots open for favored reporters who can earn an extra $50 to $125 with weekly appearances on such shows as the AFL-CIO-produced Labor News Conference. Even the United States Information Agency offers a $50 stipend to Washington newspapermen to appear on its radio news panel shows. Not to be forgotten is one of industry's oldest dodges—the annual "awards" for the best written story, a charade that enables industry to funnel money into the hands of newsmen in the name of promoting journalism.

There is no Machiavellian plot here. Industry and the government give without visible strings. The newsmen take and claim that their news judgment is in no way affected. But many newsmen can't quite free themselves from at least a twinge of guilt.

Enter Nader. If there is a love affair here, it may be because, subconsciously, the reporter sees Nader as the embodiment of what he, or his paper, should be, but often is not. Nader does not compromise. His ethics come in two colors—black and white—and Nader buys few drinks for newspapermen and even fewer lunches. Robert Wager, counsel for Senator Abraham Ribicoff's Senate Subcommittee on Executive Reorganization, complains that Nader walks the line so carefully "he wouldn't even let me pay for a hamburger I ordered him one afternoon when we were going over auto industry files at my desk." Unlike industry, Nader has never thrown a party for newsmen at a plush Washington hotel. He does not show up in newsrooms during Christmas week with a fifth of whiskey beautifully wrapped for the newsman who gave him the most lines of copy, nor does he spend his Friday afternoons sipping beer or bourbon at the National Press Club with the nest of burnt-out newsmen who frequent the 63-year-old club, once the watering spot for the capital's best journalists, but now a combination geriatrics ward and haven for second-rate public relations men. The closest Nader ever came to joining the club was to take an office on the twelfth floor of the National Press Building where, holed up behind an unmarked door and surrounded by mountains of files and newspapers, he would peck out long, single-spaced letters to cabinet officials and congressmen.

Like business, the news media were slow to understand the consumer wave. Since World War II, the Washington Press Corps, now about two thousand strong, has been almost doglike in its devotion to the concept that only institutions make news. If a story did not come from Congress, a government agency, a labor organization, a big corporation or an official spokesman for some organized group, it was seldom considered important. Institutionalized news sources made a newsman's life simple in Washington, but they left no outlet for an individual citizen with a gripe against the government or one of the other institutions. Nader was acutely aware of this phenomenon because it effectively blocked his own access to the press. But he lit upon the right tactic to force his way onto the front pages.

"I learned one thing early and it was probably the most important lesson. In a really controversial issue, especially one dealing with big business, the press will cover the story much more readily if the issues are paraded and discussed than go out on its own and investigate. When I was trying to get newspapers to name automobiles by make and models . . . for example, not refer to the Corvair as 'a medium-sized American car with a rear engine,' I learned that one of the best ways to do this was to go into forums such as the congressional committee.

"The press would not be likely to send out droves of investigative reporters to dig up a story about unsafe automobiles, but if these facts were brought to a congressional hearing then the press would cover them.

"One of the reasons for this was the fact that not only did the press lack investigative reporters, but if there was any heat from the advertisers, it was much easier for an editor or a publisher to say, 'Look, I am just doing my job—we have to cover congressional hearings,' or, 'We have to cover the courts.' If the newspaper had launched its own investigation, then it would be guilty of crusading—the worst possible sin in the eyes of advertisers.

"The reporters themselves were also woefully ignorant about the law of libel—they equated product libel with personal libel and thought that dealing with a corporation or a product of a corporation was the equivalent of dealing with an individual. In the early days of the consumer movement, newsmen thought if they ever wrote a story critical of a GM product, even though I gave them accurate information, the roof would fall in. When they finally got their feet wet things were different."

Another misconception was that people were just not interested in reading about consumer problems. "Who's interested in auto safety? Who's interested in hearing about hazards and defective products?" were the questions Nader was asked in the early days.

"Newsmen really missed the temper of the times," Nader says, "and the reason they did was that they were not listening to the voice of the people. If they had gone down to the local bar or talked to a housewife, they would have found that the conversations were about someone's lemon car or the appliance that didn't work or the high cost of auto insurance. If people talk about these things, you can be sure they are interested in reading about them." Listening to people talk is the basis of Nader's own news judgment: "If they talk about a consumer problem, I know they will support anyone who can bring it into the public arena and get action."

The press never saw this consumer revolt forming, says Nader, because of its "boilerplate type thinking about what is news; what is not news; what you shouldn't talk about; what you should talk about. The consumer movement has helped dispel a lot of this, and in fact, it has given the press more guts.

"We are getting reporters now that are increasingly able to see news as news, not news because it happens to come out of an established institution. The press is beginning to realize that poverty lawyers can make news, people in the consumer movement can make news—the fact is, news depends on the subject matter and how accurate it is, not whether it comes from the White House or an agency like the Federal Trade Commission."

According to Nader, the press, busy "watching institutions," allowed investigative reporting "to turn into a journalistic disaster area."

"I remember in 1964—two years before auto safety became a big issue—I talked to a *New York Times* reporter and tried to convince him that auto safety was a big story. I told him the industry was deliberately suppressing safety innovations and he looked at me and said, 'So what else is new? Everybody knows that!' The same thing was true of the meat and poultry contamination stories, both of which resulted in new legislation. In the meat controversy of 1967 I took a lot of my material to reporters at the Agriculture Department.

The New York Times reporter wasn't interested, nor was the *Wall Street Journal* man. They felt they had been covering the Agriculture Department for years and if there was a big story they would have learned about it from their informants on the inside." What Nader offered them was information they could have found for themselves. The basis for the meat exposé was simply a report by Agriculture Department inspectors describing the conditions in meat-packing plants that had been stashed into Agriculture Department files.

When Nick Kotz of the Des Moines *Register-Tribune*, who was not a regular Agriculture Department reporter, learned about the report, he recognized it as a great story, pushed it day after day and won a Pulitzer Prize. His paper stood behind him even though it cost $60,000 in lost ad revenue, Nader said. "A little while later, the poultry contamination story came up. When I took the information back to the same reporters, they still weren't interested, despite the impact of the meat story," Nader said.

Nader claims that reporters who cover a government agency on a day-to-day basis have been the last to see the value of investigative reporting. "They are around the agency for years; they get to be like the agency's public information office. They don't want to embarrass the agency because they have so many contacts. So they become protective. But on the other hand, these contacts feed them only routine stuff."

Before his arrival on the scene, most of Washington's agency reporters, according to Nader, "were free to ignore a story, or could work out a trade off with an agency official who would promise the reporters a leak on an upcoming story if they would lay off or go easy on an embarrassing story."

As a result, he prefers to deal with general assignment reporters who are quicker to evaluate information on a strictly newsworthy basis.

His greatest scorn is reserved for Washington's labor reporters who are "sitting on some of the greatest stories in the country."

"The Labor Department is a sinecure for old-time labor reporters or a beat editors use for training cubs whose only aim is to get out of the agency as fast as they can and go to one of the more glamorous beats."

Consequently, Nader says, the public is not getting the information it should. Labor Department reporters, for instance, have neglected the "wild non-enforcement of the Walsh-Healey Act" which sets minimum wage and safety standards for private firms doing business with the government.

"Little is being done about the corruption in union elections and the mishandling of pension funds. They've got pension reports filed by labor unions stacked seven, eight feet high over at the Labor Department and nobody even bothers reading them. But everybody knows about the manipulation of pension funds and the political basis on which they are invested and how few rights old-time workers have in pension funds."

Nader ranks automotive editors almost as low as he does labor reporters. "I learned a long time ago you just don't take auto news to the automotive editor. He thinks his only job is to write a column praising the new car models which will be run alongside an auto industry ad in the back of the paper. If the automotive editor isn't doing that, he is interviewing auto industry executives about car production or probing for gossip about who will get what job in the Detroit executive suites."

Nader cited the competition between the Detroit *News* and the Detroit *Free Press*—as an example of people's desire to read about real automobile problems—safety defects, repair gyps, poor quality control on the assembly line, and shoddy warranty work.

"For years the two Detroit papers carried the routine coverage of the auto industry. But when the auto safety controversy arose in 1965, the Detroit *News* hired reporter Robert Irvin from United Press International. Irvin was told, in effect, 'This is a new ball game. We want coverage and we are taking auto news off the automotive page. If you get a story it will be played like any other story—on the front page, if it is good.'

"The Detroit *Free Press*, on the other hand, was stuck with it's old-time auto editor and he kept writing the same old stuff. In 1966 and 1967 the disparity between the two papers began to grow immensely with Irvin writing five or six articles a week and turning into the most relentless auto writer in the nation.

"What was the result? Everybody who wanted to really know what was going on in the auto industry, the biggest business in the nation, knew they had to get the Detroit *News*. There was just no question about it.

"Irvin's investigative reporting approach to the automakers gained him a huge readership and the *Free Press*, in order to compete, had to change its style to imitate Irvin."

Does Nader have the nerve to investigate the press despite his heavy reliance on it? He says "yes," and the first target could be *The New York Times*.

"There should be a study of *The New York Times*. Why the *Times* covers what it does. What are the priorities? Why doesn't it have more investigative reporters? Why is it so poor on coverage of the way big banks manipulate the economy? What about the likes and dislikes of its editors? How high up are the decisions on editorials made? *The Times* is a world of its own and a study would be worth doing. It hasn't been done as yet because I feel that other things—such as auto safety, food, health, and safety are more pressing."

Nader's plan would be to have teams of investigators examine the press on a local basis. The only way to tackle press reform, he reasons, is to determine what a newspaper does and doesn't do in its own circulation area. For example, "the Washington *Post* will fearlessly cover issues dealing with the Pentagon, Standard Oil, and General Motors, but when it comes to its local area, it is not as active in investigating price-fixing in supermarkets or the fire hazards in Washington restaurants, which are very bad. The reason for this is advertising pressure. GM or Standard Oil doesn't support the Washington *Post*. The local drug chains, the department stores, and the restaurants pay the paper millions of dollars in advertising revenues. There isn't a memo posted in newsrooms saying not to cover some local problem, but there is a lack of sensitivity, an inbred lack of interest, in doing so."

Nader's criticism of the press, however, is tame compared to those who see Nader as a sort of Frankenstein's monster created by editors of liberal newspapers who relish an opportunity to put an antibusiness slant on the news, or embarrass a government official. "If Nader didn't exist, the eastern establishment press would have created him," says one corporate executive who feels that Nader literally has been shaped by the press into something he is not. "You read the newspapers and you come away with the feeling that Nader is a penniless underdog who is on God's side because he eats lunch out of a brown paper bag, and, according to GM's detectives, still is a virgin. That is a lot of crap. Nader is a Princeton-Harvard Law School graduate with the IQ of a genius. If you add the money he got from his General Motors law suit, I bet his income over the last three years is about the same as GM's Chairman, Jim Roche. Sure he lives in a rooming house. That is nice; very modest. But how does it square with the fact that the guy is such an egomaniac that he made more speeches last year than a presidential candidate? Why don't the newspapers print that side of the Nader story?"

Others criticize the press for being Nader's whore. Nader uses the press, this argument runs, much in the same manner as did the late Senator Joseph McCarthy. Nader will release copies of a letter or a report to the press before he sends it to a corporate chief, or a government agency. The newspapers print Nader's charge, but industry or the government is given small space, if any, for a denial issued the next day when a copy of Nader's charge finally arrives.

Federal Trade Commissioner Paul Rand Dixon, whom a team of Nader's Raiders recommended should be fired for turning the agency into a haven for political hacks and ignoring the consumer's interest, told this story in testimony before Congress: "On the afternoon of January 2, 1969, I began to receive phone calls from the press and other media requesting my comments on the Nader report which obviously had been distributed to them. By letter of the same date, I was requested by the Public Broadcasting Laboratory to appear on a half-hour program the night of Sunday, January 5, to reply to the statements in the report. I informed all requesting parties that I had not received a copy of the report and was unable to comment."

Dixon said he was called later in the afternoon and told by a Nader's Raider that a copy "had been mailed to me that day." Nader claims that Dixon did not get a copy of the report before it was released because of late mails, but Nader's critics claim that the Dixon episode is just one of many instances where the press got copies of a critical letter or report long before the victim of the attack did.

Still another charge pinned on Nader is what one government bureaucrat termed "his penchant for petty gun-jumping," which he described this way:

"Our agency is riddled with Nader's spies. Most of them are small-minded people who give him tips because they get some kind of vicarious thrill out of embarrassing the agency chief. Others are Walter Mittys who see themselves in their fantasies at a cocktail party stunning the room into silence by casually announcing 'I was a spy for Ralph Nader.' None of these people are on a policy-making level, so what they feed Nader is a tip on some report that is underway which will be released to the public when it is finished. Once Nader finds out that it is near completion, he writes a letter, cutting in the newspapers, and demands that the agency immediately release the 'secret report.' "

In the end, Nader's relations with the press will prove crucial for him. If he is, as his critics claim, simply a newspaper-created personality, he will, like all of those creatures, gradually move off the front pages until he finally vanishes into a newspaper morgue. But if he is, as his backers claim, a new force with near universal appeal, he will become a permanent fixture in the news—a sort of critic-in-residence for consumer affairs.

4

THE CENTER:
AN ASSEMBLY LINE
FOR NADERITES

You are too high on rhetoric, too short on commitment, and perhaps
too self-indulgent.

—Ralph Nader in an address to the students
at the University of San Francisco

The womb that nurtured Nader's Raiders was a great pile of
red bricks at 1908 Q Street N.W., Washington, D.C. Once an
elegant turn-of-the-century mansion where grande dames
clucked over teacups, it was in terminal decay by May, 1969,
when Nader moved in to open his Center for Study of
Responsive Law, the first of his consumer public service
units. A training school, a home away from home, and a pay
station for the raiders, the center had a Castle Dracula look
about it that added to the Nader mystique, and was a perfect
counterpoint to the antiseptic glass and steel towers used to
house the offices of corporate America.

A newly arrived raider would find himself in front of the
center wondering whether he had discovered the greatest
piece of camp in the land, or had the wrong address. Wood-
shingled turrets sprouted from one corner of the four-story
building, and half-inch thick black bars formed grids over the
first-floor windows. A creaky fire escape clung to the side of
the mansion, which seemed itself to lean over the sidewalk.

The doorway arch was framed by a two-foot thick block of sandstone. Weeds grew in the postage stamp-sized plot of ground near the door and a scraggly evergreen struggled to stay alive under the blanket of carbon monoxide that wafted over from the heavily-trafficked Connecticut Avenue. On the sidewalk, hard by the building, usually were a Volkswagen or two, symbols of Nader's few defeats since they were owned by raiders who ignored his warnings that the car was "a portable funeral parlor."

If the outside of the center was devoid of pretensions, the interior would leave a status-conscious business executive in a funk. The always-locked front door (a protection against kooks and drifters from Dupont Circle) would be opened by an overworked secretary like Sue Fagin or Karen Pierson, the wife of the *Wall Street Journal*'s White House correspondent, John Pierson, and one of several newsmen's wives and girl friends who have done hitches with Nader-spawned organizations. The tea-drinking biddies of yesteryear would hardly recognize the mansion's interior. Squatting on the landing of the main staircase was the center's Xerox machine, an advertised symbol of efficiency that could trigger ten minutes of scorn from Nader at the slightest provocation. He is convinced the Xerox machine is really more of a time-waster than a time-saver. It is a bureaucratic tool, says Nader. "You end up making copies you don't need just because it is there." Nader eventually sent the machine back to Xerox. Worse for Xerox, he is now planning an investigation of its pricing system.

To the left of the main hall was a drawing room that doubled as a reception room, but looked more like a front-line command post. Here Sue sat before an electric typewriter while an electric coil heater hummed at her feet.

Across the room, barricaded behind a foot-high stack of "to-be-clipped" newspapers, Karen manned a constantly flickering telephone console. At her feet, chained to the desk, was an overweight Newfoundland Retriever of questionable pedigree who answered, ever so slowly, to the name of "Jason."

Propped against her desk, Sue had a symbol of the center's safety campaigns—a still grease-smeared cracked motorcycle tire rim. In one corner of the room was a john, its door ajar and the seat up. Rock music from a radio sounded from somewhere in the back reaches of the house, and light poured into the high-ceilinged room through shadeless windows. Only the fireplace and its handsome mantle were reminders that this was once a rich man's home. The fireplace itself, however, was ringed with cardboard boxes stuffed with files. A few battered chairs, and a cheap cement-colored rug completed the decorations.

The message system used by the girls was a marvel of simplicity. Manila envelopes were tacked to the wall, and Nader's name, along with the names of staff members, was blocked out on the envelopes with Magic Marker. Taking messages for Nader followed a standard routine with telephone callers that went like this: "No, Ralph isn't here. . . . No, I don't know where he is. . . . No, I don't know when he will be back." The routine is familiar to executive secretaries who use it every day to protect their boss from unwanted calls while he is comfortably seated in his nearby office, but in Nader's case, it is the truth. Nader seldom tells the girls where he is, where he was, or where he is going.

On the other side of the entrance hall was another, and larger room. Again the scene was the same. The room was littered with filing cases, and battered furniture. A desk was armed with yet another telephone console, and stacked high with papers, reports, and books. Upstairs resembled nothing so much as an abandoned building. Padlocks secured some of the rooms used by staffers. Others were bare of furniture, or filled with more filing cases and worktables. In one room, the furnishings consisted of a mattress on the floor.

Nader's room, behind a padlocked door marked with a painted number "1," was no more impressive or organized than any of the others. If anything, it gave the appearance of a niche allocated to an assistant professor at a not-too-well financed college. Books were piled on the floor which was covered by a seedy rug. There were floor-to-ceiling bookshelves jammed with tomes ranging from the U.S. (legal) Code to congressional directories, and Senate and House hearings. The desk, like the others in the house, was littered with half-finished work, and was surrounded by an ancient, stuffed leather chair which the unknown, and unknowing, decorator complimented with an equally battered deep-seat canvas chair. The room was no more than twelve feet wide. A red glass exit sign on the wall behind the desk pointed the way to the fire escape outside the window, a reminder of the days not-too-long past when the mansion was a rooming house. The window itself was shielded by a large wooden folding screen. Behind the desk, pinned to a drape, was a framed picture of Thomas Jefferson, the only picture in the room.

The center held its position as mother house for Nader's movement until the spring of 1971 when the Washington Metropolitan Area Transit Authority, Nader's landlord, ordered the building demolished to make way for a subway stop. The new home for the center became a nondescript, three-story building at 1156 Nineteenth Street N.W. It sheltered a graphic arts store on the first floor, and shared the block with Speedprint—"1 to 1,000 Copies While You Wait"—and Luigi's Famous Pizzas. The rent was a little more—$1,200-a-month—but there also was more usable space. However, that was all that could be said about it since it fell far short of replacing the mansion's far-out aura. If anything, the new center has an air of a temporary student center, or a campaign headquarters for a fourth-party candidate. One half of the center's first floor is an open loft-like room. The other half is partitioned into a series of small rooms. Tucked into the corners of the building are rooms used as offices by some of the center associates. Like the mansion, the new center is constantly in a state of casual disarray with books, boxes, desks, and filing cases scattered about giving it an "after-the-explosion" look. But one secretary was only too happy to leave the drafty mansion to history. "Moving here means I can stop wearing gloves in the office this winter," she said.

The idea for the center, and even the name, were Nader's alone. The concept jelled in his mind as far back as his college days. He saw then a need for what would be basically a think tank for consumers; a place where consumer-minded lawyers, engineers, and scientists would research, write, and evolve policies and strategies. Tied directly to a permanent staff, Nader visualized the student investigating teams which a newspaper headline writer would later dub "Nader's Raiders."

Today the center is institutionalized with a board of directors. Nader is the chairman, and the members consist of his sister, Laura, Dr. Paul W. Gikas, a pathologist at the University of Michigan, Layman Allen, a professor of law at the University of Michigan, and a cousin of Nader's, Canadian attorney Edmund A. Shaker. None of the unpaid board members take any part in the center's policy-making decisions. This is done by Nader and the five or six permanent associates at the center.

The first team of students or summer interns, as Nader prefers, was on the job in the summer of 1968, a year before Nader officially opened his center. This team, whose target was the Federal Trade Commission, was heavy with Ivy Leaguer blue bloods. President Nixon's son-in-law Edward Cox (Princeton University-Harvard Law School) was a member. So was William Taft IV (Yale University-Harvard Law School), the great-grandson of President William Howard Taft. The other members were Robert Fellmeth (Stanford University-Harvard Law School), Peter Bradford (Yale-Yale University Law School), Andrew Egendorf (Massachusetts Institute of Technology-Harvard Law School), John Schulz (Princeton University-Yale Law School), and Judy Areen (Cornell University-Yale Law School), the daughter of Gordon Areen, the president of Chrysler Financial Corporation, the auto firm's sales financing subsidiary. The raider task force that probed the Interstate Commerce Commission in

77

1969 gave the elitist argument still more fuel. Along with Harvard, Princeton, and Cornell, it included students from Brown, Dartmouth, and the University of Pennsylvania. The more recent raider task forces, however, have moved away somewhat from the eastern establishment schools. The University of Texas Law School is coming on strong, recruits being funneled to Nader by one of his old raiders, Joe Tom Easley. The 1971 team included Ken Dryden, a student at Canada's McGill University Law School, and the goalie for the Montreal Canadiens. Nader has even recruited a Jesuit priest, Father Albert J. Fritsch, an organic chemist who is an expert on tobacco, mercury, cadmium, and asbestos poisoning. But the combination of good schools and upper-class backgrounds still is a common thread in the makeup of the raider teams. Cox was an example. His pedigree goes back to Robert Livingston, one of the drafters of the Declaration of Independence. He grew up on a ten-acre estate in Westhampton Beach, Long Island, and his father, Colonel (his World War II rank) Howard Cox is a partner in a New York City law firm.

Young Cox idolizes Nader, whom he met as a student when Nader was commuting to Princeton's Woodrow Wilson School of Public Affairs to teach his course on the American corporation. So strong is his loyalty that when the FTC report was published, Cox turned his $1,000 in royalties over to the newly opened center, a gesture Nader described as "nice." Cox even invited Nader to his White House wedding. In typical fashion, Nader grumped: "Can't go. Got to be in Pittsburgh that day for a speech." But for once he changed his mind under a barrage of arguments from his staff which was insistent that he not choose "Pittsburgh over the Rose Garden," and perhaps slight Cox, who, as a member of the White House family circle, might be able to help the consumer movement. So Nader sent his acceptance, and turned up at the White House gate on the wedding day between the arrival of Lynda Bird Johnson Robb and Alice Roosevelt Longworth. Tricia got the same wedding present Nader sends to all of his friends—a colonial chair made in a small Connecticut factory.

As soon as the wedding was over, Nader left for Virginia to give the commencement speech at nearby Northern Virginia Community College, a date he accepted when he cancelled the Pittsburgh trip. But it was a ten-year-old Naderite who pointed out that even at White House weddings there was work for Nader. In a letter to the editor of *Life* magazine, the girl said a picture of Tricia and Ed in the bridal car showed they were not wearing seat belts. Nader's young fan added rather testily that if Ed Cox was "such a good friend of Nader's he would wear his seat belt because Nader is trying to get everybody to wear seat belts."

If Nader is not keen on White House social affairs, he is very definitely impressed by Cox himself, and the work he did on the FTC.

"He's a very bright guy, tenacious, and factually oriented. I think he has a bright future," says Nader who is as sparing of public compliments as he is profuse in his criticism. But conservative-minded Tricia Nixon Cox is not exactly a Nader fan. Once asked by a newsman if she backed Nader as strongly as her husband, she said, carefully choosing her words, "I think we can agree he (Nader) is doing good things for the consumer."

Nader's deepest sortie in high society came when he recruited seven girls from Miss Porter's School, Farmington, Connecticut, a one-time debutante factory (Jacqueline Kennedy Onassis is a graduate) that is now struggling to trade its old playgirl reputation for one of social activism. Millionaire businessman Robert Townsend's daughter, Claire, headed the group which Nader assigned to do a study of old age homes. An anonymous donor put up the money to cover the girls' expenses, and Townsend (Princeton '41) matched this by buying a townhouse in Washington so the girls could all live together while they worked on the project.

But Townsend has contributed more than his daughter and a townhouse to Nader's crusade. He sees Nader as a kindred spirit; a younger version of his own rogue-in-the-executive-suite approach, and most importantly, a successful rogue. To back up his faith, Townsend gave Nader $150,000 which Nader put in a tax-exempt foundation he called the Public Safety Research Institute. Nader is the sole director of the institute, and it is merely a way to allow him to dispense the money for special projects. But Nader's Raiders are not above a little cattiness. "Townsend bought his daughter a raider team," is the way one raider put it. Nader doesn't like to be twitted about his predilection for Ivy League students, but it is there, nevertheless. If there is anything that impresses Nader, it is brain power. At Princeton and Harvard he found much to dislike, but he also found the intellectuals he sought, and along the way, though it brings a sharp denial from him, he absorbed just a touch of the prejudice for Princeton-Harvard Law School graduates.

Ted Jacobs is more blunt about combing the Harvard campus for recruits. "Sure there is an elitism issue. Some of the best legal talent comes from Harvard—that's the long and the short of it." The result of this incestuous recruiting is obvious at the center. For one thing, there is a shortage of black faces. The Negro is cool to Nader's Raider teams despite Nader's oft-repeated arguments that consumer problems are poor peoples' problems. It is the Negro in the ghetto who gets doctored meat delivered to his neighborhood supermarket, or is bilked by fast-talking salesmen selling shoddy consumer goods. It is the black man's health and property that are often damaged by pollution from mills and factories regularly centered around black ghetto housing, says Nader.

But the black students see it differently. They say if they are going to sacrifice a good paycheck from the establishment to become crusaders, they will work first in the civil rights movement, or in Negro job-training and Negro education programs.

In rejecting Nader's pleas, the blacks argue that Nader is not relevant to the gut issue with Negroes—their economic plight. "You have to have the money to buy a television set first before you can get screwed," is what one black told a

Nader student recruiter. Nader was so determined to woo blacks to his crusade that he even offered them up to $2,000 for a summer's work—ten times the base rate for white students. But the crusher for Nader came when one of his brightest black prospects turned him down and went to work for Wilmer, Cutler, and Pickering, the prestigious Washington law firm with a long list of corporate clients, and the firm of Lloyd Cutler, the automaker's counsel, and a long-time foe of Nader in legislative battles over auto safety.

But if the blacks are not beating a path to the door of the center, the white students are. Nader has many more than he can handle. In 1970, he got three thousand applications for about 170 spots on the raider team. In 1971, with very little recruiting, he got one thousand applications for fifty openings. But not every one is motivated by a desire to help his fellow man or to sit at Nader's feet. "Some of them think it will look good on their resume to say they worked for me when they look for a job in a law firm," says Nader. Some of the students have a complaint of their own: "It's tougher to make Nader's Raiders than to get into any of the top law schools," they claim. Tough isn't exactly the right word to describe Nader's recruiting. Careful would be more on the mark. Nader is a careful man. Careful about his friends, his facts, his privacy, his words, and his actions. When it comes to his raiders, Nader examines them like a mother sizing up a prospective son-in-law. The result of this is that the raiders tend to be a lot like their boss, or as much as it is possible for anyone to be like Nader. The better ones ape him. They push themselves with long hours of work, and vie with one another to come up with projects, documents, or interviews that will get a "well done" from Nader. But Nader is not a handholder. Any raider who expects parental-like guidance from him will be disappointed. In the course of a summer, the average raider sees very little of Nader. An occasional glimpse of him padding down the stairs of the center, or a brief pep talk at the beginning of a project, a handful of editorial conferences, and a few telephone conversations may make up the sum of a raider's contact. "I'm looking for self-starters. I don't want people who have to be constantly told to do this, or do that," says Nader. To him, the job requirements are simple. "Anybody can work for me who has the ability to dig up facts, the ability to interview, can meet deadlines, and, most of all, is self-reliant." Nader got where he is by himself. He feels his raiders should be able to do the same. If they can't, they are not his kind of people.

There are student-types Nader shies away from, however. The kid with ego-gratification problems is out. Says Nader: "My father taught me a long time ago that the highest thing after attaining a measure of progress or success is to be able to endure it. And this is what I always counsel the students—don't let that ego get in your way. Don't start getting a swollen head. Keep your eye on the objective and work harder, and harder, and harder. If they don't have that kind of personality, they can't possibly endure this kind of work because it begins either inflating or diverting them—or bureaucratizing them." He admits there are some students who come to the center with tremendous ego involvement. "They have to get credit; they have to beat the other guy; they have to constantly tell people what they've done. If the ego is associated with real accomplishment, it's not much of a problem. But usually, it's associated with not-real accomplishment, and that is a problem."

For Nader, the Weatherman-woman is another need-not-apply along with the campus Maoist, communist, anarchist, and any others who feel they can not work "on the system." The heavy drug user is definitely a reject.

"Nader is not running a home for runaways or cop-outs. This is a work place, baby," said one raider.

But Nader's barrel has its rotten apples. He admits that some of the raiders in the past "have been totally useless. All I got out of them for a summer was a ten- to fifteen-page memo." But if a raider goofs off, he is not drummed out of the center and sent to work for GM. "We are not a business organization. If someone doesn't work out, he isn't thrown out on his ass. If we made a commitment, we stick with him through the summer. No one is fired. If a kid is not just what we hoped, we try to live with it," Nader says. But the people who come to work for Nader are highly motivated to begin with, so the mortality rate is low, averaging less than ten percent a summer.

One of the problems Nader faces is the credit-giving question. The sweat and brain power a raider puts into a report is seldom noted by the press. A report Nader merely read or edited is described by the press as "A Nader Report" and the raider team is lucky if their names are listed in the news stories. Mark Green, one of Nader's youngest full-time associates and the author of a 1,100-page report in 1971 on antitrust problems, says Nader's personality helps hold down raider dissatisfaction over the lack of individual recognition. "Nader is incredibly modest. You hardly ever hear a word of self-aggrandizement from him, and this is contagious." In his case, the 26-year-old Green who gave up an internship with Mayor Lindsay of New York to work with Nader, says the lack of credit is not important compared to the other gratifications. "Where else could a guy my age have the impact I have. Everything I've done I owe to Ralph. He provided the money, the idea, and the guidance."

But some of the center's full-time associates have managed to slip out from Nader's shadow, and are becoming recognized critics in their own right. John Esposito, the author of *The Vanishing Air*, the center-backed book on pollution is one. Reuben Robertson III, the center's transportation expert, is another. Robertson has been named to head a consumer advisory board for the Civil Aeronautics Board and regularly files his own complaints with the ICC, the CAB, and the Federal Aviation Administration. James Turner, the author of the center report on the food industry called the "Chemical Feast" has left Nader to work on his own.

But unless Nader replaces his students with machines, the ego problem will remain. Robert Fellmeth, the project director for the center's investigation of the Interstate Commerce Commission, and a member of the 1968 task force sent to the Federal Trade Commission, described the problem best when he told Senator Ribicoff at a Senate hearing that he did not think the label "Nader's Raiders" was fair.

"First of all, it is inaccurate. Mr. Nader's involvement is crucial, but is not as extensive as that name would imply . . . we are not investigating for him in a direct sense," he said.

Then Fellmeth went on to give what may be one of the best descriptions of a Nader's Raider, and, at the same time, the best argument for finding another name. Said Fellmeth: "We are not raiders. That is a very inaccurate name, with an inaccurate connotation. When you are sitting there at two o'clock in the morning, going over documents page by page by page, thousands and thousands of pages, compiling things, gathering evidence, talking to people, you don't feel like a raider at all. You don't feel like you are on a foray—you feel like a scholar. Maybe you are putting together a brief of sorts—but nevertheless whatever you are doing is not really accurately described as raiding." Center associate Harrison Wellford says the raider tag is unfortunate. For one thing, it gives the students a piratical image. In a briefing to a group of new interns, Wellford was quick to disabuse them of the idea that they were swashbucklers. He told them:

"You're not to go into an agency and prove your worth by rummaging through a file that was not open to you or by seducing a secretary, or by waylaying the departmental mailman as he makes his way through the halls. We play by the rules every step of the way. And there is very good reason for doing that. In the first place, you can get what you want that way. In the second place, if you don't play by the rules, your credibility is going to be destroyed by personal attack, and the guy who destroys it couldn't touch it if he had to attack only your facts. Believe me, whenever the investigation begins to hit paydirt, they're going to be trying to find ways to discredit you, and there is no point in making it easy for them."

Jacobs, thirty-seven, is the man who takes care of the center's day-to-day operation. He keeps check on the projects, and acts as an advisor, wet nurse, in-house philosopher, and lightning rod for the raiders. Low-keyed, he has the outward air of a Talmudic scholar, but there is in him more the establishmentarian than in any of the other permanent members of the center staff. His dress, like Nader's, is conservative, but his hair is moderately long, a concession to the mod influence manifested around him by the students. When he speaks, it is in a slow, pedantic manner, but he is quick to laugh.

Jacobs works closely with Nader, but has none of his charisma. For eight years he toiled in a New York law firm earning his keep by unraveling the vagaries of real estate and business law. But he kept in touch with Nader and in 1968 he came to Washington to work as a lawyer for the National Commission on Product Safety. Finally, in 1970, he agreed to go to work for Nader, who needed a replacement for Harrison Wellford, the center's first short-term executive director. Wellford wanted to be freed from the job to do more research.

If Nader and Jacobs differ on anything, it would come under the heading of creature comforts. Jacobs says he personally tries to work a routine schedule, avoiding night sessions if he can. He also takes vacations, something Nader ignores. Jacobs also tries to keep travel to a minimum. Proud of his stamina, Nader glories in his ability to hopscotch around the nation juggling a schedule that would appall even a presidential candidate.

But Jacobs and his job smack of a fledgling bureaucracy to some of Nader's critics. Nader himself, however, has a genuine fear of bureaucracies, and reacts to the idea as if it were some kind of loathsome disease. "For our kind of work, my definition of bureaucracy starts at two," he says. The way to avoid the bureaucratic pitfall, he cautions his raiders, is to continually ask: "How do I do it better myself?"

But Nader's critics refuse to accept the idea that anyone facing the tasks Nader does can possibly accomplish anything without a highly structured organization. To back up this argument, they see Jacobs as becoming a layer between Nader and the students, Nader and the public, and Nader and the press. As it is now, the critics say Jacobs is the man who knows where Ralph is at all times. Jacobs can plead special cases and say yes or no to requests for interviews from newsmen.

Jacobs himself dubs the idea laughable, claiming no one makes any decisions for Nader, nor is that likely to change no matter how large Nader's organization grows. Most of the other permanent staffers agree. They say the center is singularly free of politics—"There is none of this 'who talked to the President last' syndrome" is the way one center associate put it. Another claimed, "If Nader is building a bureaucracy, it must be invisible."

Seated in his office, Jacobs says he is simply trying to take some of the trivia away from Nader, and make the center a more organized operation. Any prospective raider will find the furnishings in Jacobs' office not unlike the ones in his own college room. There is the ubiquitous poster with a spurious Adolf Hitler quote: "The streets of our country are in turmoil. The universities are filled with students rebelling and rioting. Communists are seeking to destroy our country. Russia is threatening us with her might. The Republic is in danger. Yes, danger from within and without. We need law and order. Yes, without law and order our nation cannot survive . . . We shall restore law and order." Several surrealistic paintings, a poster extolling the California grape workers' movement, a set of filing cabinets, a two-foot wide clear plastic ball, and the usual collection of early Salvation Army furniture complete the office. Hardly the den for a student conspiracy, but there is little doubt that Washington bureaucrats fear Nader's Raiders. Some tried to tranquilize them with pap. Others greeted them with open arms until the raiders became too incisive in their questioning. Then, as was the case of FTC Chairman Paul Rand Dixon, the raiders found themselves unceremoniously ushered out of the office. Generally speaking, many lower-level government employees welcome a raider team on the grounds that it may be able to get some action taken on the obvious ills of the agency. Other lower-echelon types, however, will not confide in the students out of fear of retribution from on high. In the upper ranks, there is often a fear that telling all to a raider could result in being pushed into one of the government's many pigeonholes and left there until retirement. "The raiders are here for a week, but I have to stay around for another ten years," is the way one civil servant put it.

Nader greases the way for his raiders with a call to an agency or department head telling him the students are coming and asking cooperation. The students are told to be polite, but persistent. "Go prepared," Nader tells the students in describing interview techniques. "Know your subject. Once the interview starts, go on the offensive and stay there. Don't let your man turn you off or turn you away from what you want, but keep your cool." To Nader, the ability to interview combined with "moral indignation," and laborious research, is what makes a good raider.

But he is the first to admit that when the students arrive in Washington they are "green" when it comes to understanding what they face in probing a government agency. "It takes them a while to break ground in a particular area they are studying. It takes them a while to develop a sense of self-assertiveness, a sense of stamina, and a sense of how to cool an indignant imagination in order to get at the facts. It is an exercise in self-control as well as an intellectual pursuit," he says.

The civil servant is an easy flash point to ignite any student's outrage, warns Nader. On the eve of battle, a group of the students crowded into Georgetown University's Walsh Building to hear Nader describe the civil servant this way:

"It's true that there are a number of very valid, very interesting, and worthwhile civil servants. But they're in the very distinct minority. The rest are, to put it mildly, drones taking orders from forces that they never wish to contend with, and they are people with considerably established egos. They really believe that because they've been working thirty years in the field that they have thirty years of experience instead of what most of them really have—one year of experience repeated thirty times. But you have to take into account these sensitivities because they are very real sensitivities. The fact that a civil servant is a drone can be as much of an issue of pathos to him as it is to you as you observe him. And he may be very sorry about what he's done and what he hasn't done, and very unsatisfied with himself. So keep that in mind. Control the outrage, but don't suppress it. Your outrage must be considered fuel that doesn't quite surface, but must be considered the metabolism of your energy. But don't spill it out until you're behind that typewriter, white-hot, putting out that memo or that final product."

But for some raiders the problem is not outrage but love. According to Nader, he has had raiders who fall flat because they want to be loved; that is, they develop a personal relationship with individuals in the agency under investigation and then get qualms about getting them in trouble by criticizing the department. "What would have happened to me if I developed a personal relationship with James Roche of General Motors?" Nader asked. But he makes it clear that he is not opposed to the emotion of love in his work. Says Nader, however: "It is better to love, than to need to be loved. If you need to be loved, you can't do this kind of work."

What is the pay scale for raiders? In a word: Low. Nader pays his full-time associates at the center between $10,000 and $15,000 a year. But the students get anywhere from $200 to $1,000 for a summer's work. If a student can show he needs more, Nader will up the ante to $1,500, his top figure. Some students get nothing from the center, subsisting on work-study grants from their universities. Jacobs put the salary problem this way: "We let them tell us the minimum they need, but if a kid is looking for money he shouldn't come here."

Before they start a summer's work, all of the students are brought together and briefed by Nader on what he expects of them. Like a newspaper editor training a cub reporter, he "psychs" them up on the importance of the deadline. Even by working at a twelve- to sixteen-hour-day, weekends and holidays included, most of them will find trouble finishing their projects. One of the raiders described the summer work load as the equivalent of doing a Ph.D. dissertation in ten weeks.

With the brief orientation period over, the students are divided up into the teams, and each team is headed by a project director, who acts as a combination straw boss and liaison with Nader. There is really nothing mysterious about the raider operation from this point—the teams simply attempt to envelop their target as well as they can.

Because of the inexperience of the students and the size of the problems they tackle, the reports have come under criticism as superficial; merely a compilation of known facts, and at worst they have been termed distorted. FTC Chairman Dixon described the student report on his agency as "a hysterical, antibusiness diatribe, and a scurrilous, untruthful attack on the career personnel" of the FTC.

In 1971, Nader got the same type of criticism for his raider report on the workings of the mammoth First National City Bank of New York. The chairman of the bank, Walter B. Wriston, said he found the raiders were prejudiced against business, careless with facts, and ignorant about banking business. According to Wriston, Nader originally did his own research and double-checked his facts, but now "franchises himself like a fried-chicken stand." The result of this dilution is "a sort of high-school essay" rather than an accurate critique of a problem, Wriston claimed. But he offered no concrete examples to back his opinions.

But Nader is convinced the concept is valid, and the investigations themselves are both detailed and accurate. Writing a foreword for the book *The Interstate Commerce Ommission,* Nader described the students' thoroughness this way:

"They began the study in late 1968 by compiling and reading all available reference material. They studied the Interstate Commerce Act and the ICC and court decisions interpreting the Act. They reviewed and outlined the agency regulations. Two students compiled an annotated bibliography of law-review articles from the past decade on the ICC and surface transportation generally; economic tests, conference transcripts, and major articles in economic journals were examined. They then gathered and read Congressional hearings, the agency's annual reports for the past ten years, agency press releases and newsletters, speeches by Commissioners over the last several years, news articles and magazine articles, including a continuous survey of the major trade press. They read and discussed government and professional studies of the agency, examined agency publications, including cost studies and formulas, job descriptions, personnel resumes, et al. They went to the Departments of Justice, Transportation, Agriculture, and Defense, and reviewed all available pertinent reports concerning the ICC.

"The students began interviewing in June of 1969, completing over 500 different interviews by September, 1969. Over 100 of those interviewed were ICC officials, and employees. Other people interviewed included truckdrivers, carriers, shippers, railroad workers, union members, consultants, government officials in other departments, and attorneys. Interviews averaged about two hours in length and some were followed up by subsequent visits." Nader went on to cite an ever-mounting pile of facts about the investigation, including mass mailings of questionnaires, and four separate statistical analyses conducted by computers.

Nader personally feels that the studies the students have done are of tremendous value.

"I think the students and the young lawyers have made a major contribution, not just in the terms of the pages they have written but in terms of style, approach, and the areas of the studies. The studies also have spinoffs. First, they establish a tradition, an investigative student tradition. The volumes will be used by their student colleagues as reading materials. This in turn will motivate them to do the same thing in their local areas or at the state level," Nader claims.

Nader's full-time associates and the directors of the student teams agree. John Esposito, Nader's air-pollution expert, said, "The students learn that the system is not as closed as many of them had believed; that there are many pressure points, and that good, old-fashioned hard work and informed criticism can have an impact."

According to Esposito, the students are extremely effective as investigators simply because they are students. "They have a great deal more credibility as critics since they evoke the confidence of many middle-level bureaucrats who really believe in the mission of the agency—people who are middle-level bureaucrats precisely because they haven't played the game of status and prestige, but actually believe the agency should be protecting the consumer."

Harrison Wellford, who led a study of pesticides and their handling by the government, argues that his student team paid off in big dividends.

The young investigators were educated in the inside workings of government; they have begun slowly to change some of the patterns of public participation in the administrative process, and even caused some changes simply by appearing in the agency and making officials discuss its problems, says Wellford. More importantly, the students found that the institutions associated with social and environmental change need not be confronted head-on. They saw, Wellford claimed, that by probing for cracks in the facade, and while working within the system, they could dismantle "the structure of institutional neglect brick by brick."

The center's output is increasing steadily, and the initial impact of each study, thanks to heavy coverage in the news media, has been sharp. If there is a problem, it would be in the area of the follow-up. Even one of Nader's associates admits that some of the reports "seemed to drop through the center of the earth after they were issued." But others have helped to bring about changes. For example, the 1968 investigation of the FTC is still having repercussions. "The Old Lady of Pennsylvania Avenue," under the leadership of its new chairman Miles W. Kirkpatrick, is showing signs of awakening from its 55-year sleep. Nader must be given a good share of the credit for this. His raiders produced a scathing report on the agency showing it was riddled with patronage and politics, and staffed by time-servers and incompetents, who did little to protect the consumer from anything or anyone. The report was greeted with disbelief. The raiders had no standing with Washington's officialdom. Then President Nixon asked the American Bar Association to investigate the FTC. The result: The substance of the 1969 ABA commission study showed the FTC wasted its funds on trivial matters; the staff was characterized by "incompetence" especially at the top; it did less work than it did ten years before, and should be overhauled or abolished. In other words, the commission of distinguished lawyers found exactly the same state of affairs as had the raiders. This was rather prestigious corroboration for the raiders, whom then-FTC Chairman Dixon liked to describe as pimply-faced kids and smart-alecky "pricks." Given a freer hand, Kirkpatrick is bringing a new spirit to the agency that hopefully may transform it into a weapon against marauders in the business world. The ICC Report was another report that was on target. Filled with bureaucrats who have been castrated by the very rail, truck, barge, and household moving industries they are supposed to regulate, the ICC is an "elephant's graveyard for political hacks," the raiders said and then documented an appalling indictment of the 84-year-old agency ranging from cosy expense-paid trips for commissioners who attended industry affairs to accusing the ICC of standing idly by while the railroads dismantled the nation's rail passenger system. The report triggered off congressional demands for reforms, and even stirred Democratic Senate Majority Leader Mike Mansfield to propose abolishing the ICC. Again President Nixon moved in the wake of a raider report and a presidential commission urged the agency be overhauled.

The center continues to grind out its reports with undiminished enthusiasm. Here is a list of what the raiders have done between 1969 and mid-1971.

THE CENTER: AN ASSEMBLY LINE FOR NADERITES

The Nader Report on the Federal Trade Commission, Robert Fellmeth, project director, Grove Press, New York.

The Interstate Commerce Omission, Robert Fellmeth, editor. Grossman Publishers, New York.

Vanishing Air, John C. Esposito, editor. Grossman Publishers, New York. (A study of air pollution.)

The Chemical Feast, James S. Turner, editor. Grossman Publishers, New York. (A study of the food and drug industries.)

One Life—One Physician: An Inquiry into the Medical Profession's Performance in Self-Regulation. Robert S. McCleery, M.D., editor. Public Affairs Press, Washington, D.C.

Old Age: The Last Segregation, Claire Townsend, project director, Grossman Publishers, New York.

The Water Lords: A Nader Task Force Report on the Savannah River, 1971. Copies available from the Center for Study of Responsive Law, P.O. Box 19367, Washington, D.C.

Water Wasteland: A Nader Task Force Report on Water Pollution. David Zwick, editor. Copies available from the Center for Study of Responsive Law, P.O. Box 19367, Washington, D.C.

The Closed Enterprise System: A Nader Task Force Report on Antitrust Enforcement, 2 vols. Mark J. Green, project director. Copies available from the Center for Study of Responsive Law, P.O. Box 19367, Washington, D.C.

Citibank: A Nader Task Force Report on the operations of First National City Bank of New York. David Leinsdorf, project director. Copies available from the Center for Study of Responsive Law, P.O. Box 19367, Washington, D.C.

Caution—This Job May Kill You: A Nader Task Force Report on occupational safety and health. Copies available from the Center for Study of Responsive Law, P.O. Box 19367, Washington, D.C.

Report on Coal Mine Health and Safety in West Virginia: J. Davitt McAteer, project director. Copies available from the Center for Study of Responsive Law, P.O. Box 19367, Washington, D.C.

Sowing the Wind: Pesticides, Meat and the Public Interest. Harrison Wellford, project director. Copies available from the Center for Study of Responsive Law, P.O. Box 19367, Washington, D.C.

Tractor Safety Report, James Williams, editor. Copies available from the Center for Study of Responsive Law, P.O. Box 19367, Washington, D.C.

Crash Safety in General Aviation Aircraft, James Bruce and John

Draper, editors. Copies available from the Center for Study of Responsive Law, P.O. Box 19367, Washington, D.C.

The Company State: The Nader Study Group Report on Du Pont in Delaware. 2 vols. James Phelan and Robert Pozen, project directors. Copies available from the Center for Study of Responsive Law, P.O. Box 19367, Washington, D.C., 1971.

Power and Land in California: A Nader task force report on land use in the state of California. Robert Fellmeth, project director. Copies available from the Center for Study of Responsive Law, P.O. Box 19367, Washington, D.C., 1971.

Damming the West: A Nader Task Force Report on the U.S. Bureau of Reclamation. Richard Berkman and Kip Viscusi, project directors. Copies available from the Center for Study of Responsive Law, P.O. Box 19367, Washington, D.C., 1971.

On the Job: Portraits of Nine American Workers, Kenneth Lasson, project director. Grossman Publishers, New York, 1971.

There are other studies in various stages of completion which will cover the following subjects:

1) Think Tanks—their use by government.

2) Supermarket practices, including pricing policies, date coding, grade labeling, and promotional techniques.

3) The impact of food companies on children—their diets, the formation of their concepts of food preferences, and the ways in which the food industry influences the consumer.

4) The National Institute of Mental Health.

5) The U.S. Forest Service.

6) The pulp and paper industry in Maine.

7) The National Academy of Sciences and its relation with the federal government.

8) The American Automobile Association and its ties to the auto industry. The study will also cover the role of the AAA in areas such as auto insurance, auto safety, and highway safety.

9) The problems associated with the sale and use of commercial blood. The study team will investigate the conditions which allow the transmittal of diseases like hepatitis from the blood donor to the patient.

5

RALPH NADER,
INCORPORATED

Even the old muckrakers like Upton Sinclair and Lincoln Steffens only did twenty percent of the job. They stopped at exposure. They didn't follow through by politically mobilizing a concerned constituency.

—Ralph Nader in an interview
with *Time* magazine

One of the many things Ralph Nader functions without is an organization chart. This staple of the business world would rate a priority below a pension fund for his raiders. But the time may be coming when one is needed; Nader-spawned enterprises are proliferating at a rate fast enough to force even his close associates to count them on their fingers. At last count, and including the Center for Study of Responsive Law, there were ten Nader-run, Nader-backed, or Nader-advised units in Washington.

Second in size to the center is the Public Interest Research Group, Nader's law firm. "Our action arm," as he calls it. Known by its initials P-I-R-G (pronounced PURG), the law firm is staffed by thirteen young lawyers and a law professor. Bright, top-of-their-class talent, the lawyers are the seeds of a legal revolution in Washington. They can be found filing petitions with the Federal Aviation Administration to end smoking on airplanes or trailblazing in areas like freedom-of-information lawsuits against government agencies. PIRG lawyers pound the halls of Congress, making contact with the young congressional aides and committee counsels. Not registered as lobbyists, the PIRG lawyers cannot go directly to the congressmen and senators, but the web they have spun over congressional staffers is a tribute to their fast growing expertise in the ways of politics.

The firm itself, like most of Nader's operations, is a lean and hungry animal. With the top Wall Street law firms paying over $16,000 to the cream of the law school graduating class, Nader offers $4,500 a year and no fringe benefits. "This is the only firm in the United States where the secretaries make more than the lawyers," says one of the members of Nader's legal stable.

So far, Nader has poured $190,000 into PIRG. To do it, he tapped his General Motors settlement money, and the funds he raised with speeches and articles. In June, 1971, the end of its first full year of operation, Nader budgeted PIRG for another full year, but he hopes eventually to finance it through public subscription. So tight is the budget, that the young lawyers cheerfully admit they hold down travelling expenses by staying with friends, bunking in student dormitories, or with sympathetic law professors. "I was on the road for three weeks, and only spent two nights in a hotel," says Tom Stanton, the managing associate for PIRG. The firm does not take cases that might show a profit, but the youthful advocates are able to contribute something to defray expenses. One source of income is speeches. Unlike Nader's $3,000 fee, however, the PIRG staffers, who bill themselves to audiences as "Ralph Nader's lawyers" are lucky to get a top price of $300.

Prospective job seekers, of which there were over three hundred in 1971, are weeded out by Nader's scouts, and those that remain find themselves facing their final job interview, not in the quiet of some firm's law library, but over coffee with Nader at a campus drugstore, or standing on line with him at an airport ticket counter. It seems a haphazard way to pick a man for a job where his every mistake is certain to rub off on you, but Nader has a sixth sense in divining who will be able to make the grade in PIRG. Stanton is a good example of that. A 26-year-old Harvard Law School graduate, Stanton spotted a notice on a law school bulletin board asking for applicants who wanted to work for Nader.

"I already had taken a job with a Wall Street law firm, but all of a sudden I had a viable alternative. It was not my style to go out picketing, but Nader seemed to offer a chance for me to translate my values into reality." Stanton's law firm offered to wait, but Stanton is hooked on PIRG, and plans to stay on with Nader. But "staying on" is a problem. Stripped of all rhetoric, the question is, how do you live on $4,500 a year? Basically, the money for the food and rent often comes from a band of unsung heroines—the wives of Nader's lawyers. If a young lawyer signs on with Nader, his wife signs on, too. She must work if her husband is to practice his idealism. In some of the husband and wife teams, it is the wife who works for the Nader firm—he has four lady lawyers—and the husband who has the more routine job. Tenure at PIRG is short. The lawyers sign one-year contracts, and may renew at the end of the year. Most of the first group still are working for Nader, but the firm is predicated on the idea that there will be a heavy turnover.

Nader even sees a fringe benefit in the turnover. Once indoctrinated in Nader's concept of public service law, the young lawyers carry it with them as they move up the ladder in old-line firms and hopefully will practice what Nader preached to them.

But Nader is blunt about what a prospect can expect if he takes a job with PIRG. Here is a notice sent to law schools when Nader was in search of law professors for the firm.

"ATTENTION: Sabbatical-Bound Professors. Ralph Nader is seeking law school faculty members who are planning quarter, semester, or year-long leaves of absence to work with his Public Interest Research Group in Washington, D.C. The pay is minimal, the work voluminous, the office decor early Salvation Army!

"The Compensations: Ralph Nader is at the cutting edge of a not-so-quiet legal revolution. Working with the Public Interest Group provides the opportunity to make a substantial contribution to the growth and stature of public interest law. It also provides a period of almost complete freedom—time to pursue an area of special interest free of the pressures of class preparation, and with the benefits of independence of choice and judgement and the 'rejuvenating' atmosphere of Washington, D.C.

"The Public Interest Research Group is presently made up of ten recent law graduates, three experienced attorneys, and one law professor on a year's sabbatical. Each has an area of special interest. The work takes many forms—litigation, publication, Congressional testimony, new course material.

"Come work in the nerve center of public interest law!

"For more information write: John Spanogle, Public Interest Research Group, 1025 15th St. N.W., Suite 601, Washington, D.C. 20005."

Like the center, the public interest law firm is not a new idea for Nader. It too has been incubating in his mind since Harvard Law School.

"Years ago I read about the leading lawyers; those who were on the frontiers of defending rights. They were always in a defensive role; they were the ones who would defend unpopular causes, defend accused people, defend minority groups. I realized that we needed the same type of dedicated and courageous lawyer to work on the institutions in society to make them more responsive to the needs of the people. We needed offensive lawyers," says Nader.

Nader has no big plans for PIRG. As he has done with all of his units, he plans to keep PIRG small, with perhaps no more than twenty lawyers.

"I'm a real believer in keeping my groups small with a high spirit, with a high initiative. Something happens to even the most creative minds when they work in an atmosphere where they don't feel they can take that imaginative or creative leap; where they postpone it or they spend their time in make-work. I haven't found the most optimum group, but it's a very small size," Nader says.

But if PIRG itself is small, Nader sees the concept flowering on a national scale with other PIRGs springing up in towns, and cities to work on all types of local- and state-level problems.

PIRG's official birth date is rather vague, but June, 1970, is as good as any. This was the month Stanton moved onto the sixth floor of the Fifteenth Street office building with his portable typewriter, propped it up against a windowsill in the barren suite, and went to work.

At this point the rest of the staff had been hired, and Nader met with them all on July 13. As always, he wasted no time with dramatics. There was no rousing rhetoric, but a simple handing out of jobs. Nader outlined the areas he wanted the firm to get involved in, and then he asked who wanted to take what. "There were areas like taxes, food and drugs, transportation, health, and safety. When it was all over we each had a field, and that was that," one of PIRG's lawyers said.

Nader tries to get as much legal clout for his dollar as possible. For this reason PIRG doesn't get into areas that have been co-opted by other public interest groups. For example, PIRG environmental experts did not get involved in the fight over the Supersonic Transport and its pollution problem because an army of SST critics were already at work to bring about the downfall of the $1.3 billion project which they succeeded in doing. Nor does Nader want to get PIRG staff tied up in many time-consuming court cases. "The minute an issue becomes a law suit, PIRG tries to find someone else to bring the suit," Stanton says. But it has sued on its own. Joan Katz, one of the firm's lady lawyers, is handling a suit against the Food and Drug Administration to force better warnings to consumers on the possible side effects of birth-control pills. She also is handling the freedom-of-information suits against the government. But in some of PIRG's major actions Nader has taken the role of the plaintiff, and pays a Washington lawyer, William D. Dobrovir, to handle the case in court. In one key case, Nader versus Volpe (Transportation Secretary John A.), Nader sued the Transportation Department to force it to issue a safety defect notice involving two hundred thousand Chevrolet and GMC camper trucks whose wheel rims could shatter under heavy loads. The Transportation Department's National Highway Traffic Safety Administration earlier had convinced GM to recall fifty thousand of the trucks. Nader then produced more information showing that the remaining trucks should be recalled, too. The safety agency backed him up by ordering GM to issue a defect notice on the other 150,000 trucks. GM refused and the government then sued. GM has replied with a countersuit of its own based on its claim that the trucks were safe and no recall was needed.

Stanton was involved in a court fight to block an Administration plan to give business a faster tax write-off that would result in what Stanton claimed would be a $3 billion-a-year giveaway to business. Karen Ferguson also took on Excedrin pain-killers in a deceptive advertising suit. But PIRG prefers to attack problems in government through the petition, and the rule-making procedure, or make itself a party to disputes. Lawyer Robert Vaughn, whose area of expertise is the Civil Service, makes PIRG's presence felt by participating in Civil Service hearings on employee firings on grievances. John Spanogle, a law professor from the University of Maine, participated in writing guidelines for the Fair Credit Reporting Act and was in the middle of a donnybrook with the government over mortgage lending forms. The forms would be required by the Federal National Mortgage Association and the Federal Home Loan Mortgage Corporation whenever they purchased conventional mortgages. With Nader carrying the ball publicly, PIRG argued that the forms were weighted in favor of the lender, and would force the borrower to pay expensive penalties if he repaid his mortgage in advance, and would provide lenders with a windfall of up to $100 million a year by allowing them to require tax prepayments in advance, but prohibiting interest payments to borrowers on these funds. The forms also would allow the lender to require full payment of the mortgage balance and foreclose if the borrower was only thirty-one days late in his payment.

One of PIRG's projects that touched an overwhelmingly responsive chord in the consumer is a campaign to overhaul the nation's system of property tax assessment. Originally organized by Sam Simon, who has since left PIRG to fill his military commitment, the property tax campaign is setting up a national network of citizens groups that will work for property tax reform on a local basis. Nader kicked the campaign off December 12, 1970, with a conference on property tax reform in Washington. He painted a gloomy picture of the inequities of the tax structure. "If all taxpayers were to bear their proper share of the property tax burden, taxes on residential and small business property could be decreased as much as twenty-five percent while increasing revenues for the local governments . . ." He flailed away at big business for not carrying its load. "In Chicago, a city not known for a lack of official abuses, nearly every major building in the city is grossly underassessed. The twin Marina Towers, the Merchandise Mart, the John Hancock Building, all multimillion dollar structures, are undertaxed by as much as fifty percent . . . In Houston, Texas, a recent study done by law students revealed that commercial property was being assessed at a rate that is approximately one-half that used for residential property . . . in Gary, Indiana, U.S. Steel's property tax assessment between 1961 and 1971 only rose from $107 million to $117 million. But in the same period the company put into its plant $1.2 billion worth of capital improvements . . . coal properties in Kentucky, West Virginia, and other Appalachian states escape taxation almost completely," he said. Then, warming to his subject, Nader went on to point out that "senior citizens are literally being forced out of their homes" because of high taxes, and financially-starved cities are losing billions of dollars a year because of the tax inequities. In the first week after the conference, Nader received seven hundred letters backing the reform drive. So far, the PIRG tax reform project has been contacted by property tax reform groups in every state in the union.

Student groups to support the project have been formed at law schools and Senator Edmund S. Muskie, chairman of the Senate Intergovernmental Relations Committee, has promised to hold hearings around the nation to examine the inequities in the tax system. Also in the files of PIRG are the records of Nader's longest running battle—his fight over the safety of the Corvair. The job of Corvair master has fallen to Gary Sellers, who with ant-like determination is piece by piece building a case he hopes will force GM to eventually admit that it knew the Corvair was an unsafe car when it sold it to the public. Along with this, Sellers, who also works as a part-time aide to Congressman Philip Burton, a California Democrat, is building a record in an attempt to show that GM officials lied in 1966 in testimony before the Senate about the safety of the Corvair. Two other lawyers, William Osborn and Larry Silverman, followed their project right out of Washington to West Virginia. The project involved three Union Carbide Corporation plants which were polluting nearby communities. The two lawyers mobilized the local citizenry, and with Nader generating the publicity over the pollution, managed to force Union Carbide into speeding its pollution control campaign. But true to the Nader tradition, Union Carbide's troubles are just beginning. Osborn has gone to Britain in a first-of-its-kind exchange program for consumer advocates. The British consumer association magazine *Which* is sending a delegate to work with Nader, and Osborn will spend a year in Britain. Osborn is already at work at one target in Britain: Union Carbide's British plants.

Lowell Dodge, the Director of Ralph Nader's Center for Auto Safety, rides to work on a bicycle. The pleasant, thirty-year-old mustachioed Harvard lawyer calmly threads his way each day across Washington's traffic-choked Fourteenth Street, and wheels up to the National Press Building where he takes the freight elevator to the eighth floor and begins work in a well-worn office suite filled with nineteen thousand complaint letters from car owners, a pile that is growing at the rate of two hundred a week. The job Nader has given

Dodge is this: Act as a citizen watchman over the National Highway Traffic Safety Administration, the agency created by Congress in 1966 to set auto safety standards. If he hadn't chosen to scatter his shot all over the consumer landscape, Nader himself might be director of the Center for Auto Safety since basically the job is an outgrowth of his original joust with the auto industry. But despite the fact that auto safety "made Nader," the center is only one among equals in Nader's circle of satellites.

Unlike the rest of Nader's units, the Center for Auto Safety did not begin from scratch, but actually is an outgrowth of his long-standing tie with the Consumers Union, which he serves as an unpaid director. In 1968, CU opened a Washington office to monitor the government's growing role in consumer affairs, but the office quickly ran through two directors, and at this point Nader and CU got together and worked out an agreement to create the Center for Auto Safety.

As part of this agreement, Dodge was put on the Consumers Union payroll via a grant from CU that carried the bumptious-sounding title of "The Ralph Nader Auto Safety Fellowship," an accolade Nader thinks "is a bit much" and would like toned down to the point where his name is dropped from the scholarship.

At first Dodge was leery of being "an auto safety expert." He readily admitted that he knew very little about auto safety when Nader approached him. But once exposed to Nader, he was infected with the virus of outrage that Nader transmits to all his converts, and in July, 1969, Dodge officially went to work for Nader. Again, Nader had made a good choice. Dodge has a quiet toughness about him. He is smart and singularly unimpressed by bureaucratic officiousness. Just as important, he couldn't be intimidated, a valuable asset, and one he showed in another kind of combat—the civil rights voter-registration campaigns. As a student, Dodge organized Negro voter-registration campaigns in Mississippi, and refused to be frightened away even after he was beaten by a band of rednecks in downtown Cleveland, Mississippi, a segregationist bastion. Today, after two years on the job, Dodge hardly qualifies as a "safety expert" in the narrow sense of the word. But he has learned to tap the technical expertise of a national network of Nader supporters who are sprinkled throughout the auto industry and the campuses of the nation.

From a standing start, Dodge and Nader have built a tight little machine capable of irritating, educating, and activating the National Highway Traffic Safety Administration. By government standards, the safety agency is pitifully small and undermanned. It has a staff of 625 to police the multibillion dollar auto industry, and its budget for fiscal 1972 was only $85 million. But it is a Goliath compared to what Dodge can throw against it. Two members of the Center for Auto Safety are conscientious objectors who, "thanks to an enlightened District of Columbia draft official," can serve their two years of required service at the center, Dodge says. The job may be far from the front lines, but it has its hazards—the pay scale, for example. Dodge pays one of the C.O.'s $40 a week and the other $70. The center also boasts one other lawyer in addition to Dodge, and three engineers, none of whom is paid more than $100 a week. One engineer has his master's degree, and experience working for TRW, the automotive and aerospace giant. His salary: $65 a week. Dodge's salary is $12,000 a year, high for a Nader associate, but again much lower than offers Dodge has had from other consumer groups who would like to woo him away from Nader.

The entire expenses for the center in fiscal 1970-1971 totaled $32,208. Nader contributes funds to the center from his speech-making tours, Consumers Union tossed in an $8,000 "expense grant," and Dodge himself produces revenue. He has been paid up to $500 a speech for appearances before groups like the New York State School Bus Owners Association, and the Automotive Parts and Accessories Convention. He also has been paid for appearances on radio and television, including a guest spot on *To Tell the Truth*, where the "real Lowell Dodge" had to stand up. The center has sold magazine articles, including one to *Popular Science*, but the bulk of the articles were bought by trade industry publications like Service Station Manager, or Automotive Industries.

Still another source of income is from information the Center for Auto Safety provides to lawyers who are involved in automobile litigation. The center gets about twenty inquiries a week from lawyers who want to know where they can get specific information on automobile defects that may be involved in a client's suit. The center doesn't charge for the information, but the lawyers are asked to send a contribution. "About every fourth guy sends a check," says Dodge. Again, Nader is the main source of much of this income. Most of the lawyers' inquiries come to him, and he refers them to the Center for Auto Safety. But the biggest money-producer for the center, and its biggest accomplishment to date is its book: *What To Do with Your Bad Car, An Action Manual for Lemon Owners.* Using letters sent to the center by lemon owners, Nader, Dodge, and Ralf Hotchkiss, a 24-year-old engineer, put together a step-by-step guide for car owners on how to protect themselves from getting stuck with a lemon and what to do if they are. The book, published in 1971, includes information ranging from the home addresses of the auto-industry lords (for the benefit of lemon owners who wish to write complaint letters) to printed copies of the pre-delivery inspection checklist dealers are supposed to follow before turning a car over to the owner. The book itself describes its purpose best when it suggests ways "consumers can help convince the manufacturers of the wisdom of altering their current patterns of irresponsible behavior."

Nader again turned to Grossman as his publisher, and the Literary Guild also chose the book as one of its selections. The book was published in the spring of 1971 and was greeted by rave reviews and sales are expected to reach the 100,000 mark. But by all standards, the Center for Auto Safety still is a shoestring operation even to the point where Dodge decided not to have the name put on the office door when he discovered it would cost a dollar a letter for the gold gilt lettering. But as Nader continually has shown, it is not how well financed you are, or how big you are, but where you push that counts in moving institutions like the United States government, or the auto industry.

The center's "pushes" have come from all sides. It produced information to help PIRG's lawyers in the court fight with GM over the defective wheels on its 200,000 camper trucks. The center's mail turned up tips on the defects in the lower control arms of 1965 to 1969 model Ford cars that could lead to the collapse of the wheel. The National Highway Traffic Safety Administration urged Ford to recall 85,000 cars used by the police, claiming the lower control arm was subject to collapse only under the stress of rough handling necessary in police work. But the fight is not over yet, and the center still is trying to force Ford to recall all 1965 to 1969 model Fords. The center has turned out a report on the safety of the Volkswagen called *The Volkswagen: An Assessment of Distinctive Hazards.* It has flooded the dockets of the National Highway Traffic Safety Administration with information criticizing the government's weak bumper standards, and has researched the problem of stronger automobile roofs and the problem of restraint seats for small children in automobiles. Dodge has even produced a report on the flammability of automobile fabrics.

As might be expected, Dodge's center is in conflict with the government as often as it is in conflict with industry. "We work hard on our research," says Dodge. "We go over all the contracts let by the government. We check the technical libraries, and we interview independent sources like professors at engineering schools. But when we go back to the government engineers working an automobile project, we find that they often don't know half of the things we have found out." According to Dodge, the staff of the National Highway Traffic Safety Administration is "with rare exception, relatively incompetent." To some government auto safety engineers, the center's staff is "a pain in the ass," as one bureaucrat put it.

But Frank Armstrong, head of the Office of Standards Enforcement for the National Highway Traffic Safety Ad-

ministration, is more kind in his estimation of the center.
Says Armstrong: "They try hard. They are not always right,
but neither are we. I appreciate their input. If we get an
occasional payoff from some of their information, it is worth
it. But sometimes I get the idea they are spread a little too
thin." Another official in the administration put it this way:
"They are gadflies and that's all they will ever be."

With Nader's blessing, the center has even produced its
first spin-off–the Center for Concerned Engineering. The man
at the helm of this satellite is the third author of the lemon
car manual, Ralf Hotchkiss. Slowed down not a bit by the
fact that a motorbike accident paralyzed him from the
waist down and left him in a wheelchair, Hotchkiss took as
his first problem hospital electrocutions. Since the advent
of the heart pacemaker and the cardiac catheterization, the
hospital has become so dangerous that it is the site of more
electrical accidents than any other industry except mining,
Nader says. He puts the yearly death toll at 1,200. Again,
Hotchkiss is like all of Nader's associates—young, but not
without experience. He is an electrical engineer, and an
inventor, whose inventions include improvements on medical devices. As for financing, Nader has put his "loaves and
fishes" formula to work—Hotchkiss is financed by his share
of the royalties from the lemon car manual. Last in the line
of Nader's automobile-oriented units is the Professionals for
Auto Safety run by Mrs. Collot Bruce, a 24-year-old Rad-
cliffe graduate and a Georgetown University law student.
In fact, the Professionals for Auto Safety is nothing more
than an information station. The basis for its existence is a
list of names of professionals around the nation—doctors,
scientists, engineers, and lawyers—who are "friends of
Ralph Nader" in the sense that they are willing to advise
him, offer him technical assistance, and tips on automobile
problems. In Nader's mind, the job of Professionals for
Auto Safety is to expand this group into a national constituency with the expertise to act as a check on the government's proposed auto safety standards as well as defective

cars produced by industry. Nader wants the group to grow, and plans to issue newsletters and hold seminars around the nation, but as yet the list of members is small, about 250.

On Saturday, May 8, 1971, an airport policeman at Logan Airport, Boston, marched over to a young student and demanded that he stop handing out purple and white fliers to airline passengers or face arrest. While the student was being harangued Ralph Nader was holding an early morning press conference in Washington at the Du Pont Plaza Hotel to announce the birth of the Aviation Consumer Action Project (ACAP), a nonprofit consumer group designed to take up the cause of the airline passenger for "better, safer, and less expensive airline service."

The student was one of a nationwide band recruited by Nader to hand out 50,000 leaflets about the new organization in an effort to woo support for "passenger power." Like the student in Boston, police ordered Nader volunteers at some other airports to stop the leafleting, claiming the airport was private property. But the student episode was a minor setback in what has been a long-running war between Nader and the airlines. "There are increasing signs that the airlines are engaging in the kind of management which may bring them to the deteriorating track run by the railroads in the past two decades," says Nader.

To counteract this, the object of ACAP will be to organize air travelers into a lobby group. Nonprofit, ACAP hopes to finance its operations with donations, not only from individual passengers but also from corporate subscribers since businessmen make up a large bloc of the airline passenger traffic. But to get the fledgling group on its feet, Nader put $10,000 of his funds into ACAP.

In announcing its formation, Nader said it was being formed "at the urging of concerned citizens around the world—businessmen, doctors, lawyers, environmentalists, aircraft owners, economists, and students as well as pilots, stewardesses, and other airline employees." But Nader also takes a deep personal interest in the airlines. As a man who travels tens of thousands of miles a year by plane, Nader knows personally all the airline passenger irritations—from suddenly cancelled flights to fare increases. His safety fetish is very much in evidence when it comes to the airlines, who are intensely proud of their safety record and highly sensitive to criticism, on safety grounds. But Nader has filed petitions with the Federal Aviation Administration to ban smoking on airliners on the grounds that it is both unhealthy and unsafe. He has criticized both the government and the Boeing Company for moving too slowly in 1970 to ferret out an engine defect on the Boeing 747 jumbo jetliners which were being plagued by a rash of engine fires. Two of Nader's Raiders, Princeton engineering graduates James T. Bruce and John B. Draper, investigated light airplanes and came to the conclusion that travel by small plane is the most dangerous form of transportation in the nation, and that the general aviation industry has ignored simple remedies that could save hundreds of lives each year. Nader has sharply criticized the Civil Aeronautics Board (CAB) for what he felt were unjustified fare increases, and has sued the agency to force the release of files on consumer complaints. Reuben Robertson, Nader's full-time associate, heads the CAB's newly-formed Consumer Advisory Board, a concession to the growing power of the consumer movement in aviation. But Nader is blunt in his demand that more must be done. There is, he says, a very definite role for ACAP. "To avoid the endless spiral of increasing rates which keeps passenger volume down, and the shortsighted subservience of the Civil Aeronautics Board and the Federal Aviation Administration, a meaningful at-the-scene action group is needed," he says. To Nader, the CAB and FAA more often behave like trade associations for the airline industry rather than sharp-eyed regulators.

"Both agencies needed to be engaged by a professional citizenship which will lead to fairer rates, planning for safety, recognition of environmental factors affected by airports and the industry—from pollution to noise—and the expansion of needed airline service in a context of effective competition nationally and internationally. At present such a professional citizenship has not been in operation. The few citizen actions before the agencies, and in the courts, have faltered for lack of sustained follow-through. ACAP, with its citizen volunteers and passenger supporters throughout the country and its student researchers, will strive to develop that stamina and close scrutiny on matters dealing with aviation practice and policy," Nader said in what for him was a mild burst of rhetoric.

But, as usual, Nader had singled out an area where the consumers had a boil. Over 200,000 passengers have their baggage "lost" by the airlines each year. It is the single biggest complaint the airlines get. Arriving in New York to find your suitcase has flown to Rome is enough to upset the most even-tempered airline passenger. If it happens more than once, the airlines have an enemy who is a potential recruit for Nader. Reservations are another sore point with passengers. Nader can tap a well of antagonism among passengers who make a reservation, and arrive at the boarding gate only to find the plane has been oversold, and they are without a seat. ACAP also plans to tackle what it terms "misleading and incorrect information" given to passengers about arrival and departure times.

To run ACAP, Nader picked K. G. J. Pillai, a lawyer from Kerala, India, and the author of a newly published book, *Air Net*, which indicts the International Air Transport Association (IATA) as a world aviation cartel designed to wring billions of dollars from the consumer in artificially rigged international air fares. Backing up Pillai as directors of ACAP are Reuben Robertson, Gladys Kessler, a public interest lawyer, and William Reisman, an associate professor at Yale Law School. ACAP's sharpest attacks to date have been on IATA, whose secret price-fixing sessions ACAP says result in international airline passengers being overcharged by at least $4 billion a year, and millions of others being denied the right to travel at all because of the prohibitive cost. Only two months after it was formed, ACAP's directors were picketing IATA's fare meetings in Montreal after they were barred admittance on the grounds that there were no provisions for consumer delegates to attend the sessions.

But ACAP delegates did manage to take a very important

first step in their war on IATA—they got publicity for their point of view. Carrying signs outside the Mount Royal Hotel that read: "Disband the Airline Cartel," and "How Fair Are Fares—End Secret Price-Fixing by Airlines," ACAP managed for the first time to get public attention for a business operation that dramatically affects the consumer, but which only a handful of airline passengers even know exists. "Getting rid of the secrecy, and getting the public to think about the role of IATA," are very important first steps for ACAP, says Robertson. But the battle will be long. The airlines are proud of the service they give passengers. There is very little recognition among top airline executives that service is a problem. How could it be? This is the area of the airlines' greatest competition, they argue, and go on to cite seating, food, and entertainment. Or they ask, "Isn't airline service better than the bus and train?" And they are right, as far as they go. But as is usually the problem with a Nader-attacked, industry, the airlines are not talking the same language as Nader. The industry is appalled at the idea of suggestions like a handbook on how the unsatisfied passenger may register a complaint. The airline industry is so closely wed to fare increases as a way to profitability that the concept of generally lowering fares to increase volume, and so profits, is not even given lip service.

The simple problem of lost baggage is not officially recognized to the public as a problem. When asked why the long-standing problem has not been solved, the airlines will argue not about the lost baggage, but concentrate on the fact that they handled 200 million pieces of luggage without incident in 1971. The same approach is taken to reservations —the industry will publicize the fact that its computers handled 330 million reservations in 1971. It doesn't want to discuss publicly those consumers who were sold tickets on overbooked flights. In the past, the industry could blow its own horn, and ignore, or respond slowly to what were considered only small groups of passengers. But in recent years these remaining hardcore problems—baggage, reservations, fares— grow faster because the number of persons who suffer grows as the volume of airline business increases. Despite this, Stuart G. Tipton, president of the Air Transport Association, the trade organization representing the major domestic airlines, could say of airline consumer advocates: "We don't need a posse of complaint seekers hunting people down to remind them of things they hadn't yet thought to complain about."

But according to Robertson, the initial response from airline passengers to ACAP showed "there was a lot of emotion build up" and it produced enough funds in two months to keep ACAP funded for a year.

Outside of Ralph Nader himself, one of the most persistent irritants in the corporate eye of General Motors is the Project on Corporate Responsibility, the sponsors of Campaign GM, a nationwide grass roots drive to force GM to think more about social problems and less about profits.

Outwardly, Campaign GM is laughable by comparison to overpowering GM. It is staffed by young lawyers and housewives. It exists on small foundation handouts. It owns only twelve of the more than 286 million shares of GM stock outstanding. Even Nader claims to have no direct connection with it. And in two tries, it has never been able to muster even three percent of the votes at a stockholders' meeting for its proposals to reform GM. But Campaign GM may be winning through losing, and if it is, the ultimate result could be a new way of doing business for GM.

Campaign GM's first goal was to create a national debate on the role of GM in society: Does the corporation have a social responsibility? Is there enough public participation in its decision-making processes? What responsibility, for example, does GM bear toward the pollution problem created by cars, or the highway traffic death toll? Should the consumer have a role in corporate policy? And the touchiest question of all: Is it the role of the corporation to decide it will take less profits to help solve social problems it may be causing? Added to the national debate, were two other goals: Put the public into the GM corporate decision-making process, and

RALPH NADER, INCORPORATED

change GM's policies in the area of minority hiring and consumer rights.

In a press conference launching the movement on February 7, 1970, Nader said:

"A basic thrust of the campaign will be alerting and informing the public about their omnipresent neighbor, GM, and how it behaves. It will ask citizens to make their views known to both shareholders and management. It will go to institutions that own GM stock and if they decline to respond, the constituents of those institutions will be contacted ... the campaign will reach to the universities and their students and faculty, to the banks and their depositors and fiduciaries, to churches and their congregations, to insurance companies and their policy holders, to union and company pension funds and their membership."

Nader kept his promise. Campaign GM by the opening of the GM stockholders' meeting only four months later had what, by GM standards, were revolutionary proposals to lay before the meeting. One called for GM to name three new directors (its nominees were former Presidential Assistant Betty Furness, Biologist Rene Dubos, and the Reverend Channing Philips, a Democratic National Committeeman) to represent "the public interest." The other called for a committee to study GM's performance in areas of public concern like pollution and safety.

The basic theory behind Campaign GM was that it was possible to bore from within GM to make changes; that it could win over the stockholders, especially the institutions in society which hold large blocs of stock, to a program of change.

To do this job, Campaign GM relied on two familiar tools of Nader's operation: the press and the power of moral suasion. For example, here is a sample of a letter Campaign GM sent to treasurers of universities it knew to hold blocs of GM stock:

"In the past twenty-five years, institutions of higher learning have become increasingly more tied to corporate America. It is crucial that the university recognize this intimacy, and not shy away from the responsibility to judge corporations according to the long-term goals that motivate educational institutions. While we address this letter to you as a representative of the university, we hope that you will consult the entire university community—including alumni, faculty, students, employees, and your neighbors—before arriving at a decision. You might consider, for example, holding a university referendum on how to vote your stock; or you could appoint a joint student-faculty committee to consider these proposals, and take the university proxy to the shareholders meeting in May."

If you were a bank president, Campaign GM sent you a letter that read in part:

"Banks own and vote large amounts of stock as trustee or nominee for numerous beneficiaries. Most employee pensions funds, for example, are managed by banks. The ultimate beneficiaries of these funds are employees, union members, and individual citizens who are concerned about such matters as air pollution, auto safety, rights of minorities, and worker health and safety."

The insurance company president got one that read:

"Your policyholders are legitimately concerned about the hazards to life and health posed by unsafe and polluting automobiles. They are also troubled by high repair bills.
"We hope that you will allow your shareholders and policyholders to help decide how to vote the share of General Motors stock held in the name of your company. The funds which your company invests, after all, are contributed by these people and held in trust for them."

When the stockholders' meeting was held, Campaign GM's proposals went down to overwhelming defeat. But Campaign GM had won a victory, too. In a little more than one hundred days from the start of its campaign, it had touched off a debate, and it had managed to win some support from the small shareholders, unions, universities, and politicians. From the moment the six and one-half hour long stockholders' meeting ended in 1970, Campaign GM began preparing for Round Two with GM in 1971. The procedure was the same as in 1970 but on a longer and more intensified scale. This time Campaign GM composed a new list of proposals for the stockholders that would 1) require GM to list on its proxy not only the management slate of directors for the board, but also candidates nominated by non-management stockholders, 2) allow GM employees, auto dealers, and purchasers of each new GM car to each nominate a candidate for the board of directors, and 3) force GM to publish in its annual report its progress in minority hiring, pollution, and auto safety.

But in the year that had passed since the first Campaign GM, GM itself had moved to placate some of its big stockholders who saw merit in some of Campaign GM's argument. Between the 1970 and the 1971 stockholders' meetings, GM appointed the first black to its board of directors, the Reverend Leon Sullivan, who promptly announced that "I know General Motors is going to use me as a symbol and sample of how liberal it has become . . . but I am going to use them." Sullivan added that "GM will have to do—if I stay on board— far more" in the fields of hiring and promoting blacks. GM got right to work on that and announced that it had deposited $5 million in black-controlled banks across the nation, and was increasing the number of blacks working at salaried jobs in its plants. To take some of the sting out of Campaign GM's charges on the lack of action on pollution, GM named Ernest Starkman, a well-known authority on air pollution, to the newly created job of vice-president for environmental affairs. It also bolstered its spending on safety research and pollution control research.

But one of the most dramatic and obvious responses to the pressure built up by Campaign GM came three months after the end of the 1970 stockholders' meeting. GM announced that it was setting up "a public policy committee" to advise the automaker on matters that affect the general public. The committee was made up of five members of the 23-man board of directors. Board Chairman James Roche said he felt the committee members were qualified to "act in the best interest of our stockholders as well as the broader community in which we operate."

Campaign GM was able to counter the public policy committee by charging that although it was a small step forward, the committee reflected GM's lack of understanding of what the public wanted. The committee, Campaign GM said, had no consumer representative, no environmentalists, no women, and no blacks.

But GM's reforms had their effect. Campaign GM went down to defeat again in 1971 by an even greater margin than 1970. But Campaign GM expects again that GM will move to adopt its 1971 proposals in some similar form before too long. The group is convinced that it has found a way to bring pressure for reform. To back up its argument, Campaign GM points to its supporters who ranged all the way from the First Pennsylvania Bank, and the giant Dreyfus Fund, to Vassar, Bryn Mawr, Brown, Antioch, and Pomona Colleges, and the Teachers Insurance Annuity Association. In between were ballots from the United Mine Workers Union and the International Ladies Garment Union. Public support came from politicians like Senators Edward M. Kennedy, Edmund S. Muskie, Harold Hughes, and Philip Hart.

Nader claims that if he is anything to Campaign GM, it is a godfather, not the father. Even on the day he was publicly announcing its existence, he stressed he was not serving the group in any official capacity. At the time, this was legal necessity; Nader's invasion-of-privacy lawsuit against GM was still in the courts. In its proxy statement, Campaign GM tried to clarify Nader's role. A paragraph in the statement said: ". . . the announcement of three shareholder proposals and of the three candidacies for director was made at a press conference held by Mr. Ralph Nader, who has been a critic of the corporation. Mr. Nader was involved in the discussions leading up to the submissions of the proposals, but he is not a member of Campaign GM or the Project on Corporate Responsibility, Inc., nor is he a financial contributor thereto."

The proxy statement went on to point out that "there is no connection between this campaign and Mr. Nader's lawsuit. There are no agreements between Mr. Nader and anyone connected with this solicitation concerning the lawsuit. . . ."

But Nader's ties are obvious. The entire concept of Campaign GM is an outgrowth of Nader's philosophy on business reform. John Esposito, a permanent associate at Nader's Center for Study of Responsive Law, is on the board of directors for the Project on Corporate Responsibility which runs Campaign GM. Geoffrey Cowan, another member of the board, is the husband of Aileen Adams Cowan, who worked with Nader on the deceptive television advertising campaign. Oddly, the chairman of the board is Philip C. Sorensen, the brother of Ted Sorensen.

Nader doesn't put any money into Campaign GM, however. It basically supports itself on grants from two foundations—the Stern and the Field foundations, both of which have contributed to Nader's Center for Study of Responsive Law. In 1970 and 1971, Campaign GM got grants totaling $30,000-a-year, $15,000 from each foundation. But like other Nader-backed units, Campaign GM doesn't plan to rely on foundation grants. It now has a mailing list of over three thousand persons who have shown support for its program, and the staff hopes to turn the list into a source of public contributions to finance its work.

Assessing what has happened since Nader first gave his blessing to the project, one Campaign GM staff member put it this way: "Yeah, we lost, but you can see for yourself, GM is turning, slowly, but it is turning, and we are going to stay on the job until it sets a new course."

One of the newest of Nader's satellite units is the Health Research Group, which will explore the autocratic world of medicine, a place where little criticism is brooked, particularly from laymen.

Like the Center for Study of Responsive Law, the doctors in the Health Research Group hope to harness the wave of idealism sweeping medical students who have finally begun to question the highly structuralized system of American medical practice, politics, and education.

Doctors and hospitals are natural targets for Nader. His mail has always carried a heavy quota of consumer gripes about shabby medical treatment, exorbitant bills, and what can only be described as contempt for the patients. To test his thesis that there is a need for medical reform, he already has made two sorties into problem medical areas. The Center for Study of Responsive Law made a study of nursing homes (*Old Age: The Last Segregation*) and also investigated self-regulation in the medical profession (*One Life—One Physician*, Dr. Robert S. McCleery, editor). But the three doctors who form the nucleus for the new group will work primarily on occupational health and safety problems and areas related to the government's Food and Drug Administration's functions, but Nader sets no limits. "These doctors can plow their own dimension. This is a pilot project designed to show what can be done," he says.

To get it moving, Nader has funded the unit, but like the other public interest groups, he expects the doctors to find their own long-range financing, perhaps through the foundation route or via contributions from the 325,000-man profession itself, one of the best paying in the nation. In Nader's mind, the group may eventually attract doctors in their fifties and sixties who have acquired more wealth than their "acquisitiveness would ever have permitted them to imagine." Men like this could afford to quit their lucrative practices and lend their aid to his medical reform drive, says Nader.

One of the most promising of Nader's satellites is the Corporate Accountability Research Group (CARG) which is headed by Mark Green, author of *The Closed Enterprise System: A Nader Task Force Report on Antitrust Enforcement.* This report attacked the failure of the government to police corporate monopolies which bilk the consumer out of billions of dollars through price fixing and shoddy merchandise. To correct the problem the report called for the break-up of most corporations with assets of $2 billion, an increase in criminal penalties for antitrust violators, a five-fold increase in the size of the government's antitrust force, and an end to political interference in antitrust cases. Funded completely by Nader, CARG's first major job will be to try to implement some of the report's recommendations. CARG will push for federal chartering laws which will set up national standards for chartering corporations, and put an end to the abuses of a state system of chartering corporations like the one in effect in Delaware, which is the corporate home to over 70,000 corporations, including General Motors. Green says CARG will spend much of its time and limited funds exposing corporate crime in areas of antitrust, pollution, and securities, using the twin weapons of the courts and lobbying for legislation. To do the job, Green has a staff of two other lawyers and an economist operating out of a suite of offices in a run down downtown Washington office building (1832 M Street, N.W.).

The Nader unit with potentially the widest constituency is called the Fishermen's Clean Water Action Project. It was organized in the spring of 1971 and hopes to recruit many of the nation's 60 million sports and commercial fishermen into a coalition which will be able to bring pressure on Congress for anti-water pollution bills. Nader's argument to the fishermen is obvious: pollution of rivers, lakes, and oceans by sewage and industrial waste is destroying the livelihood of commercial fishermen and the recreation of sport fishermen. Individually they count for little in the fight to clean up the waterways but if they band together in a national group, fishermen could become a powerful lobby group. Under Nader's plan, the fishermen would organize into five or six regional groups which would also support a national organization in Washington. The Washington headquarters will be staffed with full-time professionals lawyers, economists, engineers—who would represent the fisherman's interest before government regulatory agencies and in Congress. With its potentially large membership, membership fees would be minimal. As he usually does, Nader gave the job of running the Fishermen's Clean Water Action Project to the Nader Raider who knows most about the problem—David R. Zwick,

29, author of the "Water Wasteland," a Nader report on water pollution. Zwick says he hopes to get action on water pollution by focusing attention on the performance of public officials, by court action, and by lobbying for strong local and state laws.

One other unit, still in the planning stage, is Nader's hardest to create. He wants a black-run law firm in Washington. Despite his failure to entice Negroes to the Center for Study of Responsive Law, Nader hopes to fund a small black law firm that will stake out its own area of expertise in the public interest field. "I'll fund it, the blacks will run it. Once it gets off the ground, they are on their own," says Nader. Hopefully the black law firm will be opened for business in 1972.

Where is Nader heading with his string of satellites? To listen to him, he is only beginning. Washington is only one city. He visualizes public interest groups popping up across the nation like dandelions in a lawn. In each one he creates, he sees the possibilities of subdivision or multiplication. In Washington alone, Nader would like to see ten thousand lawyers working for the public interest. Is this legal army needed? Nader's answer: Industry has fifteen thousand lobbyists representing its side of the story, influencing legislation in its favor, and creating "a favorable climate." It is not too much to ask that the system make room for a people's lobby, says Nader. But the professional lobbyists and corporate lawyers still are prone to titter among themselves when Nader announces another new public interest law firm headed by a downy-faced lawyer fresh from a campus lecture hall whose only real assets are his brains and his still unclouded idealism. But it was Averell Harriman in his book *America and Russia in a Changing World* who said of Nader:

"He has aroused our country to think quite differently about a great many subjects. He has had enormous influence. Naturally, I don't agree with everything he and his raiders have said. Sometimes they are a bit too superficial and self-assured in their analysis. But basically he is on the right track, and it is an extraordinary thing that a young man of that type with high ideals can have the influence he has, and it gives me great heart that the individual still counts most in our country. No matter how big our institutions become, we arc as strong as our individuals are, not as strong as the state is."

6

SIDE DOOR LAWYERS

The leading lawyers of the United States ... have, to a large extent, allowed themselves to become adjuncts of great corporations and have neglected their obligation to use their powers for protection of the people.

—Supreme Court Justice Louis Brandeis

The organized bar has displayed a functional dislike of its clients. Lawyers have outpriced themselves. They have permitted the legal system to be congested, and justice to be delayed. Most Americans, in effect, have very little access to the legal system to resolve their complaints and grievances.

—Ralph Nader

In a bitterly given windfall, Ralph Nader is fattening the bank accounts of his most effective enemies—the Washington lawyers. Ever since Nader appeared on the scene with his barrage of petitions to the regulatory agencies, his court challenges and his plea to Congress for more restrictive legislation against corporate deprivations, the Washington lawyer has been there to parry, gut, or—when defeat is inevitable—simply to get the best possible deal for his corporate client.

The lawyers argue that their role is proper and ethical. They are simply advocates for the corporation, and in a democratic society it is necessary that the law provide an advocate for megacorporations as well as poor-box thieves. Nader doesn't quarrel with this. His argument is centered on the limits the lawyers may go to in fostering the private interest of a client over the public interest. He leaves little doubt that he feels too often the Washington lawyer goes beyond the bounds Nader considers proper.

Many of the Washington law firms are involved directly in preserving and protecting corporate strategies that operate in a twilight zone between the illegal and the immoral. When they do this, Nader contends the lawyers are distorting their roles, and abrogating their responsibility to the public interest, which exceeds that of their allegiance to clients. In most cases, there is no soul-searching on the part of the lawyer about this conflict. He simply follows the scent of the corporate retainer across the Nader-drawn ethical line without so much as a look back.

There is no doubt that Washington lawyers are paid well for the work the corporations ask them to do. The largest law factory in the capital, the 119-member firm of Covington and Burling, can sock it to its blue-ribbon clients at a top rate of $250 an hour. Put another way, a bill for twenty hours work by a partner in the firm would come to $5,000—that's $500 more than Nader pays the young lawyers in his public interest law firm for a year's work. But it is quite possible that it was one of these young lawyers who sent the corporate officials scurrying to Covington and Burling for help. The norm for partners in these firms are six-figure salaries, and even the fresh-from-law-school graduate can command up to $17,500.

In the pre-Nader era, the Washington lawyers performed just as efficiently and as expensively for their corporate clients, but without Nader to contend with, their job was a lot easier. Now Nader and his fellow consumerists and environmentalists have made it harder for the lawyers to work their legal magic on the government, but as a compensation, the increased work has meant increased billings, a formula the Washington lawyer is quite content with.

126

As a group, Washington lawyers are publicity shy, and the public knows little about them, and less about what it is they do for their big retainers. Occasionally one will surface—like the suave Clark Clifford who is the epitome of a Washington lawyer to the elite. Clifford's service to Presidents dates back to Harry S Truman. He also was a part of President Kennedy's brain-trust, and served a tour of duty as President Johnson's defense secretary in the ticklish period that followed the departure of Defense Secretary Robert S. McNamara. Then, like a ballet star, he whirled off center stage, and back into the recesses of the law firm of Clifford Warnke (a former assistant secretary of defense), Glass, McIllwain & Finney.

Abe Fortas, the former Supreme Court Justice, was another notable example of a Washington lawyer who operated in the Johnson Administration as a presidential confidant. Fortas, then a partner in Arnold and Porter, performed services for Johnson covering every facet of the President's life. It was Fortas who advised Johnson on how to run his personal fortune. He acted as Johnson's emissary to Washington newspapers in a vain attempt in 1964 to smother publicity over the arrest of Walter Jenkins, Johnson's special assistant, on a morals charge. It was Fortas who helped establish the Warren Commission on the Kennedy assassination, and who took part in negotiations to defuse the crisis over the uprising in the Dominican Republic in 1965.

This type of personal, unpaid, and unpublicized service to the high and mighty is the trademark of a successful Washington lawyer. Fortas was not a particular stellar example of the phenomena, either. Dean Acheson, secretary of state under President Truman, and advisor to Presidents Kennedy and Johnson, was a partner in Covington and Burling, and at the time of his death in 1971, had two hundred corporate clients. Probably the most common chore for the successful Washington lawyer is sophisticated fund-raising for politicians both in and out of power, or to take on the chairmanship of one of the government's many special commissions or task forces presidents are often wont to settle on for lack of any other solution to a problem. In return for this kind of work, Nader says the Washington lawyer is rewarded with special cues, advance tips, or simply subtle "guidance" that may be usefully translated for the benefit of clients.

Nader's shrewdest adversary in the Washington legal world is Lloyd Cutler of Wilmer-Cutler and Pickering. Cutler, a master legislative strategist, is the auto industry's first strike capability against Nader. It was Cutler who led the industry's fight in Congress against tough auto safety standards. According to Nader, Cutler's basic assignment was to prevent the 1966 Traffic and Motor Vehicle Safety Act from passing with a provision for criminal penalties against auto-industry officials who knowingly produced a product which would endanger human life. Cutler performed flawlessly, and Nader lost to a sophisticated Cutler-run lobbying campaign.

H. Thomas Austern of Covington and Burling is another famed guardian of the corporate kingdom who has jousted continually and very often successfully with Nader. Austern's specialty is the Food and Drug Administration, a regulatory thicket through which Austern leads his clients with all the confidence of Tarzan guiding the lost explorers to the edge of the jungle. It was the FDA which, in the summer of 1971, presented a microcosm of Washington lawyers at work, and revealed all the hues of their ethical cloth. What happened was this: Peter B. Hutt, a partner in Covington and Burling, was named general counsel for the FDA succeeding his personal friend William W. Goodrich, who retired. Nader pointed out rather vehemently that Hutt might find it rather difficult to regulate all of his food industry clients whom he had been representing before the FDA over the previous ten years. Not so, said Hutt, and in September, Hutt took over Goodrich's job. But Goodrich did not plop down in a front porch rocker—he took a job as president of the Institute of Shortening and Edible Oils, which happened to be one of Hutt's clients. Both Hutt and Goodrich said their job switches were coincidental, and that Hutt had nothing to do with Goodrich's selection as president of the Institute of Shortening and Edible Oils. According to Nader, the musical chairs routine was a blatant violation of the cardinal axiom of regulatory government that "an arm's-length relationship between regulator and regulatee has to be the desired norm."

It is this type of ethic-bending argument which has brought Nader to treating Washington law firms as he would any of the city's other major institutions and to investigating them to see if he can give the public an insight into the machinations of these lawyers whom he terms "the strongest power brokers in our society." Listen to Nader, as early as March 20, 1969, as he tells Senator Abraham Ribicoff's Subcommittee on Executive Reorganization how Washington lawyers bled the strength from proposed consumer legislation. Singling out first-line law firms like Covington and Burling, Hogan and Hartson, and Arnold and Porter, Nader described their lawyers this way:

"The gentlemen who run these operations are eminent specialists in cutting down consumer programs in their incipiency or undermining them if they mature. They are masters of the *ex parte* contact, the private deals and tradeoffs, the greasing of the corporate wheels, and the softening of the bureaucrats' will. They could tell this committee a great deal about the obstacles and tactics which consumer protection administration must deal with. Without such knowledge, the administrative structure cannot be devised and implemented effectively. I mean it cannot be known what to establish, and how to proceed unless you know what the opposition is like, what it has been like and what techniques it has been using, and how these techniques can be counteracted.

"I am sure that such citizens as Lloyd Cutler, Thomas Austern, and Edwin Rockefeller [another top Washington lawyer] —all of whom deal with the consumer in their distinctive way as corporate attorneys—would be pleased to come before this subcommittee and provide its members with their views and experience.

"I think you can learn more about the consumer movement and its problems by asking these gentlemen just how they go about doing it on the other side."

Nader told Ribicoff that the lawyers did not have to reveal any confidences—"just have them talk on strategies. Let them tell you how they do it and then the consumers will know how to do it to them."

Ribicoff went along with Nader's idea, and duly sent letters to the Washington lawyers asking them if they would give the committee a briefing—without endangering the confidences of clients. The results were predictable. Everyone of the lawyers circularized by Ribicoff turned him down politely, but flatly.

Most of them simply thanked Ribicoff for offering them a chance to reply to Nader, but Cutler couldn't resist the opportunity to claw his adversary with an answer that was both logical and appealing, but, lawyer-like, answered not the question raised, but another one which wasn't.

Said Cutler: "Nader's basic grievance is that capable lawyers present the views of their clients to the government on matters of consumer interest. He apparently disapproves of such presentations regardless of the merit of the case presented since effective advocacy may result in 'greasing of the corporate wheels and the softening of the bureaucrats will' and 'undermining' of consumer programs. But it is rather Mr. Nader's hyperbole which represents dangerous doctrine—one which comes close to 'undermining' the basic premises of our political institutions. The theory of our constitutional system is that public decisions can best be arrived at through the competition of ideas for acceptance. In the words of the First Amendment, each of us, large or small, powerful or puny, may 'petition the government for redress.' "

Cutler then went on to take a few more cuts at Nader. "Mr. Nader," he told Ribicoff, "has every right to challenge the merits of views he disapproves, and he is often the more persuasive. But it is regrettable that he feels compelled to cast aspersions on the very right to present views opposed to his own, or the integrity of those who do so. We do not challenge Mr. Nader's integrity and his commitment to the public interest. We take equal pride in our own and that of our clients." Then Cutler concluded with this:

"Under our system of government, unpopular individuals and institutions, varying according to the fashions of the times from Communist conspirators, foreign agitators, and security risks to the military-industrial complex, Wall Street, and Detroit, are entitled to defend themselves against attack with the help of counsel of their choice. Lawyers have been criticized for representing such clients and this can be expected to continue as long as controversies generate heat along with light. It is nevertheless disappointing that Mr. Nader, a lawyer himself with no lack of ability in a standup fight, would stoop to conquer."

To Nader, Cutler's answer was "sidestepping the issue." "Obviously, the right to represent the corporation is not questioned. What is questioned is the technique used in that representation, the quality of such legal advice, the manner in which the lawyer deals with the strain between his presumed commitment to the legal system and the public interest, and his allegiance to his corporate client, and the extent to which a lawyer has a citizen role outside his client relationship," says Nader.

Press him only slightly, and Nader gushes with examples to buttress his argument. One of the most blatant violations of the public interest centered around Lloyd Cutler, the auto industry, and a charge by the Justice Department that the automakers violated the antitrust laws by conspiring to restrain the development and marketing of antipollution devices. In 1966, the Justice Department began a grand jury investigation in Los Angeles to determine whether the automakers were keeping the antipollution devices off the market. After eighteen months of collecting evidence, the Justice Department lawyer on the case asked Donald Turner, who headed the Department's antitrust division, for permission to ask the grand jury to return an indictment. "The grand jury was even willing to return an indictment regardless of what Turner said so convinced were they that the automakers were guilty of criminal behavior," Nader said. But rather than giving the go-ahead, Turner, a Harvard Law School professor, simply dropped the criminal case without giving any explanation.

131

But on January 10, 1969, the Department did file a civil antitrust suit against the automakers, and their trade organization, the Automobile Manufacturers Association. The government asked for an injunction to bar the automakers from further conspiring to delay the development of an antipollution device. However, the suit was filed just as the Johnson Administration was coming to a close, and when Nixon took office there were rumors floated that the Justice Department wanted to get rid of what some GOP politicians saw as "a little spite work" by the Democrats to embarrass the Republicans. Finally, nine months later, on September 11, a public information man walked into the press room across the hall from the Attorney General's office and handed reporters a smoothly written news release that was designed to shove the problem into a closed file. The release said that the Justice Department had gotten the automakers to sign a consent decree—a legal device used to get offending parties to stop doing whatever it was they are charged with doing without them ever having to admit they did anything wrong to begin with.

As is usual with the government, it claimed that the consent decree was a masterful legal stroke. It avoided a long and costly lawsuit, but still brought the automakers to heel by forcing them to stop restraining the development of the antipollution devices, it said. Nader, however, was apoplectic. Here was a problem that was having a devastating effect on the entire nation. Automobiles cause fifty percent of the pollution in cities. Scientists have linked the pollutants with diseases ranging from cancer to emphysema, and government studies estimate the damage from air pollution at over $13 billion a year. Despite this, the government was allowing the automakers to snake out from under what was in Nader's mind a clear violation of the antitrust laws. Rather than avoiding a trial, Nader claimed the government had an obligation to seek one. "Can anyone deny the need and benefit for the public to learn about the nature and depth of this colossal corporate crime? The citizens of this country, who are the customers of this industry, have a right to know the extent to which the auto companies are deliberately responsible for the enormous health, economic, and aesthetic damages caused by the internal combustion machine. One of the purposes of a public trial is deterrence; but the Division [the Justice Department's Antitrust Division] has chosen to lose a grand opportunity to bring these companies and their harmful practices into the public arena of a courtroom.

"This aspect of the Division's case alone would have a greater deterrent effect than the tightest of consent judgments. Since it isn't any longer the practice of antitrust enforcement to pierce the corporate veil and hold the culpable officials responsible, a public trial would at least have shown that such corporate officials are holding far greater power over citizens in this country than they can exercise responsibly or even legally," Nader told Assistant Attorney General Richard W. McLaren.

As for the consent decree, it might as well have been written in Detroit. Particularly galling to Nader was the language of the decree—it severely restricted local governments and private persons from getting access to the information collected by the Justice Department in its investigation for use in their lawsuits against the automakers.

"The practical effect of this provision is that potential treble-damage plaintiffs would have to duplicate the investigative process which took the Department several years and several hundreds of thousands of dollars," Nader told McLaren.

Nader gave Cutler full credit for fashioning the consent decree in private negotiations with the government. "The process of secret *ex parte* type negotiations with representatives of the corporate defendants, in particular Lloyd N. Cutler, counsel for the Automobile Manufacturers Association, discourages confidence in antitrust enforcement, and facilitates sloppy, or political decision-making," Nader said.

Nader felt that Cutler was carrying the lawyer's role too far in lopsidedly favoring his client over the public interest. His feelings probably were best expressed by a group of law students who picketed Cutler's law firm carrying signs which read: DEADLY POLLUTANTS ARE OVERCOME BY LAWYER ETHICS NOT LAWYER RETAINERS. These same students, in a letter to Cutler, said: "The lawyer's duty in areas of such immense public health matters extends well beyond the narrow self-seeking of corporate clients. This broadened responsibility by the lawyer to the public interest is deeply rooted in the writings of our greatest legal scholars, including Justice Louis Brandeis, and is reflected repeatedly in the profession's canons of ethics. The canons require more than mere lip service; they require the time and energy of practicing lawyers to make them operational."

This question of "how" the Washington lawyer represents his client is in Nader's mind tied to the very weakness of the opposite side represented by the consumer interests. If the consumer had his legal expert roaming the agencies and Congress, it would redress the balance. These consumer lawyers could put the light of publicity on the dealings of their corporate counterparts; they could expose the shady deal, the profitable tip. Contrary to Cutler's claim, the consumer must be made to understand that the Washington lawyer's relationship with his corporate client is not a simple lawyer-client relationship. At times it becomes an ethically questionable partnership whose shadow falls beyond the courtroom, and reaches into fields ranging from the legislative and the political to the diplomatic. The consumer must be alerted as to how these lawyers can, and frequently do, exercise this power to the detriment of the consumer, Nader says.

The fight over the cigarette-labelling legislation is another example of the workings of a Washington lawyer in a situation where the public interest—in this instance, its health—was an issue. When the Surgeon General's report on cigarettes pointed out a correlation between smoking and cancer, the Congress was faced with a problem of what to do about cigarettes as far as the public was concerned. Frightened by the thought of the Congress acting on moral grounds, the Tobacco Institute, the industry's trade organization, opened its coffers and paid for some of the best legal advice it could buy in the person of H. Thomas Austern and Abe Fortas.

Says Nader: "What the tobacco industry wanted was men who were masters at working out quiet back-room solutions; men who knew their way around the congressional arena, and could keep a situation under control for their clients." These lawyers put on a tremendous lobbying campaign in Congress on behalf of the tobacco industry. "What you had," said Nader, "was a small group of men watering down legislation designed to protect the public from what the government's Surgeon General said was a health hazard." Was this within the bounds of legal ethics? Should Austern and Fortas supply the strategy to defeat, or shape legislation which was basically designed to benefit the public in an area of such crucial importance? Should a lawyer try to get government protection in the form of legislation to protect a client's harmful product? asks Nader.

The fight over the inflatable air-bag safety device for cars is another example of pressure being exerted by an industry to the detriment of the public interest. Available evidence indicates that the air bag is an innovation that could literally save thousands of lives now being lost, especially among drivers who refuse to use seat belts. The Transportation Department publicly supported the installation of the air bags. Transportation Secretary John A. Volpe was one of the biggest backers of safety devices, and originally set a 1972 deadline for their installation. But then the auto industry, basically Ford in this case, began putting pressure on the White House for delay. Auto industry lawyers made contact with Peter Flanigan, Nixon's special assistant, and lo and behold, the deadline for installation of the air bags began to march backward. Three times an embarrassed Volpe was forced to announce publicly that the air-bag deadline would be postponed. The newest date is supposed to be August, 1975, or in time for the 1976 model cars.

In questioning the roles lawyers play in the rape of the public interest, Nader is trying to stimulate an examination of conscience by these lawyers. Can a lawyer morally hide behind his role of the advocate when what he advocates for his client is damaging to the public interest? Doesn't the lawyer, in areas of public health and safety, have a broader responsibility to advise his client that what he may be doing is not in the best interest of the public? Or in even more simplistic fashion, does the lawyer who is involved in crucial issues affecting the public, and particularly in areas where there are few or no advocates for the public interest, have the right to remain silent, or must he speak to his clients about the public interest?

The law has always been something special to Nader. Even as a youngster, he hung around courthouses. But there really are only a handful of persons who have ever had Nader as their personal lawyer. A member of the bar in Connecticut and Massachusetts, and admitted to practice before the Supreme Court, Nader has not argued a case since he left George Athanson's law firm in Hartford where he performed his only full-time trial work. But, nevertheless, he has all the qualities of a good trial lawyer. Like Edward Bennett Williams, Melvin Belli, F. Lee Bailey, and the other superstars of the courtroom, Nader's ability to marshal facts and present them with an overwhelming rapidity impresses anyone who comes in contact with him. Nader's natural sincerity would be another plus for him in working a jury. He has a "young Abe Lincoln" look about him right down to his normally scuffed shoes. "The only thing missing is a string bow tie," cracked one reporter who watched Nader hold an impromptu news conference in the lobby of the garish Fontainbleau Hotel in Miami where he had just scolded the 173,000-member Oil, Chemical, and Atomic Workers Union for the labor movement's failure to protect workers from on-the-job safety hazards.

At Harvard, "the law students treat Nader as if he is a deity," says one of Nader's young associates. A Gallup poll taken for *Redbook* magazine in January, 1971, supported the hero-worship theme. Out of 137 graduating law students at twenty of the nation's top law schools, Nader was "the most admired" on a list of names that ranged from Supreme Court Justice William O. Douglas and Former Attorney General Ramsey Clark to William Kunstler and J. Edgar Hoover. But there are over 325,000 lawyers in the United States—five percent of them work in Washington—and obviously not all of them think of Nader as the greatest legal mind since Hammurabi. His adversary H. Thomas Austern, for example, when asked about Nader, was quoted in *The Washingtonian* magazine by writer Joseph Goulden as having said: "Fuck him."

As a student, Nader was little noted at Harvard Law School. His main after-class preoccupation was with the school's newspaper, the Law School *Record*, and his contemporaries wrote him off with a few lines in the year book saying he was a member of the "Bull and Bear," which was a student business club that was oriented to learning the workings of the stock market. Other than that, he was listed as a member of the Student Bar Association.

But if Nader was not studying his law books with all of the effort he might, he certainly was studying the workings of law schools, and what he learned, he didn't like. To this day Nader argues that to understand the legal crises that afflict areas of society like the courts, the government and the corporation, the consumer and environment, it is necessary to see what happens to law students when they come to sit at the feet of the great, the near-great, and the mediocre professors of law. According to Nader, the law schools and the law professors for decades past turned out a product that was designed to fill a particular mold which was created by the major law firms. In other words, the demands of these prestigious law firms determined what type of law would be emphasized in the law-school curriculum. Of course, the law firms hired the lawyers who were proficient in the high profit areas of law. Consequently this type of feedback produced a curriculum that reflected the profit areas over the problem areas, Nader claims. For example, he says the law student found many courses in tax law, estate planning, and the problems of the giant corporations, but criminal law, which affects many more persons and is a major societal problem, was given a lower priority since it carried a lower rate of return to the lawyers' pocketbook. There were even fewer courses offered in areas like the rights of the tenant, but the landlord's rights were well covered since he was a client of the better law firms. Fewer still were the law-school graduates who knew anything about protecting the consumer from marketplace fraud. In Nader's first specialty, the defective automobile, the emphasis in the law schools was on the law as it applied after the crash, and no thought at all was given to the law as a way of enforcing safer car designs. After all, the automobile accident business in 1971 produced over $3 billion in revenues for the legal industry and there was no great thrust to trim this pot of gold.

When it came to social questions, the law schools quietly ignored the legal problems of city slums such as the often unenforced building codes and health code. As the lawyers lockstepped out of schools, they went to work for the sellers, not the consumers, the big corporate polluters, and not those who fought against pollution. The highway lobby had all the high-priced talent it needed, but the citizen organizations who fought against it had little. The same imbalance was found in institutions like labor where the labor bosses had all the legal power they needed, and the rank and file had little or none. In Nader's case, this is what led him to the side of United Mine Workers official Joseph Yablonski who was assassinated in the midst of his effort to oust the union's entrenched leadership.

It was this massive flooding of lawyers to "one side of society" that left millions of persons without access to justice, and fueled their frustration which would finally erupt in forms ranging from city riots to the consumer revolt.

This imbalance, this lack of fair seeding of lawyers through society and the blatant encouragement of the law schools in this injustice, is to Nader a social crime that makes a mockery out of the American claim to a democracy.

"Without rights, democracy cannot exist, but without rights linked to remedies represented by lawyers, a practically functioning democracy cannot exist, and that is what the great gap is in this country."

But none of this seemed to make much of a dent on the

law school. It was not until the late 1960s that the better law schools began to add law courses on the problems of the poor, the environment, and consumerism. But even here, the impetus came from the students who recognized the problem first. Their pressure also extended to the large corporate law firms in the form of demands that they be allowed to do more *pro bono publico* work, or they would not put their brains to work for the firms, but would go to small law firms, the government, or public interest law firms. Some of the law firms responded to the pleas. In order to have their cake (the top law students) and eat it, the corporate law firms upped the starting salaries to as high as $17,500, and made promises of increased *pro bono publico* work to the law school graduate. Hogan & Hartson, number three in Washington corporate law firms, has put a partner in charge of a Community Services Department. Arnold and Porter also have a formal *pro bono publico* program, as does Covington and Burling. The same is true of many other large corporate law firms in New York. But Nader remains skeptical as to whether these are sops for young lawyers that will never have any real impact on the problem of providing legal counsel to those who have been shut out of the system. The other obvious problem with the *pro bono* program is, what happens when there is a clash of interest? It is one thing for a corporate law firm to let its staff help the indigent, but Nader is talking about a much wider interpretation of *pro bono* work. How, he asks, will law firms react to the inevitable situation where a big retainer client finds himself aligned against an opponent being served on a *pro bono* basis by one of the firm's young lawyers?

In the final instance, the drive for change in the profession of law will depend on the young lawyer. Applications for law school admission are soaring, and the 1971 total was expected to increase by forty-five percent over 1970. The most often heard argument for the rise is that the law is seen by youth as a place where the real action is; a place to make changes, and bring the big institutions to heel. Not everyone sees the trend so idealistically, however. The vast majority of new lawyers, this argument runs, still go directly from the campus to the big law firms. "Ralph Nader isn't getting anyone who has a chance at a clerkship with a Supreme Court Justice nor is he getting any of the Harvard Law *Review* editors," say the cynics, who are right on both counts. At Columbia University Law School, a questionnaire in the spring of 1971 showed that only four of the 136 third-year students said they had accepted public-service jobs. This compares with eighty-eight who planned to work for law firms alone. Mrs. Ruth Traynor, director of the school's placement office, told a reporter from the *Wall Street Journal*: "When the graduates have to choose between public service and a $16,000 a year salary, I'm cynical enough to believe that the dollar sign wins out." A survey of 375 Stanford Law School graduates in the past three years showed that 6.1 percent are working for *pro bono* legal service programs compared to 45 percent at law firms. The rest of the graduates are scattered through corporate jobs, the armed forces, the government and judicial clerkships. There is no doubt that the interest of the young lawyer in *pro bono* work has increased sharply. Nader's opponents, however, claim that he cannot realistically expect lawyers to be more self-sacrificing than any of their brother professionals or society as a whole. Unless money is provided in quantity and over the long term, Nader's vision of a widespread public interest bar will never materialize, they say. Nader doesn't dispute this. He realizes that money from foundations is not long-term funding, and government financing is too controversial and too restrictive. His real hope is that the legal community itself will supply much of the funding needed to make public interest attractive.

"It is really necessary for lawyers simply to recognize that the whole legal system is crumbling; it's archaic; at times it is downright repressive; it's not responsive to the needs of the people, it is not even expansive to meet the needs of a growing population and economy. What the legal system simply has to decide is whether it is going to let the legal system crumble even further or whether it is going to tax itself ten percent of its income and allocate this money to creating a new dimension to the legal profession—public-interest lawyers, who will, on a day-to-day basis, work on improving the overall structure of the legal system, and represent the unrepresented." This will be a major concern of Nader's in the years to come, and while most of his fellows may be content to debate the question of how, or whether to proceed along these lines, he will be in the field working.

7

MONEY: HOW TO
SPEND IT NADER-STYLE

It's always been boring to think about money . . .

—Ralph Nader

Ralph Nader's name is worth millions. It is his only real possession, and he guards it fanatically. Madison Avenue advertising men salivate just thinking of an ad campaign based on a smiling Nader standing next to a new model car, and saying something like: "The new wide-trunk Perculator-8 is the safest car on the market!" Or selling frankfurters, perhaps with this endorsement: "Ralph Nader says if you don't like animal hair in your frankfurters buy Brand-X franks today!" In their minds, the Good Housekeeping Seal would pale under a Nader-approved seal.

But the idea will stay a pipedream. To Nader, any attempt to commercialize his crusade would destroy it. He refuses to do anything that could be even faintly construed as a product endorsement, no matter how big the fee. The same rule applies to the law. A gold-lettered RALPH NADER, ATTORNEY on the door to a suite of offices would swamp him with cases. Here again, Nader feels taking cases, referring them to other lawyers, or giving paid legal advice would make him suspect. To his way of thinking, he must be the male counterpart to Caesar's wife if he is to keep his credibility.

143

GM even tried to buy Nader's name with a job offer. The bid came directly from GM's then vice-president and now president, Ed Cole, and it was made two months after Nader's book on auto safety hit the stands. Cole invited Nader out to GM's test center at Warren, Michigan, on January 14, 1966, in hopes of blunting his attack on the Corvair with a technical briefing from GM's engineers. Three times during the day, Cole threw out the bait to Nader. "We'd be getting out of cars, or walking down halls, and Cole would keep asking: 'Ralph, why don't you come out here and put your ideas to work for GM?' " Nader recalls. Having Nader on the payroll would have been an excellent investment for GM. It would have spared then GM President James Roche from the humiliating public apology he made two months later when the tawdry story of the detectives spying on Nader broke in the newspapers. And more importantly, GM might still be able to operate on its old answer-to-God-alone policy.

As for Nader, he could have, if he wished, rationalized that Cole was right; perhaps he could change GM from the inside, and along the way he could pick up a five figure paycheck and a tasteful colonial-style home in the auto industry stockade at Bloomfield Hills, Michigan. At the end of the road, there would be a comfortable pension. But to Nader, Cole's offer was simply a bribe. "They thought the job would shut me up," says Nader. When Cole made his first offer, Nader said he tried to laugh him off. But when he kept it up, "I finally told him that if he wanted to put my ideas to work he already had all the talent he needed. All he had to do was liberate it."

Some of Nader's would-be business partners never even bother to consult him. A Datsun car dealer took an ad in the newspaper and claimed that Datsun had to be good since Ralph Nader drove one. The dealer, who even ran a picture of Nader in the ad, got a call from Nader's lawyer, demanding that he not repeat the ad, and threatening a suit unless he also agreed to run another ad saying he had deceived the public. A Texas car dealer thought he had come up with the brightest of all ideas. For a fee, he wanted Nader to come to his dealership and autograph Corvairs for customers. A gas station in southern California simply put up a sign that read: "Ralph Nader Buys His GAS Here." Nader has gotten offers from novelty manufacturers promising him up to $300,000 if he will let his name be used on everything from ashtrays to key rings. Hallmark Cards, Inc., made free use of his name on a birthday card. He has been asked to endorse automobile shock absorbers, and take top billing in a travel agency. One businessman even wanted to set up a food franchise around the nation that would offer Ralph Nader Hamburgers. But if Nader is scrupulously honest, he works hard to get the money to stay that way. When he arrived in Washington, Nader was not living out of the beggar's bowl. He had some savings; the result of his frugal life-style. He had a half-finished manuscript on the unsafe Corvair in his suitcase, and the promise of a $50-a-day consultant's job from former Presidential Aide Daniel P. Moynihan, who was an assistant secretary for Labor at the time, and at work on a project to help determine the federal government's role in auto safety.

The Moynihan-Nader alliance goes back to 1959 when Moynihan, then an aide to New York's Governor Averell Harriman, spotted an article on auto safety that the 24-year-old Nader wrote for the March issue of *The Nation*. With an article of his own coming out on auto safety in the April issue of *The Reporter* magazine, Moynihan telephoned Nader and the two traded ideas. The relationship was maintained over the years, finally climaxing in 1964 with Moynihan's job offer to Nader. But even without Moynihan's job, Nader had planned to set up his base of operations in Washington in order to lobby for safety legislation in Congress.

Today Nader doesn't have so much as a suit of clothes more than he had then. But he has poured over $1 million into his consumer crusades over the last three years, and hopes to step up spending to about $1 million a year.

Where does he get his money? Who is bankrolling him? The questions fascinate his friends and his foes. The critics will tell you that Nader is personally profiting from his supposed do-goodism. His backers on the other hand, would have you believe that their "Mr. Clean" exists on contributions from traffic-accident widows, and coke money donated by students (Nader is fond of pointing out to students that they spend an average of $250 a year on cokes, booze, and cigarettes—money that could help the consumer-environmentalist crusades). Neither group is right.

The truth is that Nader is a tremendously successful money-raising machine. But he also is an open-handed spender for his consumer projects. He looks on money in the way the parish priest does—it is all to be used for God's work, and in Nader's case that work is his consumer crusades. Consequently, he has been on a continual raise-spend-raise-funds treadmill.

The first large stone in Nader's delicately built financial structure was his book, *Unsafe at Any Speed*. It produced $60,000 in royalties and was the launch vehicle for his entire movement. But selling the book wasn't easy. Book publishers, like Congress, were not all that interested in auto safety in the early 1960s. Alfred Knopf, Inc., was kinder than most who simply rejected the idea. The publisher told Nader to send in a few chapters and an outline, and they would look it over. Random House turned it down flat. A Random House editor told Nader he didn't think "anyone but the auto insurance industry would be interested in a book like that." Finally, the *New Republic*'s James Ridgeway steered Nader to Dick Grossman, owner of the Grossman Publishers, New York City. Grossman saw the value of the book. He backed it and the result was a runaway best seller. But the money from the book has long been spent and Nader now operates his center by tapping two basic sources: foundations and individual gift-givers.

To get the money he needed, Nader blitzed the foundation circuit. In 1968, the year he charted the center, his Internal Revenue filing showed a total of $5,000 in grants and gifts. By 1969, he had boosted the total to $173,117. And in 1970, the center received almost $380,000 in gifts and grants. Here is a breakdown of the 1970 contributions:

Midas International Corp. Foundation Chicago, Ill.	$100,000 (an installment on a promised $300,000)
Dreyfus Corporation New York, N.Y.	$10,000
Jerome Levy Foundation Chappaqua, New York	$10,000
Anonymous New York, N.Y.	$10,000
Norman Foundation New York, N.Y.	$25,000
Marion R. Ascoli New York, N.Y.	$ 5,000
Samuel Rubin Foundation New York, N.Y.	$10,000
Wallace-Eljabar Fund Inc. East Orange, N.J.	$20,000
Field Foundation New York, N.Y.	$10,000
Stern Family Fund New York, N.Y.	$20,000
New World Foundation New York, N.Y.	$ 9,300
Florence Roger Charitable Trust Fayetteville, N.C.	$10,000
Public Safety Research Insti- tute Washington, D.C. (Estab- lished by Nader with a $150,000 donation from mil- lionaire Robert Townsend)	$ 5,000
W-G-B-H Educational Foundation (Producer of television series on Nader's crusade) Boston, Mass.	$16,669
Mr. & Mrs. Martin Peretz Cambridge, Mass.	$14,515
Abelard Foundation New York, N.Y.	$ 7,500

New York Foundation New York, N.Y.	$ 5,000
Speiser, Shumate, Geoghan New York, N.Y. (Nader's lawyers in his invasion of privacy suit against General Motors)	$10,000
Public Welfare Foundation, Inc. Washington, D.C.	$10,000
Sierra Club Foundation San Francisco, Calif.	$ 5,000
Joseph Gluck Foundation New York, N.Y.	$ 6,000

Nader lumped the under-$5,000 contributions into a total of $61,522, bringing the overall total of contributions and grants to the center in 1970 to $380,406.

Added to this figure was another $39,245. It included $7,794 from royalties on the books published by the center. Another $15,711 came from the sale of the reports before they were put in book form. Interest produced $13,057, and the center listed $2,683 in "miscellaneous income." The money brought the center's total receipts for 1970 to $419,-651.

But Nader could hardly be said to suffer from a glut of funds. The same IRS return showed he is spending almost as much as he takes in to keep the center operating. Just paying his permanent staff, secretaries, and summer students cost the center $136,000 in 1970. The telephone and utility bill ran to $12,360. The center spent $7,571 to have its reports reproduced and another $4,945 was listed as travel expenses on research and interviewing sources. Along with these expenses were all the other normal expenses of running an organization including items like $3,375 for legal and accounting fees, and $1,926 for postage. All told, the center started 1970 with a net worth of $124,352, and finished the year with a net worth of $174,604, an increase of only $50,252, despite its receipt of $419,651 in gifts and income during the year.

There is one major missing element in Nader's foundation support—the giants of the field, Ford, Rockefeller, W. K. Kellogg, Alfred Sloan, Max C. Fleischmann foundations— have ignored his work. The biggest of all the large foundations, Ford, was the most likely source of funds based on its past record, but so far, Ford has not put a nickel into Nader's center nor is it likely to. Nader says word has been passed to him that Henry Ford, the president of Ford Motor Company, and a man who takes second place to no one in his dislike for Nader (Nader, in a letter to Ford on February 8, 1971, pointed out that the fun-loving Ford spent a good deal of time at European auto races "but no time at a single auto safety or pollution conference in Detroit or elsewhere") would try to block any attempt by the Ford Foundation to give funds to Nader's center.

But that hasn't stopped Ford Foundation President Mc-George Bundy from asking Nader's advice on how to finance other public interest groups. Bundy even asked Nader to come to New York to brief the Ford Foundation staff on how it could use its money to aid public interest groups like Nader's.

Most of the trustees of the other big foundations are connected in some way with the dominant corporations of the United States. Nader puts it this way: "The same type of person who sits on the board of GM sits on big foundation boards."

One foundation-watcher claimed that the big foundations don't want to be tied to the personality of one man. They prefer organizations to individuals. In Nader's case, "Ralph is just too much for them—he scares them.

"The easier route is to stick to the good, gray philanthropic work. Remember, the foundations still are running scared over the recent congressional investigations, and putting their prestige behind a controversial figure like Nader would bring all their enemies out of the woodwork again," he says.

But there is one exception to the hands-off attitude of big foundations. The Carnegie Corporation Foundation of New York, which ranks tenth in size of the nation's over 20,000 foundations, has given Nader's center a $55,000 grant. The money is being used to produce a citizens' guide to the government's regulatory agencies—the Interstate Commerce Commission, the Civil Aeronautics Board, and the Federal Trade Commission. To be published soon, the guide will explain how the consumer can become a part of the decision-making process in the agencies so that he will have a voice on issues like proposed rate and fare hikes for which he must pay the bill.

Nader is constantly on the lecture circuit. He thinks nothing of such stints as scheduling speeches on eight Oregon college campuses in one day with the first speech set for 7 A.M. In the course of a year, 1971, he spoke to groups ranging from the Yale University Alumni Association to the 30,000-member Japan Auto Consumers Union.

But the college campus is his prime target. Signed up with the American Program Bureau in Boston, the largest college-lecture brokerage in the nation, Nader commands $3,000 a lecture, the same price tag put on Jane Fonda, Dr. Spock, and ex-Senator Eugene McCarthy, but in Nader's case the bill never fails to startle the student government leaders who still think of idealism as its own reward. But $3,000 is his top price. He ranges all the way down the scale to nothing. Under his contract, Nader is committed for a one-hour speech. But on most campuses he will talk for an hour and a half, sometimes longer. After he is through, Nader normally will sit in a campus lounge and answer questions about his work for as long as there is interest. But his constantly tight schedule has left him with a few enemies on campuses where he has failed to keep a speaking date. Not everyone is happy to get a telephone call from Nader saying he missed his connecting jet flight when his cab, making a last-minute dash to the airport, was caught in a traffic jam. Or to be told, as was Dr. Ray Hornback, vice-president for university affairs at Morehead State University, Kentucky, that Nader's flight was cancelled and the next flight out was aboard a Convair 580 prop plane which Nader considers unsafe and refuses to ride. Left with a student convocation, and no speaker, Dr. Hornback described himself this way: "I am a very unhappy consumer."

On the speaker's platform, Nader is like the little girl: When he is good, he is very, very good, and when he is bad, he is horrid. To begin with, he is not an extrovert, and can appear very ill-at-ease if he gets off to a bad start. About to enter a lecture hall at Harvard, he once turned to an aide and said: "God, you'll never know how I hate this." He has no gimmicks in his delivery, and he starts from a low key and builds up, slowly. Bent over the lectern, seldom reading a speech, and seldom using even notes, Nader almost seems to be convincing himself as he goes along. He begins bombarding his audience with examples of corporate outrages, and if he is in good form, his genuine anger begins to well, and he starts transforming himself into the outraged consumer image the public reacts to. But Nader is only in his very best form when there is a question and answer session, and it is laced with critical questions. If he is attacked, Nader never fails to strike back sharp and fast. With his quick mind, he can hold his ground with the best of hecklers, and the most cutting critics. But if the audience is quiet and the questioning weak, Nader may never rise above a monotone, and he can leave an audience squirming in its seats or drifting toward the exits.

There is no doubt that the lecture circuit is a prime source of income for Nader. The more money he needs, the more he will speak. Between 1969 and 1971, Nader was on the road with Willy Loman-like frequency. His fee has more than doubled since he started, and even though the American Program Bureau takes about thirty percent of the speaker's fee, Nader still can earn $100,000 a year from his lecture tours.

Still another source of income is magazine articles. He was paid $25,000 in 1970 for putting his name on articles for magazines like *Saturday Review, McCall's, Ladies' Home Journal*, and a long list of trade journals. But in typical Nader fashion, he seems to take from those who can afford it, and give to those who can't. Like his speeches, his fees for articles range down to zero. He may get $1,500 from *McCall's* but he

151

contributes a regular column free to a magazine called *Business Today* which is operated by Princeton University students. But Nader, because he is juggling too many projects, is farming out writing assignments to some of the younger lawyers in his firm. They put together articles using Nader's ideas, and after he contributes editing and advice, the article goes out under his name. But this type of ghostwriting adds strength to the argument that Nader is diluting his effectiveness by taking on more than he can effectively handle.

Nader is testy about his private income. Like his rooming house, his love life, and his family, he feels strongly that this is not a matter of public concern. On one occasion he was visibly upset when photographers from *Life* magazine wanted to photograph his room for an article. He turned them down, insisting that he had to maintain some privacy. "Privacy is important to me. I have only a little left, and I am not letting go of it," says Nader. Nor will he "let go of information" on his personal bank account. Always harking back to his targets in the corporate world, Nader will argue that GM's President Ed Cole, or Henry Ford, do not reveal their personal finances. "Why should I be different? Isn't it pretty obvious how I spend what I make? I can't say the same about Henry Ford." Then Nader lapses back into the role of a very successful strategist. "Besides, if the opponents don't know how much I have to spend, they don't know what I can, or can't, do to them next," he says.

Another smaller source of income in 1971 for Nader was a $10,000 award given to him by the David and Minnie Berk Foundation for "a major achievement in prolonging or improving the quality of human life." Known as the Max Berg Award, Nader was selected because "he has, almost single-handed, made our cars safer, our food more nearly pure, our government more open and responsive, our corporations more aware of our demands." In winning the award, one of the largest cash awards of its kind in the United States, Nader joined a distinguished group, including Dr. Michael DeBakey, famed for his open heart surgery, and Dr. George Wald, the Harvard biologist and a Nobel Laureate.

But much to General Motors' chagrin, it is GM money which formed the biggest single block of Nader's personal funds. In an out-of-court settlement, GM paid Nader $425,-000 to settle an invasion-of-privacy lawsuit growing out of the private detective incident.

Nader filed for $7 million in damages in November, 1966, but GM claimed the actual total was $25 million when all the overlapping claims in the complaint were totaled. In search of a lawyer to take his case, Nader again turned to a friend for help. This time it was Paul Rheingold, a Harvard Law School classmate with the New York law firm of Speiser, Shumate, Geoghan. The question of whether of not Nader could make his charges of "invasion of privacy" stand up in court were "iffy," but the law firm took the case on a contingency basis and began a four-year court battle that compiled thousands of pages of court testimony, and cost GM an estimated $600,000 to fight the suit. It finally sputtered out in a nighttime meeting in the offices of Simon H. Rifkind, a former federal judge who represented GM, where a preliminary agreement on settlement was reached in August, 1970.

Nader's lawyers took one third of the award right off the top. Nader got the remaining tax-free $283,000 and promptly announced that he would pour the money back into his campaign to reform GM. It would be GM's contribution to the consumer movement, Nader said. "They're going to be financing their own ombudsman."

But some of Nader's backers were unhappy about what they thought was a compromise unbecoming Nader. When he filed the original suit, Nader said it would be a long, drawn-out battle. Even before the settlement there had been three appeals to the appellate division of the New York Supreme Court and one to the New York Court of Appeals. Nader took to referring to it as the "suit of the century," but in the end Nader was advised by his law firm to take the GM offer.

Speiser said at the time of the settlement that "we advised

Mr. Nader to accept because the $425,000 would be all we could likely get." If the case went to court, Speiser said the judge would have the right to cut down the settlement regardless of any eventual jury award. When it was over, Nader said he made his decision to accept because "it was a question of do you wait until the 1980s or do you start now and put the proceeds to work?" GM never admitted any wrongdoing, and contended that the settlement was "desirable from the viewpoint of General Motors to avoid the very substantial additional expense and demands" upon its legal staff. Nader, however, felt no compunctions about relieving GM of some of its cash. He calculated that the $425,000 settlement represented the equivalent of seventeen minutes gross revenue if all GM's operations were running twenty-four hours.

Nader is pinning most of his hopes for financing his crusades on the faceless American consumer. He has started a campaign to tap the huge pool of his supporters through a public fund-raising drive. To do the job, he has set up a new group called Public Citizen, a non-profit corporation, with Nader as its unpaid president. Public Citizen launched its opening drive on June 1, 1971, with a mailing of 200,000 pledge cards asking for a $10 donation. Hoping to raise $1,000,000 a year through his Public Citizen, Nader told potential subscribers in a letter accompanying the pledge cards:

"It is abundantly clear that our institutions, public and private, are not performing their proper functions but are wasting resources, concentrating power, and serving special interest groups at the expense of voiceless citizens and consumers." He told the prospective donors that "A way must be found for the individual citizen to provide an impact on government agencies and corporate board rooms. Government agencies often serve as protectors of the industries they are supposed to regulate. Bureaucrats cannot easily overcome the pressure brought by the hundreds of special interest lobbyists in Washington and state capitals. A primary goal of our work is to build countervailing forces on behalf of citizens that do not become jaded, bureaucratized, or co-opted.

"Each major company affects in some important way the lives of many thousands of people, employees, customers, retailers, the people living near company installations. Should these people not have a voice in policies that directly and adversely affect them? Must not a just legal system accord victims the power to help themselves, and deter those forces which victimize them?

"To create a voice for the individual, now ignored by these overwhelming forces, is one goal of Public Citizen. To provide strategies for citizenship action is another goal.

"Perhaps our greatest contribution may be to show the way, to encourage lawyers, doctors, scientists, and others representing all of the professions to break out of the restrictive concepts of their roles, to adapt their talents to structural change for a free and just society."

Underlying Nader's pitch for funds are two themes: His movement offers a way to operate on the system and within the system—to work to make it better, not destroy it; and secondly, Nader's movement is nonpolitical. Public Citizen "does not at all relate to any partisan political purpose. It is outside of politics, but the point is that we cannot any longer simply delegate our responsibility as citizens to institutions and vote their heads in or out every two or four years. Things happen in this country daily, not just at election time, and what needs to be done is to forge the kinds of strategies and techniques that will make the citizen more effective. He must be shown how to get the facts, how to develop programs, how to build coalitions and become an effective force," says Nader.

"It really doesn't matter what the particular citizen's opinion is in a given controversy. But he must be able to develop his own thoughts, and express them. He must make up his own mind as a citizen and not do what his employers are expecting him to do or what the government agencies expect him to say. In short, we need a freer source of citizen power," he says.

As usual, the public fund drive was not a spur-of-the-moment thing. Nader had been mulling over the idea for years, and in 1970 even tested it by running an ad for contributions in the small liberal-minded magazine, *The Progressive.*

But it was the success of the fund-raising drive conducted by John Gardner's Common Cause citizen lobby that convinced Nader that the time was right for him to move. He even got Wunderman, Ricotta, Kline, the mail-order specialists who advised Common Cause, to work free on the Public Citizen fund drive. If public subscription catches on, it can give him the nationwide in-depth support he needs to make changes.

Because of his varied financial sources, Nader is a very careful accountant. Always wary, always trying to stay that all-important one step ahead, Nader sees his finances as the first place an enemy would look for ammunition to use against him.

To Nader these enemies are very real. Since the GM episode with the detectives, he operates on the same assumption as did the rifleman on the fortress wall: He can't see them, but he knows they are out there. His files are kept locked and scattered at sites around Washington. Every critical word written about his finances, he plumbs for some sign of the author's motivation. He wolfs scraps of insider-type information given to him by contacts who, like newsmen and congressional staffers, operate on the periphery of his corporate enemies. Each fact is filed in his mind, and brought out again to be fitted with the next scrap of information on the same subject that comes his way sometimes years later. Every financial step, no matter how small, is thought of in terms of what his enemies could do with it. A casual question to Nader on where he got the legal library for his law firm instantly produces the story that the library was bought by the Center for Study of Responsive Law—which is a tax-exempt organization. But when Nader decided to send the library to his legal firm, which is financed by his personal funds, he wrote out a check to the center for $2,000—not just the amount the books were worth then, but the full amount the center originally paid for the books. He paid the full amount just so there would be "no question," Nader says. Nader is the only check-writer in his organizations. He approves everything from paper clips to printing bills, and has his own firm of accountants, A. M. Pullen & Co., Silver Spring, Maryland.

"Ralph is very careful to cross his 'T's' and dot his 'I's,' " is the way a close friend put it. "He is well aware that the Internal Revenue Service has been used as a tool of retribution."

For any of those who want to check up on Nader's income tax returns, there are thousands more who are willing to add to that income with no questions asked.

Ever since Nader first spoke up for the consumer, he has gotten unsolicited contributions in the mail. Cautious as always, he returned them until he could set up his tax-exempt center, which now receives all Nader's unsolicited contributions. Between June 1, 1970, and June 1, 1971, through-the-mail donations made up ten percent of the center's total income.

Unsolicited contributions come from everyone and everywhere. But the largest segment is sent by upper middle-class people who in their letters express one thought: They are concerned about the quality of life in the United States but they don't know what to do about it. They think, however, Nader may be their answer.

Is Nader too cautious with his finances? Is he perhaps, as his critics claim, a bit paranoid about seeing enemies and traps where none exist? Possibly. But then there is Mrs. Fabel Morrison, a conscientious civil servant at the Internal Revenue Service headquarters in Washington, who provides to anyone who asks, as the law specifies she should, the income tax returns filed by tax-exempt foundations. "Oh yes," she says, "we get a lot of requests from people who want to see Mr. Nader's file."

8

NADER ON CAMPUS

A trillion dollar Gross National Product with rotting cities, thirty million hungry people, colossal consumer fraud, a mockery of quality competition, and bureaucracies that are breaking down everywhere is the kind of paradox that is the challenge of the next generation. It's not going to be met with warmed-up versions of citizenship activity, or warmed-up concepts of how we utilize our time. It's got to be a very drastic re-utilization of our efforts and our time, and of our community organizations . . .

—Ralph Nader in a speech to the
American Institute of Planners

The red velvet curtain draped across the stage of the auditorium at Eastern Mennonite College in Virginia's Shenandoah Valley carried this biblical injunction: THY WORD IS TRUTH.

Beneath the gilded letters, standing at a lectern, his face tinted yellow with fatigue, Ralph Nader was speaking to yet another audience of college students. Over 1,000 of them jammed the old brick building at the Harrisonburg campus listening to Nader "tell it like it is, but shouldn't be." There wasn't a Weatherman in the group. Even the red eyelids of the marijuana smoker were nowhere to be seen. Only a handful of the boys affected shoulder-length hair, and some of the girls wore the white caps the Mennonites call prayer veilings. Like their parents, who were mostly farmers and small businessmen, the students did more Bible reading and beer drinking than they did worrying about politics and economics. But this night they sat in fascinated silence as Nader, looking like Cotton Mather in a three-button suit, pointed a long bony finger at them and croaked: "Do you know that you can be arrested for urinating in the street, but industry is free to pollute the nation's rivers and lakes? Do you know that water is pumped into chickens by the tonnage in this country? Do you know that General Motors spent $250 million to change its signs to read 'GM: Mark of Excellence' but spent only ten percent of that amount over the past twenty years to develop alternative propulsion systems which would not pollute the air? Do you know that the government spent more money in 1969 to protect migratory birds than it did on auto safety?"

For an hour and a half, Nader chanted his litany of corporate exploitation and violence against the land and its citizenry. The names of corporations whose dividends helped fatten the bank accounts of the students' parents tumbled from his mouth; GM, Ford, Union Camp, U.S. Steel, IT&T, Union Carbide. He painted a landscape strewn with "little people" who had been crushed by these corporate powers. Changes were needed, he said, and the students could make them if they were really willing to dedicate themselves to the job.

Only two hours before, Nader had been in Washington standing on the steps of the Capitol. He was wrung out from a day of intensive lobbying for a bill to set up a consumer affairs department, but at 6:30 P.M., a 1969 Pontiac GTO pulled to the curb to pick him up for the 120-mile drive to Harrisonburg. In the car were two Eastern Mennonite College students who had won the coveted assignment of driving Nader to the school. Excited, they were primed with a mental list of questions for Nader. But once the introductions were over, Nader carefully strapped himself in with the seat belt and shoulder harness, put his head on his chest, and only minutes after the car drove away from the Capitol

160

grounds, was asleep, leaving the two students to ponder the ways of Ralph Nader, whose speech-making schedule in April, 1971, left him with only 120 hours sleep for the entire month.

The students sat in silence as the car snaked out of Washington, drove across northern Virginia, and headed into the hunt country of Middleburg where a gas stop brought Nader back to life. The students began peppering him with questions: Can they work for him? What can they do while still in college? Where can they get a public-interest type of job when they do graduate, and still make enough money to get married? And the one question which is constant: How safe is my model car? Nader cross-examined each of them. What do they know about the problems in the Harrisonburg area? In the state? What has the college done about them? One of his questions uncovers the fact that the students staged a fund-raising drive on their own to build a library and collected enough in a week to start construction. Why, says Nader, couldn't the same tactics and enthusiasm also be used to help raise money to finance an investigative task force?

Back in the car, Nader munches on a candy bar to replace the dinner he missed, but ten minutes later is asleep again, leaving the students to debate with each other the merits of starting their own investigation team à la Nader's Raiders.

The trip to Eastern Mennonite is typical of Nader's one-night stands at colleges around the nation. Like a jet-age Paul Revere, he scurries from campus to campus shouting warnings about the corporate enemy, and the problems of consumerism and ecology. Several weeks earlier, fresh from a full day in Washington, Nader stepped down a ramp of an Eastern Air Lines jet at Raleigh, North Carolina, in the evening to be met by a professor from tiny Campbell College, which is hard by Buie's Creek, a Carolina hamlet where the population in the summertime reaches 300. The professor tells Nader "he looks just like he does on television," and the two men leave the airport for the college in the professor's 1965 Firebird, but Nader keeps the window open a crack because the car "is one of the models that leaks combustion gas." As the Firebird races through the tobacco country toward Buie's Creek, Nader fights to stay awake as the professor tells him that his son wants to quit his job with the Secret Service and become one of Nader's Raiders. Then the talk switches to a television show done by Nader on the evils of the Cannon textile mill town of Kannapolis, N.C., which is run as the personal fiefdom of Cannon Mills. The show appeared locally the night before and the professor admits "it created a lot of talk hereabouts." Nader, who has never seen the show since it was filmed, probes for the professor's reaction. Did he think it was effective? On target? Could it have been wider in scope? He presses for any comments the professor may have heard from blue-collar mill workers in the area. The professor tells him that "a lot of people around these parts have worked in those mills, and they say you're right. They say something has got to be done about it." To Nader, the arrogance and insensitivity of the millowners to the housing and health problems of the textile workers is, to use one of his favorite words, "outrageous." He promises the professor that the television show will not be "a one-shot affair," and the professor seems to accept this promise as if it were holy writ.

At the college, a Baptist stronghold, Nader starts the wearily familiar pre-speech routine. He is ushered into a dining hall for a steak-potato-and-pecan pie dinner with the dean and the student leaders who make bad jokes about the quality of the food not being up to Nader's standards. But "small talk" is not a Nader specialty, and there are long silences. Most of Nader's fans and critics alike usually are puzzled by his shyness. Expecting an extrovert and a man full of opinions, they find a low-keyed, pleasant man who speaks in answer to questions, and is neither a lapel-grabber, nor an egotist.

When the dinner finally ends, Nader and his escorts troop to the auditorium. As usual, the hall is packed, but Nader is upstaged immediately by an old white dog who ambles across the stage. When the dog finally curls up, Nader begins his exhortation to the students to turn the nation around. In any Nader speech, there is always plenty of talk of "violence," but it is the violence being done to the land, the air, and the consumer's pocketbook by corporations of which he speaks. There is even more talk about "radical changes"; the kind that will force corporations to live up to the antitrust laws, or make them take on more social responsibilities even at the expense of some profits. The "bombs" Nader throws usually come in the form of questions like: Why didn't General Motors tell the public that its tests showed the Corvair was unsafe? Why must 15,000 workers die in industrial accidents every year? Why is industry allowed to pollute the air and the water when there are laws, which, if enforced, could stop them? Why are food prices more expensive in ghetto stores? Why, if America believes in a free enterprise system, does the government use taxpayers money to shore up bankrupt firms like Lockheed and the Penn Central?

Once the speech is over, there is a trek to the student lounge where Nader slumps on a couch and fields questions from a ring of students who trailed after him. After an hour more of questions, and having made a roomful of converts, it is back into the car for the drive to Raleigh, and the airport's Triangle Motel, a grudging stop for Nader who feels he is wasting time when he must lay over because there is no late-night plane back to Washington. In the lobby of the motel he grabs the evening paper just as the room clerk spots him and sings out "Don't worry, Mr. Nader, I've got a room for you!" (Nader made no reservation, nor did he carry even a toothbrush.) How, Nader is asked, did the room clerk know him? "I was in Raleigh last night to give a speech to some students," he says in the matter-of-fact tone he uses.

The mammoth state universities, the Ivy League, the black colleges, the all-girl colleges; Nader stumps them all. To him the 8,000,000 students in the nation's 2,000 colleges and universities represent the raw material for the new type of citizen Nader would like to see people the United States.

"They are at an age when it is easiest to cultivate an awareness, a sense of right and wrong, and a desire to control one's destiny. This is the time when the fibre of citizenship can be most easily developed," says Nader. But he has no desire to become a Pied Piper for the students. "I simply want to challenge them to match their rhetoric to action."

And Nader makes his challenge quite blunt. Unlike the politician or the school administrator, he doesn't fawn over the students. If anything, he ridicules the gap between what they say they want, and what they are willing to do to achieve it. He lards his speeches with sarcasm about students who prattle about the need for social reform programs, but give more financial aid to the record industry. He worries aloud that the current student idealism may be short-lived, but he is also convinced that if properly directed, the student force could shake society.

What is different about today's climate, says Nader, is that the majority of students is willing to give all-out backing to the activists among them, if the cause is right. "That doesn't mean that the great bulk of students will eventually become activists themselves, but it does mean you do not have to persuade them there has to be change. In the past, you had to begin at that basic level; there wasn't even an awareness level."

In Nader's mind, there are other subcategories of students. "There are a lot who have a very fine sense of values, but they are basically dropouts. They are more interested in cultivating their personal freedom in a commune or in Greenwich Village than they are in reforming the establishment. They reject the route I have taken, and want to build their own little enclave of maximum freedom. These kids are not going to bring about a social reform movement; they are just interested in getting society to leave them alone.

"Then there are the students in the drug world. That is a distinct problem, and not part of what we are doing. They are incapable of being reached at the present time."

Nader's strategy is to form an alliance between "the small minority of students who have a sense of awareness, and are willing to work hard to make a contribution," and the much larger group which will back them morally, financially, and with part-time help or, as Nader says, "to simply avoid obstructing the idea." "I am talking about the guy or girl who thinks what we are doing is great, but wants to be a sculptor; he wants to do his own thing, but would also like to give a helping hand to a new movement to reform society."

The tool Nader hopes will give the students the power they need is this: A public interest law firm, one that would be staffed by full-time professionals hired by the students; a law firm which would be fully financed by student contributions, and a law firm which would operate in areas the students choose.

This hardly sounds like a revolutionary idea, but Nader feels it could be if the students are made to realize its potential for power. Basically, what Nader visualizes is an extension of the concept behind his own Washington-based Public Interest Research Group. Rather than operate against the federal government and the Washington-based corporation lawyer-lobbyist, the student public interest firms would become a hub for a reform movement aimed at state and regional problems. Nader is not talking about a penny-ante operation which would be a sop to the students, but a nationwide chain of student-run public interest firms whose combined budgets would run into the millions of dollars.

Specifically, the concept works like this: The students petition the school to assess each student at a rate of about $3 per student per year. The assessment is made a part of the tuition fee, but any student who doesn't want to contribute can get a full refund from the school after the term begins. The assessment sounds relatively small, but multiplied by seventy thousand students enrolled at a state-run university system, the fee provides a tidy yearly expense fund.

Once the financing is assured, the students can begin hiring a full-time professional staff to operate what would be a student public interest research group. Nader has outlined a general plan for building the firms—it calls for a staff of ten to fifteen, mostly lawyers, but also including engineers, ecologists, consumer experts, or accountants—persons whose skills would be needed in the areas the students felt were most pressing.

"When you think of lawyers working for a student public interest research group, don't think of them in the traditional sense of someone going into court and litigating a case; that will be the last resort. Think of these lawyers as people who are trained advocates; who will advocate student views before the state legislatures, who will be participating in drafting legislation students favor, who will do the kinds of investigation and exposure that the Center for Study of Responsive Law has done, who will act as catalysts for organizing citizen groups to lobby for things like zoning changes that will make an industrial practice illegal, or will force an industry to clean up its pollution. This is the kind of action we are talking about," says Nader, who foresees the day when a student public interest research group might support its own television show which would report on consumer problems or corporate irresponsibility. The firm could use its advocates to try to force unwilling television and radio stations to give equal time to conservation groups, or to critics who dispute the auto industry's safety claims, or the firm could bring charges of sex discrimination or race discrimination before the Equal Employment Opportunity Commission, Nader says.

As Nader sees it, a student public interest research group would have to have a set of rules designed to fit the desires of the students at each school. But here is a model plan used by the students of Oregon, the first university system to set up a student public interest research group.

Once the State Board of Higher Education approved the petition to assess students $3 each to finance the firm, students at the schools elected delegates to sit on local boards at each of the campuses which make up the Oregon university system. The job of students on the local boards is to cull information from the campus student body on which problem areas they wanted their public interest research group to attack. One student representative for each four thousand students on campus is sent by each local board to sit on a central board of directors, where they serve for one year without pay. The job of the board is to control the student

166

funds and to make a final decision on projects for the student public interest research group. Another key power for the board, however, is the right to hire the professional staff to run the firm. The payroll for an ideal-sized fifteen-man firm would run about $100,000, the obvious emphasis being on young idealistic professionals who are more interested in service than in money. Added to this would be another $18,000 for secretarial help, $32,000 a year for rent, travel and phone, and the firm would be in business. If enough funds are available, Nader sees the firms spending $35,000-a-year to fund a fifty-student raider force as part of a summer project. Here is a model budget for a student public interest research group.

A MODEL BUDGET

(Estimated Operating Expenses for one Fiscal Year for A Public Research Group with a support base of between 70,000 and 80,000 students. This model may be expanded or reduced to fit different size student bases.)

A. *EMPLOYEE COSTS*

10 Professionals (for example, 9 professionals— $ 9,500.00, average; 1 executive director— $13,500.00, approximate)	$ 99,000.00
4 Secretarial and clerical employees (for example, 1 administrative secretary—$550.00 per month; 3 secretaries—$425.00 per month, average)	22,800.00
2 Full-time equivalent community-workers (at $6,000 average)	12,000.00
Employee benefits	14,700.00
Total Employee Costs	$148,500.00

B. *OCCUPANCY COSTS*

Space rental (2100 sq. ft. at $4.50 per sq. ft. per year)	$ 9,540.00
Electricity ($40.00 per month)	480.00
Total Occupancy Costs	$ 10,020.00

C. *OFFICE EQUIPMENT*

4 Electric typewriters—$390.00 each (for example IBM—Model C—factory reconditioned)	$	1,590.00
14 Desks and Chairs		
10 desks and swivel arm chairs—$210.00 each		2,100.00
4 secretarial desks and chairs—$240.00 each		960.00
24 Side Chairs—$30.00 each		720.00
8 File Cabinets—4 drawer		
3 legal size—$95.00 each		375.00
5 letter size—$85.00 each		950.00
10 Bookshelves—$95.00 each		
Total Equipment Costs	$	7,115.00
Equipment cost amortized over 10 years	$	712.00
Typewriter maintenance—$42.00 per machine		168.00
Total Equipment Cost per year		$880.00

Nader has tried to insure that any plan adopted by a school has a series of checks and balances. In the Oregon plan, any campus could pull out of the program, "if, during any academic term, fifty-one percent of the students" request a refund of their assessments. The plan also has provisions for removal and recall of the board of the directors.

Nader singled out the Oregon University system for his first big campaign for two main reasons: It was big—seventy thousand students—which makes it easier to collect the needed money, and it was not split by the radical politics that have scarred other West Coast campuses. But Nader does not feel that size should necessarily be a barrier for small college participation. There is nothing to prevent small private colleges from banding together to support one student public interest research group even if the schools are spread over a wide geographical area. As for the divisive effects of campus politics, there are few schools where the students could not be brought together on the issue of ecology.

Once Oregon was settled on Nader sent, as advance men, a pair of smooth, dedicated, supersalesmen, Donald Ross and James Welch, both of whom are lawyers—Welch from the University of Texas, and Ross, a New York University alumnus. For months, they combed the fourteen-college Oregon system for on-campus drumbeaters. They themselves made speech after speech hammering home the value of an Oregon public interest research group. Ross, who earned his organizing spurs working for former Robert Kennedy-aide Adam Walinsky in his unsuccessful campaign for Attorney General of New York, lost eight pounds in a one-week round of speeches. The pair wrote and distributed pamphlets on the idea, appeared on radio and TV talk shows, and organized petition-signing campaigns.

Welch and Ross got reaction; plenty of it. The students took to the idea immediately and the first step, the petition to the state Board of Higher Education to approve the fee to finance the idea, got over 30,000 signatures in a short time. Nader made three barnstorming trips through the state starting in October and November of 1970. He drew enormous crowds for a college speaker, and kept a schedule calculated to wear down the best of iron men. In one note written to Nader to brief him on his November 16 sortie, Ross began by saying "Ralph, you are not going to like this, but I have scheduled you for eight speeches in one day." Nader didn't like it, but he made each one of them. At 7 A.M. on the sixteenth, he was in the dining room of Lewis and Clark College near Portland urging eight hundred sleepy-eyed students to take time out from their cereal and coffee to sign a petition for a public interest research group. At 8 A.M. he was at Portland Community College. At 9 A.M. he gave a speech at Portland State University. At 10 A.M. he gave a second speech at Portland State College. From there, he made an hour and a half drive to Oregon College of Education for his fifth speech. Then it was on to Willamette College in Salem. After that, he held a press conference at the state capitol building. When it ended, he raced to Oregon State where seven thousand students packed a hall to hear him plead: "Who is going to do this, if you don't?" From Oregon State, he went to the University of Oregon for his seventh speech. Then as a finale, he drove three hours to Bend, Oregon, to give a speech to the Bend Community College.

Ross and Welch had done their work well. The arguments

they fed the students to present to the college administrators were hard to turn down. "The students told them we want to work within the system and we want to spend our own money to do it—how could they reject an argument like that," Ross said. But the concept was not without opposition.

The first and most persistent criticism came on the issue of the mandatory payment of the fee by all students even though a refund would be obtained later. The conservative Young Americans for Freedom fought the plan on this issue, terming the fee coercive. The Students for a Democratic Society (SDS) attacked the plan on the usual grounds: It would work within the system. Others thought they saw Ralph Nader's hand in the till, or at very least, orchestrating the entire project for some dark gain. But the bylaws of the project prevented Nader, even if he wished, from exercising any control, or using the funds in any manner. In his usual blunt manner, Nader spelled out his role in a background paper distributed on the campus. He said:

"What is in this for Ralph Nader? Nothing. The most the Nader group in Washington, D.C., can gain from this plan is an ally in their fight for the adequate representation of the public interest. The group in Oregon will be funded with Oregon money, it will be controlled solely by Oregon students, and presumably it will concentrate on Oregon problems." He told the students he merely conceived the idea and passed it on as something of value. But the largest hurdle of all was the state's conservative Board of Higher Education which had the final say. The argument here was whether the Oregon Student Public Interest Research Group could be considered a part of a student's education process. But there were other pressures on the board. In a state like Oregon, one of the key targets for a student public interest research group would be the lumber industry and its use of the land. Student organizers in the drive claimed that lumber lobbyists were exerting none too subtle pressure on the board to turn down the project. One of the members of the board, Becky Johnson, was more outspoken than most. To her, Nader was a radical trying to disrupt the free-enterprise system, and the Student Public Interest Research Group was simply another part of his plot.

The fight came to a climax in March, 1971, when the board took its vote. The result was a victory for the students, but not one without pain. The board approved the idea of the Student Public Interest Research Group, but it forbade it to litigate. Everything else—the right to lobby, to investigate, to research—was approved. But the loss of the right to go into court was a severe blow to Nader's concept of what a student public interest research group should do. It was not, however, fatal. The obvious route around this roadblock would be for the Student Public Interest Research Group to give a case it felt should be taken to court to a public interest law firm or perhaps stage a separate funding drive to finance legal costs. No matter what strategy is finally decided on, the establishment of a permanent annual income of over $200,000 a year for the Student Public Interest Group assures it a permanent place on the Oregon scene. With the fifteen full-time advocates at the service of the students, it also assures there will be some changes made in the state.

But Oregon is not the only spawning ground for Nader's student power concept. Nader-Ross-Welch, Inc., conducted a hopscotching campaign to campuses in the midwest and the south at the same time they were organizing the Oregon fight. Minnesota fell in behind Oregon to become the second school to set up a public interest research group. Ross and Welch used the same tactics they did at Oregon and were even more successful. By January, 1971, a statewide petition drive was underway in Minnesota. At the University of Minnesota, sixty percent of the school's 53,000 students signed the petition in less than two weeks. By the end of the spring term, over fifty thousand names were on the petition representing students on eighteen campuses across the state. The State Board of Regents gave its approval, and the Minnesota Public Interest Research Group became a reality with each student in the school system paying a fee of $3 a year to support the firm. Wasting no time, the students went right to work, and in September, 1971, this ad appeared in a national magazine:

NADER-STYLE public interest research group, funded through student fees, is seeking professional scientists, and lawyers to work with students in areas of public concern. Should have working knowledge of environmental problems. Priorities geared to environmental quality, consumer protection, and corporate review. For more information write to Minnesota Public Interest Research Group, 225 Coffman Union, University of Minnesota, Minneapolis, Minnesota 55455. Send resume c/o Staff Selection Committee.

From Minnesota, Nader took the idea to campuses across the nation. Students in West Virginia, Washington, Hawaii, Utah, Illinois, Missouri, Massachusetts, and Georgia began planning petition drives. In California, a student group at Berkeley plans to set up its own public interest law firm without Nader's help, and call it the California Advocates.

To Nader's mind, this concept of the student public interest research group is the answer to the lack of continuity in the student movements of the past. With a full-time staff there will be no breaks for summer recess, or time out for exams. The firms will operate on a regular year-long schedule with long-term financing. Like any good idea, Nader's concept is simple. If it catches on, it could be tremendously effective, and Nader is certain it will. His faith in the ability, the drive, and the idealism of the students is unlimited. He is utterly convinced that their power can be harnessed to bring change. Writing in a manual he published ("Action For Change—A Student's Manual For Public Interest Organizing," Grossman, New York, 1971) on how to organize campus campaigns to win approval for the student public interest groups, Nader put his faith this way:

"Who began the sit-in movement in civil rights which led to rapid developments in the law but four black engineering students a little over a decade ago? Who dramatized for the nation the facts and issues regarding the relentless environmental contamination in cities and rural America other than students? Who helped mobilize popular opposition to the continuance of the war in Vietnam and turned official policy toward withdrawal? Who focused attention on the need for change in University policies and obtained many of these changes? Who is enlarging the investigative tradition of the old muckrakers in the Progressive-Populist days at the turn of the century other than student teams of inquiry? Who is calling for and shaping a more relevant and empirical education that understands problems and considers solutions?"

All of these things were accomplished by "a tiny minority" of students, Nader says. "The vast majority of their colleagues still are languishing in a colossal waste of time, developing a fraction of their potential, and woefully under preparing themselves for the world they are entering in earnest." But student public interest research groups can end some of this lethargy, Nader claims. He sees the students being drawn into the project undertaken by the campus law firms, and shows that with the proper tools, they can have an impact on society. Once "the direction has been forged," the students will carry the idea with them that it is possible to do what seems impossible.

9

WHISTLEBLOWING

Today the large organization is lord and master and most of its employees have been desensitized, much as were medieval peasants who never knew they were serfs.

—Ralph Nader in a speech to the Conference
on Professional Responsibility, Washington, D.C.

Ed Gregory was fed up. The feisty little assembly line inspector at GM's Fisher Body plant in St. Louis had tried his damnedest but no one listened. Those shiny new Chevrolets still were rolling off the line and if he was right, any one of them could be a potential coffin for the buyer. For weeks Gregory had been buttonholing foremen, and sending reports to plant officials about a possible deadly defect in the Chevrolets—a carbon monoxide leak. Colorless and odorless, the deadly gas entered the passenger compartment through a defectively sealed panel in the trunk compartment, Gregory claimed. It took little imagination for him to conjure up visions of drivers on high speed highways slipping into unconsciousness from carbon monoxide poisoning, and the police duly recording their deaths as simply another case of a driver who fell asleep at the wheel. But if the peril was obvious to Gregory, it was less so to the GM plant managers. It would be three years before they became convinced of his argument.

Gregory's fight with GM began in a gravel pit in La Grange,

Missouri, where Gregory, a rock hound, spent his off hours scouring the pit for new additions to his rock collection. On one of these expeditions, a chance meeting with a geologist he knew led him to the carbon monoxide leak.

The geologist was an unhappy consumer. He had bought a new 1966 Chevrolet only to find that dust from the quarry roads would seep into the trunk and cover his instruments with a thick film. Irritated, he spotted Gregory at the quarry and asked him to check the trunk.

"He knew I worked for Fisher and knew I was an inspector," Gregory said recalling the encounter. Listening to the angry geologist, Gregory thought first of the seams in the trunk panels which were welded closed in the assembly-line process.

"There was this old pump down the road a ways from his car, and I told him to drive down there," Gregory said. When he got to the pump, Gregory found a rusty bucket, filled it with water, and poured it along a welded seam in the trunk. "Sure enough, the water seeped through the seam and dribbled out on the ground."

Gregory was a career blue-collar worker, a ham-fisted wrench-and-hammer man, who came to the assembly line after stints as a railroad brakeman, a shuttlecar driver in a limestone mine, and a cement plant worker. But when the water seeped through the welded seam, he didn't feel the need of an engineering degree to convince himself that this could be a death trap.

"I got to thinking about it all the time after that day in the gravel pit. The dust flowing in there was the thing that bothered me. If dust could come through that seam, then carbon monoxide could, too," Gregory reasoned.

Gregory was no novice at spotting safety defects. He had then thirteen years experience in the Fisher plant and had earned a reputation as a "nit-picker" on safety items. He did not even quake at the thought of recommending the assembly line be shut down, a drastic step in any auto plant because of the expense involved.

Slowly, almost torturously, Gregory pondered the problem

of the leak. What was wrong with the sealing process? How could it be fixed? If it was not fixed, what was the danger to the driver?

Convinced that the leak had to be fixed, Gregory went to his foremen, who promptly gave him a brush off. The chances of enough carbon monoxide, if any at all, finding its way into the passenger compartment were too remote to worry about. Sure, it was a possibility, but not a very likely one. Forget it, Gregory was told. But the more he was told to forget it, the more he became convinced he was right. If the foremen would not listen, maybe the supervisors would, so Gregory took his plea to them.

"Every supervisor I met I told about the leak. I tried and tried to convince them it was dangerous. But it didn't do no good. No one did anything." The argument Gregory got from the supervisors was that there were no field reports of any problems with carbon monoxide in the 1966 models. Translation: If the customers had not complained about carbon monoxide seepage there was no need to make an expensive change in the manufacturing process to fix a defect they were not even aware of.

By management's standards, Gregory was an agitator. He was a militant union member who went by the book. He knew the language of the United Auto Workers contract and could recite it and interpret it with the confidence of a labor lawyer. But the union itself was as bureaucratic as management when it came to doing anything about the carbon monoxide leak. "Under the contract there is nothing that can be done," the UAW officials of Local 25 somberly told Gregory when he carried his plea for action to them.

By now Gregory began to pay the penalty for bucking the system. His constant harping on the defect had turned the disinterest of the foremen and the supervisors into an annoyance that was translated into the petty and vicious harassments that would eventually climax in GM assigning a guard to follow Gregory around the plant. "Did you ever try to go to the bathroom with the door open and the guard watching you? I couldn't go to the telephone to call my wife without the guard listening. He even sat at the cafeteria table with me," Gregory said. The guard, assigned to follow Gregory ostensibly because of a work rules fight in which GM claimed Gregory was working at a job he was not entitled to under the contract, trailed him so closely Gregory had to warn him about stepping on his heels. But before the guard incident, Gregory began to get an unmerciful riding from his foremen and supervisors. He became that "little jerk" who thought he knew more than the plant engineers. In his Missouri twang, Gregory admits he began to have "cuss fights" with his bosses over their failure to do something about the carbon monoxide leak. "All they did was tell me I'd get fired if I didn't shut up," Gregory said. With the threats came a barrage of obscene phone calls to Gregory's wife who was home alone since he worked a night shift.

But Gregory refused to back off. He began filing formal written complaints to the plant safety committee. The records show that one of these suggestions filed on April 18, 1966, outlined a new procedure to seal the defective panel to "eliminate safety hazards from fumes and dust leaking into the rear compartment." Again, no action. Gregory filed more reports, and all the while "was raising cain about these cars going up the line." One of the formal complaints warned prophetically that "if one unsafe car gets out of the plant" it would be too many. Another urged that GM "recall all these cars immediately."

The only reaction Gregory got was a notice that he was being taken off his job as an inspector and sent back to his old job in a metal finishing gang "due to cutbacks." To Gregory, this was simply GM's way of gagging him. But what could he do? He had already done more than most men; he'd used the chain of command; he'd put his complaints in writing. Now if anything happened to the owners of those Chevys, it would be on the corporate soul of GM, not Ed Gregory's. But Gregory, a World War II veteran who collected three battle wounds fighting his way across North Africa and Italy, was plagued by his conscience. No matter how logical an argument he raised to justify ending his crusade, he could not forget the specter he saw hanging over each of the Chevrolets moving along the assembly line. Because of this, Gregory's Hamlet-like debate with himself was short-lived. He went to the phone and called Ralph Nader.

"I'd been watching Nader on television testify before the Senate. I thought here is the guy who can help me," Gregory said. His phone call was put through to Sen. Abraham Ribicoff's subcommittee, and Gregory left a message with a secretary. "I told her I had a problem that I knew was dangerous and I wanted Mr. Nader to see if they could do something about it." In fifteen minutes, Gregory's phone rang and the voice on the line said: "This is Ralph Nader."

Once he checked out the facts, Nader teamed with Gregory and began publicly hammering away at the threat. But nothing happened until four corpses entered the argument. On July 11, 1968, Chief Petty Officer Charles L. Hunt, his wife, and their niece Susan Koehler were found asphyxiated in a 1968 Chevrolet parked by the shoulder of a road near Heber City, Utah. The day before, the Hunts damaged the underside of the car when it hit a bump. Hunt took the car to a Chevrolet dealer who was supposed to repair the damage, but apparently overlooked a damaged or misaligned exhaust pipe. Carbon monoxide fumes from the pipe leaked into the passenger compartment and the Hunts drifted into unconsciousness and death. Three days later, in Baton Rouge, Louisiana, Mrs. Charles Dunaway's car was hit in the rear by another car in a low-speed collision. Later she was found dead of asphyxiation. A damaged exhaust pipe sent exhaust fumes seeping into the car, the accident report showed. In the same period GM got thirty other reports from the field on exhaust fumes seeping into the passenger compartments of the Chevrolets. Finally on February 26, 1969, GM capitulated. It recalled 2.4 million Chevrolets—1965 through 1968 Biscayne, Bel Air, Impala, and Caprice models. The reason? "For inspection and service to the body areas adjacent to the exhaust tail pipe to prevent the possibility of exhaust emissions entering the vehicle." On the same day, GM awarded Ed Gregory $10,000 for his suggestion on how to seal the side panels.

Despite the recall, GM refused to admit any negligence on its part, and law suits filed against the automaker on behalf of the four dead persons were settled out of court. GM claimed the recall was ordered mainly to correct a problem caused by plastic plugs used to fill holes in the car body left by the manufacturing process. The plugs were deteriorating under heat from the exhaust system. If the plugs dropped out, carbon monoxide from a defective or damaged tail pipe could enter the trunk compartment. This had nothing to do with Gregory's original suggestion for sealing the side panel on 1965 and 1966 models. But GM also admitted that a sealing method similar to the one he suggested was being used on some of the recalled 1967 and 1968 Chevrolets to seal trunk seams. "Our Fisher Body Division wished to eliminate any possible suggestion of unfairness and therefore awarded him $10,000 for his suggestion," a GM spokesman said.

Gregory's bonus was small change compared to the expense of the recall. The postage bill to notify each of the 2.4 million Chevrolet owners by certified letter cost over $1.5 million. When the recall was announced, GM had to set up an emergency telephone system to handle the queries from car owners, and the repair bill to fix the cars came to a whopping $50 million.

GM said that recalling so many cars to correct a relatively few was "like calling in the haystack to find the needle," but it said the step was taken because "General Motors regards excellence as a constant objective and safety as its first requirement." Gregory says simply that there would never have been a recall if "I hadn't raised a stink."

"Not a single one of my supervisors shook my hand after I got my award, and they tell me privately I'll never get another dime for a suggestion. But I don't care what they say, I'm still turning in safety suggestions when I find something wrong. I want to see the car buyer get the car he should be getting," says Gregory. But Gregory also thinks he is living on borrowed time. "GM would fire me tomorrow if it weren't that they're scared of Ralph Nader." As it is, Gregory says GM will not allow him to work in sections of the plant where crucial safety inspections are made. "I am so far away from the important jobs, I couldn't make waves with an outboard motor," he says.

Was Gregory right in doing what he did? Or was he a stool pigeon, a fink, a traitor to GM, the company that gave him a job and a good paycheck? Gregory's critics, both on the assembly line, and in the executive suite, claim he should not have taken his plea "outside the company." But Ralph Nader says Gregory was a hero, and Nader wants to see more Gregorys, particularly among the ranks of the nation's scientists, engineers, lawyers and accountants—those who call themselves society's professionals, but who, in fact, have presided over the birth and growth of more of the problems of society then they have exposed. Blue-collar workers like Ed Gregory are not often in a position to see and document abuses, but the professionals are and Nader wants them "to come out from the shadows," and blow the whistle in the tradition of Ed Gregory.

Nader is harsh in his indictment of the professional man's lack of courage. He blames automotive engineers for not alerting the public to the lack of designed-in safety for cars. For twenty-five years, Nader claims, engineers sat on their slide rules and allowed style to take precedence over safety. These same engineers also kept silent while the auto industry effectively blocked the development of an automobile exhaust control system to curb air pollution, Nader claims. But engineers were not any worse than some of their brother professionals. Where were the chemists when industry was dumping mercury into the nation's rivers and streams? Or for that matter where were the accountants of these same corporations? They knew how much mercury the firm bought, and where it went. But it took a Canadian university student to sound the alarm with his "discovery" of the rise in mercury levels in Great Lakes fish, says Nader.

In Alloy, West Virginia, thirty miles south of Charleston, a Union Carbide plant dumped 28,000 tons of pollutants a year into the air—one third the amount poured annually into the air over New York City whose population is five times greater than the entire State of West Virginia. The pollution blotted out the sun, and covered towns as far away as Charleston with soot. But it was not until environmentalists, including a Nader Raider team, entered the fight that Union Carbide made drastic changes in its anti-pollution campaign. But Nader asks where were the voices inside Union Carbide. Why didn't they speak out years ago? In 1970, Nader says the citrus juice processors stole $150 million from the consumer by adding from ten to fifteen percent water to their product. Why didn't someone in the industry blow the whistle? He asks the same question about the sale of dangerous drugs, the overuse of DDT, brown lung—byssinosis—a disease plaguing textile workers, cost overruns at the Pentagon, auto insurance frauds, shoddy housing industry practices, exploitation of the land by mine operators and timber interests, the quality of medical service, the misuse of economic power by big banks, the sale of potentially dangerous toys, and water and air pollution. "It is clear that hundreds and often thousands of persons knew about these things, but chose to remain silent. By their silence, they became in fact instruments of private and public policy which contravenes the public interest, destroys the environment, and defrauds the taxpayers," Nader says.

In testimony before the Senate in 1966, Nader described the professional in the auto industry as a man "with invisible chains" who surrendered his independence for security. When Nader approached these automatons for information he said he found "a profound reluctance, in not a few cases it could be called fear, to speak out publicly by those who knew the details of neglect, indifference, unjustified secrecy, and suppression of engineering innovation concerning the design of safer automobiles by the manufacturers.

"I soon realized that the stifling of candid expression . . . was the key reason why auto design safety took until 1965-66 to receive public attention instead of 1936, or 1946, or 1956." The price society paid for this silence was "needless death, needless injury, and inestimable sorrow," Nader said.

Historically, the whistleblower has played a key role in

great events. When he tacked his Ninety-five Theses to the door of the church, Martin Luther was blowing the whistle on the excesses of the Vatican. The United States was built by Americans who blew the whistle on Britain's King George the Third. General Billy Mitchell was a whistleblower who was forced to take his case against the battleship admirals to the public in an effort to win recognition for the airplane. My Lai would have stayed an obscure dot on the map of Vietnam if an American GI had not blown the whistle on Lt. William Calley. Robert Townsend, the former president of Avis Rent-A-Car, and the author of *Up the Organization*, thinks President Eisenhower should be dubbed the father of the modern whistleblowing movement for warning the nation in his 1959 farewell address to beware of the military-industrial complex, an ogre he himself helped build as both a soldier and a President. "But too often whistleblowers have been demoted, ostracized, discharged or suppressed when, in fact, they frequently may be heroic figures," Nader says. How then are these chains to be struck? How can a professional find the path that will allow him to remain loyal to his company, but do what his conscience dictates? Who will protect him if he speaks out? Must it always take, as Nader claims, "a terrific act of courage in order to utter a simple statement of truth?"

The law is vague about the whistleblower. There are examples where whistleblowing is actively sought and rewarded. The Internal Revenue Service will pay a tipster a share of the take if he provides information on a fellow citizen cheating on his income-tax return. Rewards are provided for information leading to the arrest and conviction of criminals. The Army has its Inspector General, Congress has the General Accounting Office, which glories in its newspaper title of "watchdog" of federal agency spending, and private corporations themselves make use of internal audit departments. But most incidents of "condoned" whistleblowing involve the government urging citizens to do their duty by blowing the whistle on other citizens. There is little in the way of legal or moral encouragement for anyone, either in government or industry to blow the whistle on the consumer's behalf.

183

No less a corporate giant than GM's James M. Roche sees whistleblowing as an attempt by antibusiness critics to erode the free enterprise system. In a speech to the Executive Club of Chicago, Roche spoke for many of his fellow industrialists when he said: "Some of the enemies of business now encourage employees to be disloyal to the enterprise. They want to create suspicion and disharmony, and pry into the proprietary interests of the business. However this is labeled—industrial espionage, whistleblowing or professional responsibility—it is another tactic for spreading disunity and creating conflict."

To Nader, it is fear that motivates Roche's attack. "When the professional does break through the corporate chains, the impact is powerful—which may explain the corporation's dogged determination to keep the professional in his place," says Nader.

Despite Roche's charge, Nader insists his call for an uprising of whistleblowers is not antibusiness. "I am not suggesting an employee be disloyal or subvert his employer. But if a professional man is privy to information that shows his superiors are mulcting or endangering the consumer, then the superiors are the disloyal employees and the whistle should be blown."

Nader recognizes the need for rules of conduct in what is essentially an uncharted moral ground. "We've got to develop an ethic of whistleblowing. We've got to develop a kind of common law of whistleblowing," he says. But even without a rulebook, Nader is convinced he is morally right to recruit whistleblowers.

"I think every individual whether he's a professional, or a technician, or a floor sweeper has got to have fixed in his mind where the line is going to be drawn. There has to be some sort of initial determination that the individual employee will only go so far in obeying the dictates of the organization. Beyond that, he will have to blow the whistle." To Nader, this concept was firmly embedded in law. "It is basically the principle established by the Nuremberg war crime trials," he says.

To set standards for whistleblowing, Nader is not relying on himself, but on professional and technical societies like the American Chemical Society, the American Society of Safety Engineers, the American Society of Mechanical Engineers and the American Society for the Advancement of Science—groups which already claim to be the keeper of the professional's ethics but which in fact have been little more than house pets for industry, or as Nader puts it: "Professional societies have been excessively beholden, if not dominated, by industry." In most professional societies, the code of ethics is kept in a frame on a wall where it can be admired and ignored. The societies have become social organizations and meeting places to make contacts or pass out resumes. Little or no effort is made to develop policies on controversial issues in the profession—especially one which would be contrary to the corporate line.

To trigger a rebirth, Nader suggests that the professional societies might start by asking themselves this question: "What issues in our profession, if openly discussed, would get the greatest number of persons fired?"

This fear of being fired for speaking out is a real problem for the professional. Unlike the union worker, he has little or no job protection. The fact that his argument is based on issues like the health and safety of the consumer are no guarantee he can buck company policy. Fired by one of the major automakers, an engineer can expect to be blackballed in the industry. In the case of other scientists, loss of their jobs in a fight over corporate decisions can mean the end of a lifetime research project. Seldom can an industry scientist take his work with him or find another firm with either the need or the facilities for his work.

But if this is the way it is, it is not the way it has to be, Nader contends. A professional society with backbone, whose members would support the right of dissent and perhaps even provide a shelter for an outcast professional to continue his research, could become a countervailing force against the arbitrary use of power by the corporation. As a model, Nader suggests that other professional societies look to the example of the American Association of University Professors, an organization with a strong tradition of defense of its members against pressure from college administrators, trustees, and public clamor.

In government, Nader is finding some support for his plea that the whistleblower be given legislative protection. Senator William Proxmire (D-Wis.) is backing a bill designed to protect the federal employee from retaliation if he follows the federal employee code of ethics and puts "loyalty to the highest moral principles and to country above loyalty to persons, party or government departments." Proxmire says "blowing the whistle, or raising a hue and cry, or living up to ethical standards that are already embodied in various codes of conduct is part of the antidote to the poisonous abuses of power that are infecting our society." Senator Edmund Muskie (D-Me.) is another lawmaker who agrees on the need for protection for whistleblowers. His water-pollution bill bars a corporation from firing an employee who reports a violation of the water-pollution standards. If the employee is fired under some other guise, the bill provides for an investigation of his case by the Labor Department.

Nader himself is moving against this same fear with a unique idea of his own—a sort of mission house for whistleblowers known as the Clearinghouse for Professional Responsibility (P.O. Box 486, Ben Franklin Station, Washington, D.C. 20044).

The job of the clearinghouse is just what its name implies— to collect information on a confidential basis from whistleblowers. But it will also help develop a whistleblowers' bill of rights, and prod Congress and the professional societies into action. To run the clearinghouse, Nader picked Pete Petkas, a 25-year-old graduate of the University of Texas Law School who operates out of a Nader public interest law firm in Washington. To Nader's critics, the clearinghouse is simply a "fink tank." But Nader, always short-tempered when he feels his point is missed, repeats at every opportunity that he is not collecting personal information, he is not interested in office or factory quarrels, gossip or vendettas, nor is he planting the seed for a new wave of McCarthy-era informing. What he wants is information on problems that directly affect the welfare of the consumer, nothing more.

Nader is aware that the concept can be, and probably will be, abused by some. But to Nader it is a risk worth taking. It is no different from the exercise of a constitutional right— they all carry the risk of abuse, but it is an acceptable risk, he says.

The real problem, as Nader sees it, is for the whistleblower to exercise the proper judgment. At a Conference on Professional Responsibility called by Nader in Washington on January 30, 1971, the consumer advocate urged those who would blow the whistle to ask themselves such questions as these:

1) Is my information right?

2) What will be achieved by blowing the whistle?

3) Did I use all the avenues of complaint provided by the corporation?

4) Are any laws violated by taking information outside the corporation?

Petkas, sifting through mail in a rabbit warren of an office, is beginning to see what type of people are traveling along what Nader terms "the pathways of anguish and courage" that led them to the conclusion that their allegiance to society supersedes their allegiance to the corporation. According to Petkas, the information ranges from executives griping about being forced by their corporations to make contributions to political causes to engineers detailing how their corporations make exorbitant and illegal profits from government contracts. One whistleblower turned over information involving a major chemical firm he claimed was padding its balance statement by as much as $40 million. In this case, Petkas, and the staff of Nader's public interest law firm began a close analysis of the data. If it indicates that the whistleblower is on to something, the next step will be to take it to the Securities & Exchange Commission, the government agency most interested in violations of this sort.

But Petkas says that in some instances the clearinghouse will take the verified information back to the corporation or the government agency and try to stop the abuses by winning a private agreement from the guilty party. If that fails, Petkas says the clearinghouse will rely on formal complaints and lawsuits.

So far, the clearinghouse has found whistleblowers to be surprisingly compartmentalized. They are unable to see that abuses in their corporation or area of expertise may be simply more than a microcosm of an industry-wide consumer abuse. If a pattern is indicated, the clearinghouse will funnel its findings to Nader's Center for Study of Responsive Law which may use the fragmented information for the basis of an industry-wide study of the abuses.

To Nader, the clearinghouse is a key way station on the road to a whistleblowers' ethic. It will allow the whistleblower to function in secrecy, if he wishes, and will lift the fear of losing his job or of being branded a spiteful malcontent. The revengeful corporation is not a creation of Nader's sometimes purple rhetoric, but is a very real threat to any whistleblower. Ernest Fitzgerald, the Pentagon civilian who blew the whistle in testimony before Congress on the $2 billion cost overrun for the Lockheed Aircraft Corporation's C5a transport, can attest to that. Fitzgerald, an industrial engineer, was nominated by the Air Force in 1967 as a candidate for the Distinguished Civil Servant Award. But in 1968 when he told the Senate Subcommittee for Economy in Government about the Air Force attempt to cover up the cost overruns he was fired, not immediately but in a manner only a vindictive bureaucracy could contrive. After his testimony, the Air Force reassigned Fitzgerald to checking the costs on bowling alleys. Then it revoked his job protection status, claiming that it had been given to him by mistake. Air Force gumshoes "were unleashed in an unsuccessful attempt to find something in my personal life which could be used to discredit me and my testimony," Fitzgerald said. Finally, the Air Force "abolished" Fitzgerald's job. The reason for this massive overkill: Fitzgerald says it was because "I committed the truth."

In a word of advice to a potential whistleblower, Fitzgerald says he must "be prepared, financially, and psychologically to become an outlaw. If you must work for the government, big business, or major banks to make a living, forget it." It is true that civil servants are protected by law from retaliation, but Fitzgerald puts the problem in proper perspective when he asks: "Who is going to enforce the law? Would Attorney General John Mitchell put Defense Secretary Melvin Laird in jail?" Congress would seem to be the natural protector for government whistleblowers, but according to Fitzgerald, the congressmen who have the power to act refuse when faced with the strength of agencies like the Pentagon, and its allies, big business and big labor. Despite his experience, Fitzgerald still believes the whistleblower can act as a check on the Pentagon. "If enough well-intentioned, tough, and skillful people take stands inside the Pentagon, the deterioration of stewardship can be slowed, at least temporarily." The second way to blow the whistle is to become what Fitzgerald calls a "secret patriot"—someone who writes anonymous letters or makes phone calls to congressmen, newspapers, or organizations like Nader's clearinghouse. "This is a safe and prudent way to surface information the public should have. I believe our secret patriots are making indirect but worthwhile contributions to the education of the taxpaying public. This, in turn, will have a wholesome cumulative effect," Fitzgerald claims.

Fitzgerald's battle with the Pentagon was well-publicized and argued on a national level involving a full cast of luminaries from Air Force generals to senators and top industry officials. But for most would-be whistleblowers, the fight will be lonely and without glamor, and overwhelmingly frustrating. Take the case of the government poultry inspector who wrote to Nader's clearinghouse with this tale:

As a veterinarian, he uncovered a practice in the poultry industry he considered to be a serious danger to the consumer. Dutifully he reported it to his immediate superior, but got no action. This didn't thwart him, however, and he continued right up his agency's chain of command—but his plea for action was turned down at each higher level. Finally, in desperation, the inspector wrote to Mrs. Virginia Knauer,

President Nixon's special assistant for consumer affairs. Mrs. Knauer immediately wrote back to the head of the poultry inspector's agency, but to protect him, omitted his name when she questioned the agency head about the inspector's complaint. The letter was then passed down the chain of command until it arrived back on the inspector's desk with a notation from his immediate boss.

"Answer this," it said.

10

THE CHAIRMAN
OF THE BOARD
OF GENERAL MOTORS
SPEAKS:
RALPH, YOU'RE WRONG!

Some critics are like chimney-sweepers; they put out the fire below, and frighten the swallows from their nests above; they scrape a long time in the chimney, cover themselves with soot, and bring nothing away but a bag of cinders, and then sing out from the top of the house, as if they had built it.

—Henry Wadsworth Longfellow

James M. Roche,* the seventh chairman of the board of directors of General Motors, and its then chief executive officer, is the man who made Nader a public figure. He did it when he told Senator Ribicoff's Senate committee in 1966:

"I am not here to excuse, condone, or justify in any way our investigating Mr. Nader. To the extent that General Motors bears responsibility, I want to apologize here and now to members of this subcommittee and Mr. Nader. I sincerely hope that these apologies will be accepted. Certainly, I bear Mr. Nader no ill will."

That apology took a lot of guts since Roche is not a man who relishes humble pie. Like Nader, he has a strong sense of

*James Roche retired as chairman of the board on December 31, 1971. He was succeeded by Richard C. Gerstenberg.

191

duty and he did what he felt he should do. But in the six years since Roche could honestly tell the Senate he bore Nader "no ill will," his attitude has changed.

Roche now has a thorough dislike of Nader and his tactics, and he sees spokesmen like Nader as a danger to the free-enterprise system. He classifies them as masters of exaggeration; people who masquerade as the voice of the mass of consumers when in fact their support is narrow, and their issues often are not valid. To Roche, Nader cannot possibly understand business because he is not a businessman. When Nader rants about criminal prosecution of businessmen who turn out shoddy and unsafe products, Roche is sincerely puzzled and angered. "Some of the critics equate a businessman with being a crook, and that business people ought to be put in jail. I certainly don't subscribe to that—any business people I know are trying to do a good honest job of running their business successfully," he told the author.

Roche is not a sophisticated product of a Harvard School of Business Administration or any other college. Nor did he make it to the top on family money, or by marrying into money. His is the classic Horatio Alger story. Left orphaned at the age of twelve when his father died in the 1918 flu epidemic, Roche managed to finish high school in the Illinois prairie town of Elgin, and find a job with a gas and electric utility company in Aurora, Illinois. Married to a hometown girl, Roche plugged away at correspondence courses. Soon he was able to title himself a "statistician" and by the time he was twenty-one he had a job with GM in its Cadillac Division. From then on it was one slow, steady step up the corporate ladder until finally Roche's drive and analytical mind put him in the chairman's chair at GM.

The view from the chair is staggering. GM's $18 billion 1970 net sales figure was larger than the gross receipts of all but two nations in the world—the United States and the Soviet Union. GM employs almost 700,000 persons, and in 1965 produced a record-setting 5,696,000 cars. Roche's salary is $250,000 a year, and in 1969 his bonus and stock credits ran his pay up to $790,000.

The figures are enough to bring out a touch of arrogance in most men. But though there is no doubt as to who is the boss, Roche remains courtly in his dealings with others. His critics liken him to Babbitt, and claim he is a vacuous personality once he leaves the confines of the auto industry. True, Roche is not a "swinger" like some of the other GM executives. He is a practicing Catholic and a near-daily communicant. He is, in sum, what GM is: conservative in his politics, cautious in his speech, proud of his accomplishments, and if the need be, contemptuous of those who question, challenge, or sneer at GM's walled-city mentality.

He is also a man who is delighted with his 14-year-old grandson's "healthy interest" in the problems of pollution, and who argues that the American businessman has a responsibility to listen to the voice of the critic. But for all his candor and honesty, Roche can see no value in the approaches to the consumer problem offered by Nader. He has his own concept of what the consumer movement is, and what it should be. And, like Nader, Roche leaves little room for deviation.

To begin with, Roche doesn't see the consumer movement as new. To a man "who came up in the selling end of the business" (he was general sales manager for Cadillac), Roche believes that the consumer movement "goes back a long way," and that Nader is a late-comer to the field even if he has vocalized the consumers' problems.

"It is quite obvious that if we didn't satisfy our customers at least reasonably well we wouldn't last very long in the automobile business. . . . We've tried to please the consumer with the type of product we built; we've tried to build the kind of products we thought he wanted, and would sell to the best advantage. So the consumer movement, from the standpoint of trying to provide the consumer satisfaction with his purchase, has always been a very important factor in the scheme of things. What is new is the criticism that is being directed toward the manufacturers, and toward the people who are merchandizing and selling products. The criticism is based on difficulties that you experience in the use of the product. This has been given a great deal of attention; it has gotten wide coverage in the press and it has attracted attention among the politicians," Roche told the author in the carefully measured phrases he favors. Like a professor lecturing a skeptical class, Roche argues that certainly there is a problem, but not one the size the consumer critics picture. Proof: Roche says "this so-called consumer dissatisfaction is not being registered with GM in the number of letters we receive from our customers." The complaints are actually no higher than they have been in the past years, he claims. (According to GM's figures, complaints amounted to 2.5 percent of sales, or approximately one hundred thousand complaints a year.)

Even though Roche is convinced that Nader is a paper tiger who could be crumpled with heavy blows of the truth as GM sees it, he is concerned that a wayward consumer movement headed by antibusiness critics will do enormous damage to the economy. A Nader mouthing simplified economics from podiums across the land, a Campaign GM infecting stockholders with untried concepts are threats that could be more dangerous than any book of Mao's sayings, or Marxist dialectics, he feels.

Because he feels so strongly about this, he has begun to speak out, ending a period of silence that began when he finished his public apology to Nader. In the intervening years, Nader has had the field to himself. Hidden behind the walls of its grim-looking headquarters building in Detroit, Roche and GM sat out barrage after barrage fired by Nader, each one more damning that the last. At first, GM took the unofficial stand that it was beneath its dignity to reply to a man whose only real claim to fame was that he had written a book criticizing the auto industry. The corporation's well-paid public-relations staff saw Nader as only a temporary apparition. They believed he would vanish shortly, killed off by his own repetitiveness which, they advised their corporate chiefs, was considered deadly by news editors whose cry, they said, is always for the new, the fresh angle. But as Nader began to balloon in strength, GM's silence strategy began to crumble. Nader constantly forced GM to answer by turning his information over to government agencies which would in turn query GM, forcing the corporation to say something publicly. Then GM moved to a campaign of trying to get its denials publicized in time to water down every Nader charge. Finally it switched to a campaign design to get its story across to the public via intensive press briefings, lobbying, and advertising.

Even though Nader had shown GM that it could be costly to use private detectives to investigate its critics, there still are a gaggle of Nader-watchers in GM's executive suite. His television and radio appearances are monitored. Copies of the reports produced by Nader Raider teams find their way back to Detroit, and Roche himself carefully reads Nader's speeches—so much so that he can even quote what he considers some of the more blatant examples of Nader's distortions. In Roche's mind, part of Nader's attack on GM is a personal vendetta; revenge for using detectives to pry into his private life. The other reason is simply that GM is number one in the industry. He has apparently decided that General Motors should be the target, says Roche, who also is candid enough to admit that "I suppose if I was in his place, I would look at it the same way. If Nader were to go after U.S. Steel, Alcoa, or a large petroleum company, it wouldn't give him the kind of a platform that he has with General Motors. We are a big company; we sell products that are used intimately in the lives of people—cars, trucks, appliances. They are mechanical products that require service; they are products that deteriorate with age and use and have to be replaced; this is a natural [for a consumer critic]."

But Roche feels the constant carping of the consumer critic is damaging the free-enterprise system, and that some of the damage is being done deliberately.

Seated in General Motors' Washington office, Roche said, "I think in some cases some of the critics of our society today are based on the destruction of our society. I think they are using things like consumerism, things like pollution, things like minority issues, unemployment—any cause that may come along to attempt to carry out those ends. I think there are a lot of people in the country today who would like to see us change from a so-called free competitive enterprise society to a socialist society—to be, perhaps, charitable."

Roche was quick to add that he does not think that critics who feel this way are in control of the consumer movement. "Definitely not, but they add to the momentum of the movement through their espousal of the cause," he claimed. But when pressed on the question he also admitted that he feels "some of the leaders would like to see the system changed." This change, at least, "would be a lot more control over the things we do in society," he said.

Nothing in a corporation the size of GM is done quickly or without careful planning. The decision to counterattack the consumer critics was no different. There were policy meetings starting in the summer and fall of 1970. There were the usual staff recommendations for and against the idea. But one argument that carried real weight was the impact made by Campaign GM's first campaign to woo institutions and individual stockholders to its call for changes in the way GM was run. True, the campaign failed but Roche and the rest of GM's management were agreed that the time was at hand to staunch the slow erosion of confidence in GM's management, and the moves must be taken before the May, 1971, stockholders meeting. Once the decision was made, Roche carefully picked his spots and began slowly to build his attack.

On December 14, 1970, he made a speech at the Waldorf-Astoria in New York before the Advertising Council in which he said: "No institution today is free of loud public criticism —not the government, not our churches, not our schools, certainly not the business community. The critics of America are many, and they are skilled at defaming. They move from place to place, bitter gypsies of dissent. They seek out audiences rather than truth. Responsible to no one, their true motives are best known only to themselves."

On March 10, 1971, he was back on the podium; this time before the Economic Club of New York: "Irresponsible criti-

196

cism makes big headlines but little headway. The sensational accusation is newsworthy, and has a self-reinforcing quality. More harmful, the search for scapegoats leads away from personal responsibility and into self-excuses. It is the other fellow who is at fault. It is the government. It is business. It is, in short, 'they'—the mysterious 'they'—who pollute the air and water, who sell poorly made products, who are guilty of intolerance, indifference, or inaction. It is 'they' who are responsible—never 'I.' "

Then on March 25, 1971, Roche, speaking to the Executive Club of Chicago really laid it on. He said:

"Much of the modern criticism of free enterprise is by no means idle, nor is it intended to be. Many of the critics have the professed aim to alter the role and influence of the corporations and corporate management in and upon American society. Their philosophy is antagonistic to our American ideas of private property and individual responsibility . . .

"These critics whose aim is destructive are following the basic tactic of divisiveness—and with considerable success. They are endeavoring to turn various segments of our society —government, labor, the universities—against business. They are trying to make America in the 1970's a society at war with itself.

"Their ultimate aim is to alienate the American consumer from business, to tear down long-established relationships which have served both so well. They tell the consumer he is being victimized. New products are being foisted upon him, whether he wants them or not. These products are not as good as they should be—that is, they are less than perfect. Businessmen are greedy, and uncaring. Corporations are beyond reach and above response to the consumer's needs. Advertising is false. Prices are padded. Labels are inaccurate. Therefore, the consumer, many would have us believe, is helpless and unprotected when he shops, and is really not responsible for what he buys."

According to Roche, this concept—that the consumer cannot trust his own free choice—strikes at the heart of the free-enterprise system. "To destroy the concept of consumer supremacy is to destroy free enterprise. If the consumer can be convinced that he really does not know what is good for him—and this is what the critics try to do—then freedom leaves free enterprise," Roche claimed.

Roche was particularly bitter about what he considers to be the self-serving motives of some of the consumer critics. They claim they are exercising the American right of outspoken criticism. But according to Roche, the nation's past critics were constructive—"doers as well as doubters." But he said the current lot is different.

"Too many today seek less to correct a wrong than to condemn a system. Too many critics focus on a particular fault for no more than a moment, and offer few if any solutions. They jump from cause to cause, going wherever popularity or expediency lead, using whatever means are at hand, inflaming any issue that promises attention.

"Each of their criticisms may seem inconsequential by itself. Yet taken together, these criticisms, in their number and in their intensity, are an indictment of economic America that can do lasting damage to our system. The criticisms themselves are a form of harassment unknown to businessmen in other times. They tend to mislead the courts and government into other forms of business harassment. This unjustified harassment—and much of it is unjustified—is a covert danger we can no longer ignore," Roche said.

Erect, silver-haired, his voice still deep, at sixty-four Roche was at the apex of his career. His prestige in the business community was enormous—but more importantly what he said accurately reflected the feelings of corporate America toward those who challenged it.

Certainly it did the feelings of the other auto barons. To Henry Ford, the moralistic approach taken by critics distorts the consumer movement, and simplifies to the point where it is reduced to "the good guys"—the consumers—must go and punish the "bad guys"—the business community. President of Chrysler, John J. Riccardo, a week before Roche was to make his speech before the Chicago Executive Club, made a speech of his own urging businessmen to "move off the defensive."

"I think it is important that we once again respond to the generalizations about the soulless corporations, and—by extension—about how the profit-motivated free-enterprise system rejects basic human values and stifles cultural achievement." According to Riccardo, the successful businessman in the United States is seldom the candidate for a hero role. But "I don't feel good about it when a number of people who ought to know better think he's the enemy of the people," he says.

The biggest single weapon in the consumer critic arsenal—and all the auto chieftains agree on this—is the press. "You'll have to ask them [the press] why they give Nader so much publicity," says Roche, but he is convinced that the nation's communications network has multiplied the influence of what he has termed the "doubters and the naysayers." With the news media as their public-address system, the critics have covered the nation with what he feels is a cloud of pessimism that is not supported by the facts.

Industry is doing a much better job than the critics would have the public believe, says Roche. "If you could get to individual consumers they would agree—not that they haven't had a problem; you can have a problem with anything that is mechanical. For example, the life of a car is about eleven years, but many cars, perhaps the majority of them, from the time they leave the factory until the time they go to the junkyard, are never to see the inside again—they are outside; they are driven in all kinds of weather; they are exposed to the sun, to salt, and ice. Very few receive any preventive maintenance even though there are 15,000 pieces in an automobile . . . we think the automobile does a pretty good job of providing the kind of service people expect. Prove this to yourself, go out on a freeway and see the traffic jams, but see how infrequently you see a disabled car," says Roche who defends the industry with the same arguments offered by the salesmen in the showrooms, and feels their logic is incontrovertible. In sum, his argument to the critics is that, given its size and the possibility of mistakes and errors, the auto industry is giving the consumer more, not less, than can be expected.

"We make no claims whatsoever that we are a perfect industry. We make no claims that we give the customer the kind of service in every instance we would like to give him. We recognize this, and we're trying to solve the problem," he says. But Roche feels the critic is taking advantage of this small hardcore of unresolved complaints. The critics home in on these and are welcomed by the dissatisfied consumers, says Roche.

"The critic, whether it is Mr. Nader, or anybody else, has one very great advantage going for him—that is, the average person never objects to anyone sympathizing with him no matter what kind of problem he has," is the way Roche explains the intensity of support for the critic.

Beyond the irritation that an outsider would presume to tell business that its products are shoddy, unsafe, or that it thinks too much of its profits and too little of its social responsibility, is a genuine fear that entrenched power historically has had of new ideas.

The fear is centered on the consumers' influence on government which can result in what business feels is profit-stifling legislation, or meaningless restrictions which actually rebound against the consumer by making him pay more for a product to offset the manufacturers' cost in complying with federal regulations.

"Make no mistake, the results of irresponsible harassment have added significantly to the cost of doing business. The higher taxes are costly. Adapting products to new regulations is costly. Meeting daily harassments, answering criticism, defending against public attack, all of these carry costs," explains Roche.

Roche sees the restrictions stifling business incentive, the element which provides the needed force in a free enterprise system. With incentive lacking, business suffers a downturn with all its resultant effect on society, Roche claims.

To protect its profits and its power, business can be

expected to strike back even harder in the future. Roche himself says "It's my opinion that the thing has reached such proportions that somebody should try to place it in its proper perspective. I think one of the jobs we have to do is accentuate the positive for a change instead of the negative. I think that we are facing such serious problems that unless we start to do that, we are going to be in very deep trouble.

"I've been in the automobile business a long time and we've always had service problems—they are nothing new. We've worked at them and tried to fix them. But I suppose as long as we ever make anything mechanical we are going to have them. But you don't condemn the automobile; you don't say the automobile is a vicious beast because you have a problem with the transmission once in a while. We should look at what the automobile does beyond the occasional repair job."

Roche is circumscribed in what he can say by his very position, and he feels other businessmen are too. "There is a great deal of difference in the ability of a businessman to speak and the ability of a critic to speak. The businessman has to speak from the standpoint of responsibility. He can't speak without having the facts to back it up. With the critic, if he isn't right, well, he just forgets it and goes on to the next thing. But the businessman has complete responsibility for what he says." It is this speaking from ignorance that Roche claims is most frightening. "What happens is that they do not fully understand some of the things they are talking about." This is why they alienate business and retard progress on solving consumer problems, Roche indicated.

As part of its arsenal for the counterattack, business is building a list of its own instant oversimplified arguments against Nader and his consumerites. Seat belts are an example. Nader billed seat belts as a lifesaving device, one that was simple and effective. But what happened once the government legislated seat belts into law? Only one third of the drivers use them. But the belts cost the auto buyer $250 million a year to buy. DDT is another argument. DDT boomed the world's food supply, wiped out disease-bearing insects, and made hundreds of thousands of acres of land useable for mankind. The critics argued that overuse of DDT was destroying wildlife, and finding its way into the food chain. But the critics were never able to prove conclusively that it was harming man. Despite this, DDT is being phased out. Now, say the anticonsumer groups, insects will return en masse, and cause food crops to drop.

One of the sharpest attacks on Nader came from that friend of old ladies in distress, the American Automobile Association. As might be expected the AAA struck after Nader announced in July, 1971, that he planned to investigate the thirteen-million member AAA. As its first target, the AAA chose the Nader-backed Center for Auto Safety. In a petition filed with the Federal Communications Commission, the center sought equal time under the FCC's fairness doctrine to reply to Ford Motor Company commercials which claimed the air-bag safety device could be dangerous for drivers if the government forced the automakers to install the air bags without an extended period of testing. The center argued that the air bags were reliable and supported early installation on cars. The AAA, however, backed Ford's stand, and claimed the Transportation Department was forcing the automakers into an unsafe action. In a letter to FCC Chairman Dean Burch, John de Lorenzi, the AAA's managing director of public and government affairs asked the FCC to deny the center's petition and proceeded to attack its credibility, its expertise, and its motives.

"The Center for Auto Safety is a self-proclaimed 'auto safety and consumer advocate.' In the news media it has been identified as either being supported by or backed by Ralph Nader. Mr. Nader has defined for himself the role of a consumer advocate. Is this the basis on which the center makes its claims?

"Who does the center really speak for—is it the consumer, and, if so, how do the consumers participate in the decisions of the center? Or do a handful of men decide the policy for the organization? Where do the funds for the center come

202

from? If the majority of funds are based upon large grants, were any strings attached to these grants?

"Specifically, how many consumer members does the center have and where did it obtain its mandate to speak on behalf of the consumer on the air-bag issue?" De Lorenzi asked.

Lowell Dodge, the director of the center, replied immediately with a detailed financial statement, and an outline of who the members of his staff were, and their qualifications. In return, he asked the AAA for a breakdown on who paid the major part of the $1.5 million AAA made in advertising fees in 1969. He also asked the AAA to list the names of the insurance companies which paid the AAA $2.7 million in commissions, plus a list of the companies that produced $5.8 million in travel agency fees for the AAA. The AAA remained silent, however.

The AAA attack was apparently designed to put Nader on the defensive in the same manner Nader put corporations he attacked on the defensive. It was also part of a strategy designed to block Nader from skewering the AAA management in front of the public. The AAA made no effort to conceal its contempt of Nader. It even went to the extreme of providing "guidelines" to its employees on how to handle Nader's Raiders, and then promptly labeled the guidelines secret when Nader asked to see them.

The man who has marshalled the national AAA headquarters for a fight against Nader's Raiders is Executive Vice-President James B. Creal, who feels that the AAA's role is not that of a consumer-action group but a service organization. According to Nader, AAA has opted for the service organization theory because it is more profitable for the executives and guarantees that there will be no boat-rocking that could bring about changes in the AAA management.

The war between the two really began to heat up when Nader found that his raiders were being shut out of AAA clubs around the nation, and Creal himself asked Nader to submit to an interview by AAA officials so that they could assess what Nader had in mind before any further interviews would be given to his raiders.

Nader replied with a stinging letter to Creal pointing out that the AAA had originally promised to allow its top officials to be interviewed.

"Your reversal of this agreement constitutes one more evidence of bad faith, along with the invectives in your public commentary that have utterly no redeeming value in an iota of fact or insight." Nader then asked to address the AAA's annual convention so he could tell his story directly to the delegates. But Creal blocked the end run. In a testy letter of his own to Nader, Creal told Nader his refusal to be interviewed by the AAA staff "means to us that you want one-way communication—your way." Creal then told Nader flatly that he was shutting the door on any further cooperation with the Nader's Raiders.

From this point, the argument descended to petty slurs with Creal claiming that Ron Landsman, Nader's project director for the AAA investigation, had used obscene language over the telephone. And Landsman proudly admitted he said "shit" when he was being passed from one AAA official to another without having his questions answered.

But Creal's approach to Nader is another indication of the growing strike-back philosophy being adopted by institution executives who would rather fight than reform. To Nader, his fight with the AAA is evolving in the same way the battle with the auto industry did. The AAA is not listening, or prefers not to hear what he is saying, and is concentrating on repeating over and over again what it has done to satisfy its members.

But Nader is concentrating on what it has not done. He ticks off facts like these: The AAA was officially opposed to any federal regulation of auto safety features until 1966 when he arrived on the scene and Congress passed the first auto safety legislation. With an income of $900 million a year, the AAA has never made any attempt to rate automobiles as to safety or value for its members, nor has it ever made any attempt to pressure the auto industry for design changes in automobiles which would have improved safety, or cut repair bills and insurance rates for members. When it has taken a stand, says Nader, the AAA has usually been on the wrong side as far as its consumer-members are concerned. It supported the highway lobby's campaign to protect the $4 billion highway trust fund from being used for any purpose other than road building, and, as in the case of the air bag tends to accept, without investigation, the automakers' view on critical safety innovations.

Thomas R. Shepard, Jr., publisher of the now defunct *Look* magazine, is another who makes anti-Nader arguments. To him, Nader is bad for the nation. He sees the consumer movement as stunting progress, and, as do most of his fellow businessmen, destroying the consumer's marketplace freedom. He puts his argument this way in a speech to a meeting of the Soap and Detergent Association:

Members of the consumer movement are "libertarians who champion the cause of freedom from every podium, who insist on everyone's right to dissent . . . to demonstrate . . . to curse policemen and smoke pot and burn draft cards, and fly the flags of our enemies while trampling our own—these jealous guardians of every citizen's prerogative to act and speak without government restraint are also the most outspoken advocates of eliminating freedom in one area. When it comes to commerce, to the making and marketing of goods, our liberty-loving critics are in favor of replacing freedom with rigid controls."

To Shepard, Nader is one of the worst examples of intolerant consumerists. "I have heard many businessmen dismiss Ralph Nader and his associates as well-meaning fellows who sincerely want to help the consumer by improving business methods. Forget it. Mr. Nader isn't interested in seeing American industry clean house. What he wants is the house—from cellar to attic. His goal is a top-to-bottom takeover of industry by the government, with Mr. Nader, himself, I would guess, in charge of the appropriate commission."

According to Shepard, all business has to do to undercut the consumerists and win back the American people "is acquaint them with the facts."

Shepard's view has even won some support in Congress, long a friendly forum for Nader. Congressman Bob Wilson (R-Calif.), chairman of the Republican Congressional Committee is one of Nader's most searing critics. His line parallels Roche's almost identically. "Under the guise of consumer interest, business is being tarred in a manner which, at times, almost makes one think that business and industry are un-American. Sure, there are problems in our industrial life. But it is still the lifeblood of the nation. And it is one segment of our society that is providing the people with the goods and services they need and want. I would be the first to acknowledge that every item off every production line isn't perfect and that we all should be striving to improve quality. But, with all of the faults within the business community, I ask you, does it rate the type of abuse which is being heaped upon it?" asks Wilson.

Nader's answer to this obviously is yes. Only by exposure will there be correction, he feels. But Wilson, like Roche, feels Nader is throwing the baby out with the bathwater, and he goes so far as to compare Nader with the late Senator Joseph McCarthy, the master of innuendo and half-truth.

Wilson said in a speech to a group of advertising men: "Today, business is being hit with a newer and even more refined strategy. This one could justly be called Naderism. I realize that speaking of Ralph Nader in anything but reverential tones nowadays is somewhat less than a popular undertaking. As a matter of fact, he has all the earmarks and the trappings of a sacred cow. As an observer of the business scene today, it is obvious that many of Nader's charges are specious and unfounded. As a matter of fact, rather than being a sacred cow, in my opinion a better description would be an expert at throwing the bull." Again, Wilson cites what is the continuing cry of business—Nader and the consumer critics are more interested in tearing down the system than in correcting it. In the case of automobile industry, Wilson says that Nader "has gone beyond a consumer crusade and is trying to destroy the entire industry."

Over in the Senate, Nader has stirred the ire of Senator

THE CHAIRMAN SPEAKS: RALPH, YOU'RE WRONG!

Ted Stevens (R-Alaska) by his barbed rhetoric. In testimony before the Senate Commerce Committee on May 11, 1971, Nader accused the auto industry of criminal fraud by designing cars that are easily damaged and can be repaired only with so-called captive parts available solely from the automakers. This device assures the automakers a "parasitic" multibillion dollar market in parts, Nader said.

That was too much for Stevens. Pounding his desk with his fist, Stevens hit back at Nader: "You look for the worst in people, and not at what's good that's happening in this country." Nader's reply to Stevens, and indirectly to all those in the business community who offered the same argument was—"Do you give credit to a burglar because he doesn't commit burglaries ninety percent of the time?' This was pure Nader. It shows sharply the divergent approaches to the consumer movement by the Naders and the corporate chieftains. Nader wants business to face up to the ten percent that is bad. Business wants to talk about the ninety percent that's good.

Intellectual business students see the very fact that business needs, at this late date, to explain its role to the American public as its biggest failure, and the reason why the consumer critics find willing adherents. The nation's corporations spend millions of dollars on public relations each year, but the money is an obvious waste when men of the business stature of Roche are forced to explain what the philosophy of business is in regards to profits, social problems, and the free-enterprise system.

Given the tenor of the times, critics' arguments for more social responsibility from business seem perfectly logical to many consumers and stockholders. Why shouldn't business do more? If it creates pollution, why shouldn't it clean up its own dirt? If its product is shown to be dangerous, why shouldn't it be punished by government, and restricted from repeating its sin?

In defense, business spokesmen have mouthed weak-worded replies about their lack of expertise in handling social problems, and their lack of a clear mandate to spend stockholder profits on societal problems.

Many businessmen agree with economist Milton Friedman that business has only one social responsibility—to use its resources to multiply its profits. But in general, business itself is confused. Even those corporations who want to defuse public resentment find little in the way of concrete guidelines. Part of the answer to the problem may lie in the advice given by C. B. McCoy, the president and chairman of the board of Du Pont. Said McCoy of the critics: "Maybe it would pay us to argue with them less and confide in them more."

11

THE SECOND
MAYFLOWER COMPACT

Because the leaders of large organizations are distracted and corrupted by luxuries and the trappings of corporate success, they have no time to consider fundamental values like honesty, truth, and justice.

—Robert Townsend, author of
Up the Organization, and former President
of Avis-Rent-A-Car

For Goodyear Vice-President Robert H. Lane, this was to be, if everything went well, a good day for the rubber lords of Akron; a day they did what their corporate soul brothers in Detroit could never bring themselves to do: deal face-to-face with Ralph Nader in a hotel room.

Lane, a smart, one-time newspaperman who parlayed brains and natural charm into an upper five-figure salary, was by rubber industry standards a sophisticate who prided himself on knowing his way around. He had scrambled from the city room of the Pittsburgh Press to a vice-presidency in Carl Byoir, a prestigious public relations firm where he toiled at sprucing up the image of Byoir's clients in the auto and chemical industries. By 1958, he had made the jump to the upholstered suites of Goodyear's executive row and quickly won the ear of Russell DeYoung, Goodyear's chairman, and Victor Holt, its president.

In the summer of 1969, DeYoung, Holt, and Lane had

problems—big ones. Smarting from the recent defective tire recalls, the tire industry was still being pummelled on the same subject by Senator Gaylord Nelson, the Wisconsin Democrat who worked in tandem with Nader, and worse, the industry itself was on the verge of a bloodletting over the value of the polyester versus rayon tire. Goodyear, which accounted for thirty percent of the 200 million tires produced annually, was using its power in an effort to drag the other major tire manufacturers—Firestone, Uniroyal, Goodrich, and General—along with it in a changeover away from rayon. Eight million dollars had been poured into advertising Goodyear's Polyglas tire which combined polyester, a petroleum product used to make tire cord, and fiber glass belts into what Goodyear argued was a safer tire that gave more mileage and better traction. Goodyear had the support of General Motors, which had promised to make polyester tires standard equipment on their next year's models. With the two giants pulling together, there appeared little doubt they could force their competitors to join them in what was the biggest production change in the tire industry in thirty years.

But if there was money to be made from the more expensive polyester tires, the rayon cord suppliers had a stake of their own in the game: a cool $95 million worth of rayon had gone into tire cord the year before. To protect this investment, the rayon suppliers, who had the tacit support of some of the smaller tiremakers, were fighting back tooth and tire iron. They claimed the new polyester tire was subject to sudden deterioration at high speeds and suffered what tire engineers quaintly describe as "catastrophic failure"—a massive blowout that would shred the tire into spaghetti-like strips almost immediately. To prove this argument an organization known as Tyrex, which was made up of large rayon tire cord suppliers, produced a fourteen-minute film that showed with awesome clarity polyester tires undergoing "catastrophic failures."

Between the film, Nelson and Nader, and the confused consumer, Goodyear was getting panicky. Its Polyglas tire could conceivably end up in a consumer goods graveyard along with the Corvair, which only two months before had been officially pronounced dead by General Motors when sales had plummeted ninety-three percent following the Nader-sparked controversy over its instability. GM still contends the car was safe but the consumer decided otherwise. Goodyear was not planning to accept a similar defeat. Too much money was at stake, not to mention the possibility that if the polyester decision boomeranged it could put new faces on the executive row. Operating under that somewhat dubious American business principle—if one is good, two are better—Goodyear produced its own film to answer Tyrex. It accused the Tyrex group of filming blowouts on polyester tires under test conditions that would cause any tire to fail, and with a barrage of facts and charts it stoutly maintained that polyester did not deteriorate faster under heat than rayon.

In the first week of July the pressure on Goodyear and General Motors increased when a letter showed up on the desks of GM President Edward N. Cole and Goodyear's President Holt. "Disturbing information has come to the Bureau's attention to the effect that tires constructed with polyester ply cords and polyester cord tires with glass fiber belts may fail catastrophically. Further information received by this Bureau indicates that tires constructed with cords of other material such as nylon and rayon do not fail in the same manner or under similar conditions." The letter went on to point out that polyester tires were available as optional equipment on some 1969 model GM cars and were planned as original equipment on some 1970 models. Cole and Holt were told to forward the data on polyester tire performance immediately. The letter was signed by Robert Brenner, Acting Director of the National Highway Traffic Safety Administration, the agency created by Congress to watch over the auto industry and enforce tire safety standards. The same week, Nader, who had never seen the Tyrex film but was getting a steady stream of complaints from owners of polyester tires, delivered a speech in Atlanta citing the reports. Nader did not support the rayon side of the argument, but his stand was critical of Goodyear and General Motors for forcing the polyester tire on the public without, in Nader's opinion, sufficient testing. Lane was a candid man. It was his contention that there were few problems the tire industry, and in his case, Goodyear, could not work out to its own benefit, if it sat down with the critics. But to some Goodyear executives, the idea of meeting with Ralph Nader in a hotel room was akin to asking Yippie-leader Abbie Hoffman to chair Goodyear's annual stockholders' meeting. Should the $3 billion Goodyear Corporation, with facilities stretching from Ypsilanti, Michigan, to Dolok Merangir Estates, Indonesia, meet with what one company official termed a "self-serving, opportunistic man"? If it hadn't been for Nader, they argued, the industry might not have to contend with government test standards or labelling regulations, not to mention the expensive operation of tire recalls that chipped away at Goodyear's profit margin as well as its public image.

Then there was another problem. What would GM think? Nader's name was an obscenity to GM President Edward Cole, "the father of the Corvair." Would it be wise to rub his nose in another apparent Nader victory, especially since GM was backing Goodyear? In the end, however, Goodyear president Holt and chairman DeYoung felt it was necessary to stamp out the brush fires spreading around the polyester tire. If the tire became suspect in the eyes of the consumer, GM would not hesitate to go back to rayon, leaving Goodyear holding a polyester bag. Lane's argument was simply this: Nader was arousing public opinion against polyester. The only effective solution was to find out what would placate him and try to do it. The result would be an easing of his pressure on Goodyear. "I did it, it was my idea," says Lane who rejects the notion that the meeting was anything less than a sincere attempt to solve a consumer problem.

To Nader, the idea of meeting with Goodyear's top level management was intriguing. It represented a chance to get immediate action, but he was also afraid Goodyear might attempt to turn the meeting into a public relations gimmick that would trade on his name and benefit Goodyear's image, but do nothing for the consumer. His wariness sprung from the fact that he had never before met in such a peace conference with officials of a corporation, nor has he met with any since. Not surprisingly, executives had become cool toward Nader in 1966 at the sight of GM President James Roche humbly apologizing to him.

What finally swayed Nader to Lane's idea was the hope Goodyear really wanted to listen to his suggestions. Nader didn't expect Goodyear's presentation on polyester to be anything but a flood of engineering data that would take time to assess, and in any event, was not likely to be conclusive. But there were more immediate things Goodyear could do for consumers.

Nader's "yes" set in motion a give-and-take that would have brought a smile to the face of Talleyrand, the master diplomat. America's major corporations have long had unwritten rules for meetings between friendly and even unfriendly competitors. They apply to anything from the supersecret hotel-room price-fixing sessions such as those that sent General Electric officials to prison in the early 1960s to the casual, "accidental" meetings on country-club patios, where, between sips of gin and tonic, and just out of earshot of onlookers, executives carve up markets, trade information, and settle grudges.

But in Nader's case, none of the normal rules would do. Nader was not interested in "dealing," nor was he a member of the business establishment. Because of this, Lane, kept on a short leash by DeYoung and Holt, carefully laid out an agenda and set the ground rules. Goodyear would limit its team to Lane himself, John J. Hartz, vice-president of tire development, and Goodyear's manager of tire engineering, J. F. Hutchinson. One of the touchiest points was the status of the meeting: Would it be public, secret, private, or what? Even though Goodyear hoped the meeting would tone down Nader's attacks, the company was not, as one official put it, "interested in putting out a press release to tell the world we are meeting with Nader.

"We weren't doing anything illegal. We simply wanted to

find out if there was anyting we could do to get Nader off our backs. We wanted to do the right thing."

But there were other considerations. Not every one of Goodyear's 68,469 shareholders thinks Ralph Nader should be treated with deference or for that matter even be recognized to any degree. "As for the customer, he might be convinced there was something wrong with our product simply because we were associating with Nader. After all Nader's name is associated with criticism, not quality," the official said.

Nader never considered the idea of a secret meeting. He refused to accept any condition that would prevent him from openly discussing what was said and done, should he choose to. To Nader's way of thinking, a secret meeting would smack of the very thing he had so often accused industry of doing. In the end, there was no agreement one way or the other on the status of the conference. "We didn't register under false names, and Nader was free to say anything he wanted to about the meeting," was the way one irritated Goodyear official recalled the arrangement.

For the site, Lane chose his favorite Washington hotel, the Mayflower, an aging, but respectable establishment on Connecticut Avenue that claims as its most ardent admirer J. Edgar Hoover, who for decades has been chauffeured from his office in the Justice Department to eat quietly in a corner of the hotel's Rib Room.

When Nader climbed out of a taxi in front of the hotel, Thursday, July 10, he had with him one of his raiders, a young Princeton engineering student named Jim Bruce, whom Nader brought along for a practical lesson in dealing with corporate executives, and Edward Heitzman, a Princeton engineering professor and automotive consultant. Lane had asked Nader "to keep his group small, not so that it would go unnoticed, but because it would be more manageable." For Nader, keeping a group small has never been a problem. On most occasions, especially when rendezvousing with sources, Nader's group consists of one: himself. It is rare when he will either share an assignation, or delegate a stand-in. Once the door to Lane's hotel suite closed, it stayed shut for six hours, and when it finally reopened, Nader and Goodyear had reached a new "Mayflower Compact" that would have been as hard for Goodyear to imagine in pre-Nader years as it would have been for the Pilgrim Fathers.

As Nader expected, Lane, Hartz, and Hutchison flooded him with data on polyester. They ran a film to refute, point by point, the Tyrex film. Nader was impressed by the Goodyear argument, but not converted. He preferred to wait and keep an ear tuned for complaints about polyester. His criticism would escalate if the consumers' criticism did.

But Nader's real coup came in securing the kind of immediate gain for the consumer that he had counted on. Under Nader's prodding, Goodyear agreed to publish a pamphlet which would be called "It Must Be Right Or We Make It Right." The pamphlet outlined specifically how a customer gets an adjustment or files a complaint if he is not happy with the performance of a Goodyear tire. Nader has long contended that many major corporations obstruct complaint channels. The man who buys a defective product often finds that the warranty is designed more to thwart than to serve him. To get a corporation the size of Goodyear to recognize the need for a new approach to consumer complaints was for Nader a significant development.

The form the pamphlet finally took was Goodyear's own doing. Specifically the work was approved by O. E. Miles, an executive vice-president who retired in 1970, and John P. Kelley, Goodyear's director of advertising. Nader wanted the pamphlet to mention possible defects that the consumer should watch out for—such as bulges on the sidewall, signs of tread separation, cracks, excessive wear—but Goodyear turned this idea down, and would not consider suggesting that the customer forward a copy of his complaint to the National Highway Traffic Safety Administration. Instead, it took the normal public-relations approach to the matter. For example, the pamphlet began, "Although it is highly unlikely that you will not be satisfied with the performance of your Goodyear tires...." Nevertheless, it gave the consumer something he had not had before—a simple three-step guide on how to make a legitimate complaint.

The pamphlet told the tire buyer that if he was not satisfied with his dealer's decision he could: 1) Leave the tire with the dealer to be inspected by a Goodyear district service representative, or 2) Write or phone the local Goodyear district office "listed in the white pages of the telephone directory under the Goodyear Tire & Rubber Company, and direct his letter or phone call to the attention of the district service department." If Goodyear did not have a district office in the customer's community, the pamphlet advised him to call any Goodyear dealer and ask for the address or telephone number of the closest district office. The pamphlet wound up by counseling the customer that "if, in some rare instance, you are not satisfied with the adjustment proffered" to write to H. Fox, the manager of Goodyear Service Department in Akron, Ohio. As a result of its meeting with Nader, Goodyear has printed two million of these pamphlets without fanfare and is planning to print four million more. A simple service, perhaps, but before the Mayflower Compact, there was nothing like it, and there should have been. An effective procedure for making complaints is an absolute necessity, Nader feels. For a corporation, the lack of genuine "consumer feedback" leaves it without a true reading on its quality control system. Nader is completely convinced that the complaint letters he receives are an accurate gauge of the seriousness and extent of a defect. Between 1969 and 1970 consumers sent Nader's newly-created Center for Auto Safety over six thousand letters complaining about tires and automobiles, but sent only two thousand to the National Highway Traffic Safety Administration in the same period, a possible indication of which one they feel is more effective.

The second concession from Goodyear related to a pet peeve of Nader's, a man who has more peeves than most. The tiremakers agreed that in all future Goodyear ads based on road tests, Goodyear would offer to the customer, or anyone else who requested it, the engineering data to back up the claims in the ad. A subsequent ad for its Polyglas tire said:

216

"Two cars, identical except for the tires, were braked from 45 m.p.h. to zero on a wet macadam track. The average stopping distance for the car with bias ply tires was 226 feet. The car with the Polyglas tires had an average stopping distance of 194 feet. So the difference was 32 feet, almost two car lengths—and that can make all the difference."

The ads went on to claim that Polyglas tires gave more "starting traction on a wet track than the bias ply tire—and more cornering grip, too." But the crucial paragraph, as far as Nader was concerned, was the following:

"A fact book, describing the type and extent of testing behind the Custom Power Cushion Polyglas tire referred to in this advertisement is available on request. Write to: The Goodyear Tire & Rubber Company, Dept. 805N, Akron, Ohio 44316." To Nader this concept of a manufacturer backing up advertising claims is the only way to prevent fraud and deception.

A year after Goodyear agreed to his requests, Nader filed a petition with the Federal Trade Commission urging it to issue a rule requiring all advertisers to furnish scientific proof of claims. In answer to Nader, the FTC in 1971 began ordering individual advertisers on an industry-by-industry basis to produce documentation for claims in their advertisements.

How important is a policing of tire claims? The industry spends $60 million a year on advertising, ample criteria of its value in influencing buyers.

But is there really a need for such close scrutiny of tires? Is Nader overdoing it? Is he using his power with the press to crucify Goodyear and the tire industry which has been forced to recall over 378,000 tires since 1969? Nader says no, and insists that the watch on the tire industry should, if anything, be closer. In his book *What To Do with Your Bad Car—An Action Manual for Lemon Owners*, Nader states his case very succinctly: "Tires tend to be more defect-ridden than any other single part of a car, and the defects generally have more disastrous consequences than other car defects." To back up his argument he uses statistics: "Eighteen percent of the tires tested by the National Highway Traffic Safety Administration up to May, 1969, failed to meet the minimal standards in one or more ways." And he points out that "because of cost squeezing by the automakers, the quality of 'original equipment' tires is generally lower than many replacement tires."

In 1970 the National Highway Traffic Safety Administration disclosed that some of the tires which failed to meet the government's standards were finding their way back into the market through a simple racket. The manufacturers stamped the tires "For Farm Use Only," but somewhere along the way the labels were buffed off and an unknown number of the tires ended up in the hands of unsuspecting consumers who bought them from dealers innocently assuming they were getting a tire fit for high-speed highway driving. The same tires were also being sold to used car lots and put on second-hand cars to make the customer think he was getting a new set of tires. Government investigators uncovered instances where the restrictive labels were not even removed; the tires were simply sold as a first-grade item to the many customers who never bother to read a tire label.

What is the punishment for a dealer who would deliberately sell an unsafe tire? In December, 1969, a tire dealer in Wichita Falls, Texas, paid a $600 fine; another dealer in Brighton, Colorado, was fined $400. Hardly a deterent in hopes of breaking up the racket, the government took the not too revolutionary step of requiring manufacturers to stamp the defective tires "Unsafe for Highway Use" and attaching a label warning dealers of a $1,000 fine for selling the tires for use on a passenger car. Critics contend, however, that the tires must be destroyed if the racket is to be squelched.

If Nader has one overriding asset, it is that he is what he says he is. He never masquerades, he doesn't pretend, cheat, or manipulate. The fact that the American corporation will do any one of these things is its weakness.

In that summer of 1969, as Goodyear pretended to sit at the feet of Ralph Nader and ask for absolution for its sins against the consumer, it was also busy hatching a plot to undermine Nader's tire safety campaigns. Lane, who carried the white flag to the Mayflower, was the advance man for this plan, too. The plan was simple: Hit back at Nader and his fellow critic, Senator Nelson, whose thunderbolts were landing on the industry with jolting regularity, and do it with a well-financed industry front organization.

The industry had already won its battle to water down the government tire safety standard known officially as Federal Motor Vehicle Safety Standard 109. Effective for tires manufactured after January 1, 1968, the standard was so weak when industry lobbyists finished their job that even the Rubber Manufacturers Association (RMA), the trade organization representing the major rubber manufacturers, agreed it was simply based on "long-established practices by the tire industry." But then something happened that the tire industry had not bargained for. When government inspectors checked the tires under the new standard, as bad as it was, a substantial number of tires failed to pass the test. This finding became fodder for Nader and Nelson, and the news media trumpeted their charges across the nation. By the beginning of 1969, the industry was ready for any plan that would muzzle them.

What it got was a scheme devised in the Washington office of the Rubber Manufacturers Association by five vice-presidents, one each from Goodyear, Firestone, Uniroyal, Goodrich, and General Tire, each one a director of the RMA. The RMA, run by Chairman Ross R. Ormsby, is the Washington mouthpiece for the rubber manufacturers, and like most such organizations, its job is to lobby for or against legislation, and generally cultivate politicians who may be of help to the industry.

The RMA scheme was to set up an organization that would attack Nader and Nelson whenever they attacked the tiremakers. When Nader was not pursuing the industry he was "feeding" information to Nelson. A hit on one would damage the other, the reasoning went.

The idea was sold to eighteen tiremakers in a 28-page confidential memo. Titled "To Call, Or To Be Called," the memo showed the type of thinking characteristic of executive rows in some of the nation's biggest corporations. The thrust of the document was that Nader and Nelson were crucifying the industry unjustly, and it was time for the industry to be let down from the cross.

The vehicle for this counterattack was to be called "The Tire Industry Safety Council," an officious sounding name which was needed because of "the climate and arena in which it would operate," the memo said. The major job of the council would be to answer Nader or Nelson's charges immediately so its comments would be carried in the same newspaper stories devoted to the charges. The memo described what it expected the council to do:

"After some future abuse at the hands of Nelson or Nader, the Council might release a story which would begin like this:

" 'Washington—"Irresponsible statements by Sen. Gaylord Nelson and Ralph Nader are seriously hampering the tire industry's efforts to implement a tire standards program sought by the Department of Transportation," Ross Ormsby, Chairman of the Tire Industry Safety Council said today.'

"Thus, the industry would be lending support to the Department of Transportation effort and depicting Nader and Nelson as the bad guys, who, for a change, would be on the defensive.

"Or, the Tire Industry Safety Council could put Nelson on the spot by nudging him into the politically ticklish area of state motor vehicle inspections.

"Following is a purposeful story in which the good guys in the white hats represent the rubber industry:

" 'Washington—Sen. Gaylord Nelson was urged today to get behind a movement to persuade states to ban driving on public roads with worn-out tires.

" ' "Without such support from the states, all of the present programs on tire standards are an exercise in futility," said Ross Ormsby, Chairman of the Tire Industry Safety Council.

" 'Ormsby made his plea in a letter to Nelson, long a propo-

nent of safer motor vehicles and equipment, and pointed out that the Senator's home state of Wisconsin was among those states which currently do not have such a law, etc.' "

According to the memo, "the Nelsons and the Naders pose as dragon killers. To play their role, they must paint their dragons as exploiters of the consumer, the public. They compete best with mute dragons who never return their fire. Such inaction on the part of their targets actually encourages the Naders and the Nelsons to greater activity at the expense of others."

The memo went on to describe how it believed Nader and Nelson operate. "These men have been adept in seeking out 'leaks' from the Department of Transportation and the National Highway Traffic Safety Administration (and possibly from the industry itself), and then going to the news media with announcements, demands, and disclosures of a sensational nature.

"Often their 'revelations' to the media involve a step or a program already being taken by the government and the industry in an orderly, cooperative manner. The Naders and the Nelsons 'demand' what already is being worked out, thus claiming credit for the deed or action sure to follow.

"Nelson also has demonstrated complete irresponsibility as evidenced by his recent use of a spurious, unattributed quote that two-thirds of all new tires sold may have serious and potentially hazardous defects in a letter to Transportation Secretary John A. Volpe, in a news release, and even in the wording of his tire bill."

The memo suggested that the United Rubber Workers be encouraged to "take offense" at Nelson's charge as a reflection on the skill of the union workers; a subsequent news story might read:

"Akron—The United Rubber Workers protested to Sen. Gaylord Nelson his allegation in a recent bill that two of every three tires built may be defective.

" 'This is an insult to skilled workers everywhere,' a URW spokesman said."

221

The memo recommended that the Tire Industry Council be given more freedom than the industry had allowed its trade organizations in the past. "The council should be allowed to issue industry rebuttal statements immediately upon cause or need without a complicated approval requirement within the industry." This method had been used by the tobacco industry and by the Nixon "truth squads" during the 1968 presidential campaign and was a necessity, the memo insisted, because rebuttals "must be done within a few minutes after a Nader or Nelson outburst."

Moreover, Congress should be cultivated with a vengeance. "Eight tire companies have 49 tire plants located in 43 cities and towns in 22 states, 12 of which have more than one company and multiple plants. This means there are 44 Senators and some 61 Representatives who could logically and reasonably be expected to have an interest in knowing about at least the particular segment of the tire industry that is part of their political constituency.

"The individual approaches should be varied: Drop in at the Senator's or Representative's office after arranging an appointment because of being in Washington today; dinner; a luncheon; attend a breakfast meeting of the Rubber Manufacturers Association.

"Every effort should be made to keep these initial meetings casual, but to get across the message that the tire industry and company representatives are ready to be of service in their particular areas of expertise whenever necessary.

"The important thing for top management to accomplish is to set the proper tone for the continuing involvement of the industry on the Washington scene and to do so with the 105 members of Congress from tire-plant states as soon as is practical and feasible."

Nor did the memo leave out the Department of Transportation and the National Highway Traffic Safety Administration. "There should be involvement of top management where possible and continuing liaison with appropriate government representatives by their opposite members in the industry—public relations people with government agency public affairs people, engineers with engineers, etc. The industry should seek out and get to know government people with whom they share a common occupational bond and should do so on a regular and continuing basis." It cautioned the industry not to consider the Transportation Department and the Safety Administration as being "in the enemy camp." This also applied to Democratic Senator Warren Magnuson, the head of the powerful Senate Commerce Committee, "to whom Nelson and Nader are thorns in the side."

"Where an individual company would be wise to avoid taking sides, the Tire Industry Safety Council could look for ways to help Magnuson in his role as chairman of the Senate Commerce Committee," the memo said.

Such a brisk propaganda operation would require money, of course. The memo said the council's first year of operation could be financed for about $1,159,000 with most of the funds being spent for advertising designed to present the industry's "story precisely as the industry desires to have it presented." The final proposal was a very old one by Washington standards: hire an influence salesman. The memo called for "a public affairs counsel, who would be a 'Washington Professional' with a Clark Clifford-type of relationship to the Nixon Administration [Clark Clifford was an unofficial advisor to President Johnson before he was named Defense Secretary and a man generally known for his clout in high places]. This man would be expected to open the right doors in Washington, make top-level contacts in government on behalf of the industry and catalyze situations which would provide for a dialogue between leaders of our industry and legislative and executive members of government, when necessary." The pay for that kind of service? The memo recommended $50,000.

The presidents of the five major tire companies all approved the idea, and while Goodyear was working out the final details of its concessions to Nader two months before, the Tire Industry Safety Council took a suite of offices on the seventh floor of the National Press Building and went to work.

12

CONSUMERISM

A great deal of thinking is going into computer applications in the defense area, in the space area, and in the production-merchandising area. One has to search far and deep, however, to discover some thinking on the other side of the aisle, that is, for computer uses for consumers.

—Ralph Nader in a speech to the
National Conference of the Association
for Computing Machinery

As a consumer, Ralph Nader is a flop. He doesn't own a television set, a summer home, an air conditioner, a car, a motorcycle, an electric blanket, a surfboard, or a stereo set. He survives in a materialistic society without a single credit card, department store charge account, or an installment loan payment book. His "dining out" is done mostly on airliners, and he drinks little, and smokes not at all. His suits, ties, and shoes are worn long past the average throw-away time, and he doesn't allow himself the luxury of an expensive hobby. In terms of money spent on himself, Nader in 1971 contributed only $5,200 to fuel the nation's trillion-dollar economy, and that included his expenses for both room and board.

"We grew up in a family where 'things' were never important," says Nader's sister, Claire. "No one in the family collected possessions. We were more interested in ideas."

But if Nader contributes little in the way of consumption of goods himself, he has almost single-handedly done more for the consumer and the consumer movement than any clutch of Presidents, politicians, or corporation chiefs. Since 1966, he has been responsible almost entirely through his efforts for the passage of seven major consumer-related laws— the Traffic and Motor Vehicle Safety Act (1966), Natural Gas Pipeline Safety Act (1968), Wholesale Meat Act (1967), Radiation Control Act (1968), Wholesale Poultry Products Act (1967), Coal Mine Health and Safety Act (1969), and the Occupational Health and Safety Act (1970).

He has been a force behind the drive to set up a consumer protection agency in government, and has lobbied fiercely for legislation to permit consumer class action law suits. Since 1966, he has testified before Congress almost forty times, peppering the lawmakers with examples of dangers to the consumer ranging from radiation leakage from color TV sets, to the hazard of monosodium glutamate in baby food. It was Nader who prodded the Food and Drug Administration to force the railroads to stop what Nader termed "their repulsive corporate practice" of dumping two hundred million pounds of human excrement along railroad tracks every year. It was Nader who gave public exposure to the threats of poisoning from mercury in fish, cadmium in water, and asbestos in ventilation systems. It was Nader who charged that non-tobacco elements like glass fibers and rock wool were finding their way into cigars and cigarillos. It was Nader's petition which pressured the Interstate Commerce Commission into ordering segregated seating for smokers who ride the nation's 23,000 interstate buses. And it was Nader who warned that the Volkswagen bus was "so unsafe" it should be permanently barred from the road.

But it was in December, 1970, that Nader's value was illuminated for even the skeptics to see. Statistics released by the Transportation Department showed that 55,300 persons died in highway accidents in 1970. This was 1,100 fewer than 1969, even though Americans drove five percent more miles than they did in 1969. Why the drop, which was the largest

226

decline by far in twelve years? In a word: Nader. Government officials, industry experts, and medical highway safety specialists are almost unanimously convinced that the automobile safety standards that exist mainly because of the pressure catalyzed in Congress by Nader and his book *Unsafe at Any Speed* have begun to pay off in human lives.

Seat belts and shoulder harnesses, head rests, collapsible steering columns, improved windshields, padded dashboards— all of these "voluntary" and government-ordered improvements resulted from the great auto safety debate of the 1960s which Nader triggered. But even this supreme accolade dragged only this comment from Nader—"What's happened so far is nothing compared with what could be done." To Nader, the entire consumer movement to date still is "feeble" despite its growth and its victories.

Consumerism does not carry any real weight with many politicians, and less still with the White House where "the consumer gets far less attention from our President than the University of Texas football team, or any of a host of golfers, comedians, and actors," says Nader. The best that can be said for Nixon's Administration is that "it has been creative in its proposals that would undermine legitimate consumer protection. It has not just stood by silently, it has made the kinds of proposals that would further delegate public policy to private interest, and place a veneer of activity and concern . . . over the consumer abuse area.

"I don't think it's prepared to commit the funds, to engage the enforcement resources, to ask for the sanctions, or to promote the disclosure of unsavory facts about the marketplace and various industries that's necessary," Nader told Senator Ribicoff in testimony on a bill to create a consumer protection agency. The pitifully small budgets of supposedly consumer-oriented agencies like the Food and Drug Administration ($95 million a year) and the National Highway Traffic Safety Administration ($69 million a year) show Nader has a strong argument.

"The veneer of activity" Nader talks about could take in the politicians whose old gambit of kissing babies for votes is rapidly being replaced by "hugging the consumer." So fast is the political seduction developing that Nader has warned that the consumers are endangered of becoming a "gaseous verbal balloon floating over the heads of do-nothing senators."

In 1971, Betty Furness quit her job as the first consumer advisor to New York's Governor Rockefeller. Why? "I don't think I have accomplished anything," she said. Miss Furness was right. As chairman of the State Consumer Protection Board, she had a title and nothing else. Bowing to the special-interest groups, the New York State Legislature made sure the board had no power to sue, fine, or revoke licenses of businesses mulcting consumers. The board was allowed to test products and conduct investigations, but how far could it go on a budget of $250,000 a year? New York City's Commissioner of Consumer Affairs, Bess Myerson, summed it up nicely with a remark that there was "the danger that we will be fooled by fake reform."

The danger is real. Government and industry are busily building a Potemkin village of consumer agencies. Virginia Knauer, President Nixon's consumer adviser, is a good example of the trend. A bouncy, Betty Boop-ish-type woman, she is a hard-working but powerless representative for the consumer. The fact that she has a job that was non-existent seven years earlier is not enough to satisfy. Nader terms Mrs. Knauer as nothing more than "window dressing." "She is not in charge of her own office. Peter Flanigan, Nixon's special assistant, and Commerce Secretary Stans, tell her what she can and cannot do," says Nader. On a day-to-day basis, Mrs. Knauer doesn't even get as high up as Flanigan. She reports to thirty-year-old Jonathan Rose, a lawyer and aide to Flanigan, who himself is a former investment banker, and could hardly be expected to defend the consumer with any great zeal.

Even writing to Mrs. Knauer can be a problem. One consumer, in a letter to the Washington *Post*, gave a vivid example of how the White House can rival the automakers in its lack of sensitivity to consumer problems. According to a Hyattsville, Maryland, man, he called the White House telephone operator to get the address and proper title for Virginia Knauer to whom he was writing a consumer complaint letter. He said the telephone conversation went like this:

I would like to write a letter to Virginia Knauer. Could you please give me her title and address?
White House Operator: I'm sorry, we're not permitted to give titles over the telephone.
Well, how can I get this information?
Operator: Call her office in the morning.
What's the name of her office?
Operator: I'm sorry I cannot give you that information.

Following the lead of the White House, consumer offices are popping up like toadstools in a forest of government agencies. The Transportation Department now has a lady advisor for consumer affairs. She is Ann P. Uccello, the former mayor of Hartford, Connecticut, who was named to the $32,546-a-year job in April, 1971, after she was defeated in a race for a Connecticut congressional seat, and faced an uphill battle to retain the mayor's chair. Six months after she took the job as director of consumer affairs, Miss Uccello had done nothing more than put out a handful of press releases. When asked what she had done for the consumer, an aide replied "She's still organizing her office." The Food and Drug Administration, which by law is supposed to be a consumer protection agency, has set up a consumer affairs office, apparently to do the job it was supposed to be doing all along. The Justice Department has followed suit with a legal office designed to handle consumer cases referred to it from the FTC. But as yet the office, despite the fanfare given it by the Justice Department, has failed to show any appreciable increase in either its work load or its aggressiveness. In the Department of Health, Education, and Welfare, Barbara M. Burns, a fortyish, green-eyed blonde, was named deputy assistant secretary for consumer affairs. Miss Burns' background in consumer affairs? She was a GOP fund-raiser and worked as an organizer of businessmen's conferences con-

229

ducted by the School of Advanced International Studies at Johns Hopkins University. But the most remarkable of the government consumer organizations is the National Business Council for Consumer Affairs. The advisory council consists of eighty businessmen whose job it is to identify and recommend solutions to "current and potential consumer problems." On August 6, 1971, in the historic Indian Treaty Room of the old State Department building, Nixon gave the council a dramatic send-off. Surrounded by his consumer advisor Virginia Knauer, FTA Chairman Miles W. Kirkpatrick, Food and Drug Commissioner Charles C. Edwards, Assistant Attorney General Richard W. McLaren and Special Assistant Peter Flanigan, Nixon said that the "council will allow businessmen to communicate regularly with the President, his Office of Consumer Affairs, the Federal Trade Commission, the Justice Department, other government agencies as appropriate and private organizations which are directly concerned with consumer affairs."

Fine-sounding rhetoric. Giving businessmen a vehicle by which they can have an input into consumer problems theoretically could only be good. But was it? A look at the roster of appointees, all of them named by Commerce Secretary Maurice Stans, turned up items like these: One member of the council is Hobart Lewis, an editor of the *Reader's Digest* and a friend of Nixon's. Lewis could perhaps discuss with the FTC the agency charge that the *Reader's Digest* was misleading the public with its promotional sweepstakes games which paid out less than half as much as advertised. Lewis also might have some added clout in his dealings with the FTC based on his $3,000 contribution to the GOP plus the $40,101 contributed to Nixon's election campaign by his boss DeWitt Wallace, the founder of the *Reader's Digest*, and a long-time Republican fat cat. Lewis isn't alone with his FTC "problems." Take council member Stuart K. Hensley of the Warner-Lambert Pharmaceutical Company. The drug firm merged in 1970 with Parke-Davis, and the FTC is now trying to get Warner-Lambert to divest itself of the drug firm. During the Johnson Administration, the Food and Drug

Administration also seized shipments of a Warner-Lambert prescription drug, Peritrate SA, on the grounds it was mis-leadingly labelled and the FDA urged the Justice Department to prosecute on criminal grounds. Warner-Lambert also was a client of President Nixon's old law firm of Mudge, Rose, Guthrie & Alexander. Added to this list of pluses for Warner-Lambert was still one other. The honorary chairman of the drug company—Elmer H. Bobst—is a close friend of Nixon's and was the man who convinced Mudge, Rose, Guthrie & Alexander that it would be a good idea to take Nixon on as a senior partner in the wake of Nixon's disastrous defeat in the race for governor of California, the all-time low point in his career. But not only was Bobst there with encouragement when Nixon needed his ego massaged, but he gave $63,000 to Nixon's 1968 presidential campaign. Another director of Warner-Lambert, William S. Lasdon, contributed $27,000 to the campaign.

Still another member of the council—Justin Dart of Dart Industries—was listed for a $9,000 donation. The president of Atlantic-Richfield—Thornton Bradshaw—won a seat on the council. Robert O. Anderson, chairman of Atlantic-Richfield contributed $48,000 to the GOP, and fifth member, Robert G. Dunlop, is the chief executive officer for the Sun Oil Company. The Pew family, which controls Sun Oil, gave the GOP $84,000.

One of the major toy manufacturers—Mattel Toy Company—has a representative on the council. This is the same toy industry, Nader says, whose products cause seven hundred thousand injuries a year as the result of "the ignorance, callousness, or downright venality of the product manufac-turer." The toy safety act was never even enforced by the Health, Education, and Welfare Department until the agency was sued by the Consumers Union in 1970, but Nixon continues to give an industry like this "a preferential access to the inner councils of government" and to finance the access with consumers' tax funds, Nader continues.

The list is long enough to plant doubts among the most ardent believers that the men on the council may not, as

President Nixon claimed they would, take an interest in "assuring equity in the American marketplace." Rather, they may be more intent on seeing that their favors are returned by the Administration in the form of having their views on consumerism prevail.

Nader is the most cynical of all when it comes to accepting at face value any of the government-industry-created consumer agencies. He believes that industry still does not accept the consumer movement for what it is—a genuine plea for changes in the marketplace. Since industry doesn't, government can't because of the ties between the two.

According to Nader, even the term "consumerism" was given vogue by business spokesmen to describe what they believe "is a concerted, disruptive ideology concocted by self-appointed bleeding hearts and politicians who find that it pays off to attack the corporations. Consumerism, they say, undermines public confidence in the business system, deprives the consumer of freedom of choice, weakens state and local authority through federal usurpation, bureaucratizes the marketplace and stifles innovation. These complaints have been made in speeches, in the trade press, and in congressional testimony against such federal bills as truth-in-lending, truth-in-packaging, gas pipeline safety, radiation protection, auto, tire, and drug safety legislation, and meat and fish inspection.

"But what most troubles the corporation is the consumer movement's relentless documentation that consumers are being manipulated, defrauded, and injured not just by marginal businesses, or fly-by-night hucksters but by the blue-chip business firms whose practices are unchecked by the regulatory agencies." What was the result of some of those "practices" Nader talks about that would create the angry climate which fostered the consumer revolt? Part of the answer was found in the pages of a report issued in June, 1970, by the National Commission on Product Safety. Here is what the report showed: Each year thirty thousand persons are killed and 110,000 injured in accidents in the home "as a result of incidents connected with consumer products." What are some of these consumer products? Over 100,000 persons walked through doors with no safety glaze over the glass. Over ten thousand television sets caught fire in 1969. Power mowers injured 140,000 persons, and six hundred died in accidents involving ladders. Outside the home, there were other massive failures in quality control. Mechanical problems have forced GM, Chrysler, and Ford to recall 24 million cars and trucks since 1966. In 1971, eggs and soups were plucked from grocery shelves by FDA inspectors (250 field inspectors must police sixty thousand food processing plants) hunting for suspected chemical sprays on the eggs and botulism in canned soup. And the agency banned 150 toys as "hazardous."

These statistics are not new. Over the years, politicians have approved a steady stream of legislation that has been outwardly designed to cure these same ills. There is the Hazardous Substances Act, the Flammable Fabrics Act, the Radiation Control for Health and Safety Act, and so forth. But the problem, as the politicians well know, is that the funding and enforcement of the legislation is a joke, and business is well aware of this.

But the corporations are now beginning to proclaim that they have been "born again" and have nothing but love in their hearts for the consumer. Proof: Since 1970, more than a dozen major corporations have named high-ranking company officials to consumer affairs jobs. Some of these like Chrysler, Pan American World Airways, and RCA, carry the title of vice-president. Chrysler took full-page newspaper ads to woo the consumer with honeyed phrases like: "Your Chrysler man in Detroit really cares what you think . . . Write Byron Nichols . . . about your concerns, your comments, your questions, your complaints—and he will act promptly." Says Nader: "The whole thing is a fraud. Nichols is doing nothing more than funneling complaints back down through the bureaucracy to Chrysler dealers where they are serviced in the same old inept way."

In the Chicago area, General Motors set up a hotline for a ninety-day test starting April 5, 1971. James Roche himself kicked off the fanfare for the toll-free telephone service which would put an angry car owner in contact with a GM official in Detroit. "We will invite the public to call, to comment, to make suggestions, to ask questions, to discuss any problem they may have about the GM product they own," said Roche. GM's complaint system is a three-stage affair that starts with a consumer complaining to the dealer, then moving to the GM zone office, and finally to the headquarters of the appropriate car division. The system is not new. But GM insists that it is the best way to handle complaints, and in advertising its hotline, it harped on the fact that a car owner with a complaint should follow the system. The problem is that the customer still ends up at his dealer, who, as one GM official put it, is not overly concerned that "some fink from the general office called and said fix the car." In effect, GM still is not exercising all the clout it can to bring the dealers into line to improve service. At this late date, the company "is thinking about" revolutionary ideas like printing decals that would be pasted inside the car in some unobtrusive spot and would outline the present three-step complaint procedure. "We've even thought about having dealers sit down and lecture every customer on the complaint procedure after a sale is made, but this idea was discarded because we all had the sneaky feeling that once the salesman closed the deal it was 'Goodbye, Charlie,' as far as the customer was concerned," the official said in an uncharacteristically blunt fashion for a GM man, but not so uncharacteristic as to let himself be quoted by name. As scheduled, the plug was pulled on the hotline in July, 1971, after recording only 6,750 calls from an estimated 1.8 million owners of GM cars and trucks in the area covered by the test. Even GM had expected to receive about 24,000 calls, but it proclaimed the test a success anyway. John C. Bates, director of the service section of GM's marketing staff, put GM's thinking this way: "The open-line test reconfirms our belief that car owners must get their vehicles back to the local dealers who are equipped to handle them." The logic of this may escape many car owners who rightfully feel that they are

234

being shuffled back to where they started without any more visible leverage to use on the dealer than they had when they tried to go over his head in the first place. The only hotline service consistently given good marks is the one operated by the Whirlpool Corporation's consumer division. The first of the major toll-free services, Whirlpool claims it solves seventy percent of the callers' complaints over the telephone. For the rest of the complaints, Whirlpool has developed a network of servicemen around the nation—none of whom are on Whirlpool's payroll—but who are contacted and asked to do the special jobs needed to soothe an irate consumer.

Some consumer advocates think Nader paints too dark a picture. The gains may be small, but they are gains, nevertheless, this group argues. When in the past, for example, would the consumer have found one firm attacking another's marketing procedures because the procedures were cheating the consumer, they ask? It has happened, however. The Bohack Corporation, a New York-based food chain, stopped stocking Lady Scott tissues when the Scott Paper Company began placing only 175 tissues in a box that formerly had two hundred. The paper company claimed the only alternative was to raise prices. But Bohack argued the action was a fraud since the company's competitors continue to put two hundred tissues in similarly sized boxes. Not too long ago, a vice-president of RCA asked at a conference who handled the giant firm's complaint department, but today consumers have heard the late RCA President David Sarnoff make a speech to the Poor Richard Club of Philadelphia in which he said: "Life styles may differ, but a $5 lemon is just as sour as a $5,000 lemon, and double-talk is no more welcome in a Main Line home than in a Harlem flat or on a Kansas farm. Young or old, dove or hawk, square or hippie, one tie that binds us all is irritation at being had . . . This is the age of the articulate consumer. The buyer is demanding a more active voice in determining the nature and quality of things available to him. Business will have to spend less time talking and more time listening—and responding to what it hears."

Nader agrees there are exceptions. "Some 'business statesmen' and even the National Better Business Bureau, which is emerging from its 'past, passive slumber,' are trying to make genuine efforts to ease the consumer's plight. But movement inside corporate America for consumer relations reform is glacial," he says.

What exactly is the plight of the consumer in Nader's eyes? There is one set of figures he uses time and time again to emphasize what is happening to the consumer. The figures were plucked from the mound of information collected by Senator Philip Hart's Antitrust and Monopoly Subcommittee and show that in 1969 the consumer spent $789 billion, but $200 billion of that money purchased absolutely nothing of value. How is it possible to cheat consumers on a scale of that magnitude? According to Nader there are "discernable sub-economics of consumer exploitation, and each of these sub-economics avoidably wastes the consumer dollar or prevents the use of this dollar in ways that should be the right of all citizens."

The first of these is what Nader calls the "involuntary" sub-economy. This is money the consumer would not have spent if he knew what he was getting. Nader is not talking about the tastes of individuals. "If a consumer wishes to buy a purple-covered toy wagon with cookie-type wheels, that is a matter of taste. But involuntary expenditure is money spent which the consumer would not have to put out if corporations observed elementary standards of honesty, safety, and utility in selling things to the consumer." As examples, Nader says "fragile, recessed ornamental bumpers on cars generate about $2 billion a year of involuntary expenditures. This staggering bill is the result of collision of under ten miles an hour where damage could easily have been prevented with an effective bumper."

"Worthless auto repairs is another high-cost area," Nader said. "Congressional investigations have shown that consumers are spending up to $30 billion a year on auto repairs, but up to $10 billion of that went for shoddy, unneeded repairs, and repairs paid for, but simply never performed. This expenditure, therefore, is 'lost' money for the consumer.

"The consumer lays out another $1 billion a year for drugs that are basically worthless in terms of delivering what the manufacturer promises. The Federal Trade Commission estimates that fraudulent home improvement sales skim off another $1 billion," Nader claims. "Added to the list are items like adulterated food which cheats the consumer of the value he paid for, worthless beauty aids, mouthwashes, and diet pills. Even that long-time enemy of the housewife—the short weight—is costing the consumer $1.5 billion a year," says Nader.

His second category is "the transfer" sub-economy in which costs are added to goods that are sold to the consumer in a way that the consumer has no control over. As examples, Nader cites price hikes that resulted from the recent phenomenal increase in thefts from airline, railroad, and truck cargo, which has mounted into the hundreds of millions of dollars yearly. Writing in the *New York Review of Books*, Nader said:

"Most of these losses are being passed on to consumers who do not realize that they are paying for the cost of such pilferage and yet would be unable to challenge it in the courts or anywhere else if they did. Thus there is little pressure on the corporations to increase efforts to stop pilfering, instead of transferring the costs to the consumer." In testimony before the Senate Subcommittee on Priorities and Economy in Government, Nader used as an example of transfer costs the ploy used by the airlines and the Civil Aeronautics Board in 1970. Without a public hearing, the CAB granted the airlines what amounted to a fare increase by allowing them to round off the cost of tickets to the next highest dollar. Billed as convenience to the passengers, the move actually would have put $50 million into the coffers of the airlines, but the CAB ordered a revision months later. The railroads and truckers are another example. These industries get the ICC to approve a rate increase on foods and vegetables and the large supermarkets and other retail chains passively transfer the cost to the consumer with only the rarest of formal opposition before the ICC. Nader sees some hope in easing the transfer costs, however. He said the auto insurance industry, under pressure from customers over soaring rates, has finally begun to criticize the automakers for failure to provide efficient bumpers and safer cars.

The third sub-economy on Nader's list is the "controlled market" and here the basic threat to the consumer is antitrust violations such as price-fixing, product-fixing (i.e., freezing the development of more efficient but lower profit products), and shared monopolies. This is the sub-economy where arrangements are made by manufacturers to avoid competition over the price and quality of an item. This results in the consumer paying an outrageously higher price for a product than he would have if the market was not controlled by the manufacturers.

What kind of price does the consumer pay as a result of this lack of true competition? According to Nader, the Federal Trade Commission has estimated that if concentrated industries were broken up by enforcement of the antitrust laws to a point where the four biggest companies in any industry would not control more than forty percent of the industry's sales, prices would drop by twenty-five percent or more. Nader says this formula would apply to major industries like autos, steel, copper, aluminum, and chemicals. The power of these same concentrated industries is used to smother changes that might be beneficial to the consumer, but would mean reallocating capital or changing ways of doing business. Because of this situation, Nader says the nation doesn't have auto engines that cause less pollution, nor can it have can openers that prevent tiny metal fragments from falling into the can, or typewriters which increase the typist's speed by up to forty percent—all of which are available now.

The fourth sub-economy is one Nader describes as "corporate socialism." "This is of enormous magnitude, and can be described as the corporate use of government power to either transfer public funds to unjustified corporate control or the withholding of proper payments or obligations from government. The tax system is a weapon of the corporate socialism and is used by business to skim off billions of dollars from the public. To Nader, the tax loopholes used by business are, in effect, huge payments by government of money that business otherwise would not have received. As an example, he cited the oil and mineral depletion allowances. Because of the oil depletion allowance, combined with other tax loopholes, the Atlantic-Richfield Oil Company "had a net income of $797 million, while paying no federal tax whatever, from 1962 until 1968, when it paid at the rate of 1.2 percent," Nader said.

Nader's fifth sub-economy is one he calls "compulsory consumption." "I am referring to such compulsory consumptions as environmental pollution and occupational health and safety hazards with clear economic costs that reduce the quality of the gross national product and the citizen's dollar. We know that in the aggregate, pollution costs people and the economy billions of dollars yearly in health, cleaning, property and agricultural crop damage."

The last entry on Nader's list is the "expendable" sub-economy. Or, in his words, "the poor Americans." These are the people who are being cheated out of services by business. "This phenomenon goes far beyond the practice of the poor paying more. It goes to the refusal of business to sell at all," says Nader. In every large city in the United States insurance firms and bankers "red line" sections of the city where they will do no business. "But," says Nader, "by cutting off the funds needed for housing, for financing businesses, and for floating municipal bonds, the moneylenders are actually causing the decay of the inner cities and injuring the well-being of millions of people. Government is manipulated or becomes a willing partner in such discriminations against consumers by providing quick tax write-offs for manufacturers of everything from airliners to computers. This causes money from lenders to flow in those directions and not toward the poor. It even provides tax inducements to slum landlords who are allowed to depreciate slum property at an accelerated rate and to pay capital gains taxes on profits from sales—a process which is quickly repeated by the next slumlord." To Nader, these "sub-economies" are subverting the values of American life.

He is particularly bitter at those who argue that the existing sub-economies actually support industries, generate income, and provide jobs for people. He puts it this way: "A safer automobile traffic system would certainly weaken or diminish the so-called accident-injury industry—the jobs and money generated in the form of everything from medical services to auto repairs—but there is no doubt that the safer traffic system is the route which should be chosen." What is tragic, Nader says, "is the failure of the American people to understand some of these problems and what they mean to them in terms of lost value."

One weapon Nader has in mind to help put the consumer on more equal terms with the seller is the computer. Nader is the champion of the idea that the computer can be put to work to give the consumer the information he needs to make an educated decision in the marketplace.

"Rapid disclosure of the facts relating to the quantity, quality, and safety of a product is essential to a just marketplace. If companies know their product can quickly be compared with others, the laggard will be goaded to performance and the innovator will know that buyers can promptly learn about his innovations," Nader says. On the other hand, buyers must be able to compare products in order to reject the shoddy and reward the superior producer. But in fact, Nader says, manufacturers try to avoid giving out such information and instead rely on packaging or advertising.

In Ralph Nader's consumer world of the near future, computers set up in shopping centers could provide the consumer with the information he needs to compare products. For example, the computer would give the housewife a store-by-store comparison of food prices in the area. A prospective camera buyer might get not only a comparison of camera prices, but the same computer could give him a comparison of the strengths and weaknesses of a particular make of camera. In a nation that bought over six million air conditioners in 1971, 2.5 million dishwashers, 2.3 million dryers, 4.5 million washing machines, 2.4 million kitchen ranges, and 5.5 million refrigerators, the value of this type of information is obvious. But product information would not be the only type of information available from the computer. A consumer looking for the best insurance policy for his needs could extract a rundown on available policies, or find a list of available jobs.

Nader held the first conference on computer and consumers on June 19, 1971, in Washington, D.C., but the computer already is at work in some consumer areas. In the office of the Attorney General of Wisconsin, the computer was used to get a clearer idea of the types of consumer problems affecting state residents. Complaint letters were analyzed and categorized to determine whether a deceptive practice is statewide or confined to a specific county or area. The Consumers' Association of Canada wants that government to fund a consumer computer system which would provide citizens with updated information not only on consumer goods and services, like housing, and new and used cars, but also educational opportunities, and social services available from the government.

Industry likes to argue that the consumer already is king in the marketplace; that he is equipped with some mysterious divining rod which allows him to go straight to the supermarket shelf and pluck the best product from a line of competing items. The truth is, the consumer knows very little, and the reason is that he lacks information, says Nader. "A fuller and freer flow of information from business to the public is critical both for the consumer and for a competitive market system. Business firms repeatedly tell us they believe in competitive enterprise and the open market. This is preaching not practicing. For, if this belief is held, certain principles should follow. One is that buyers have a meaningful choice of products from which to choose. Another is that these buyers are provided with enough information to make their choice in a way to reward the better product and penalize the shoddier one by rejecting it.

"Unfortunately, in far too many instances, what business says is not what business does," Nader continues. As an example, he cites the automobile—one of the most expensive items purchased by consumers. "Until recently, the manufacturer provided virtually no specific information about the safety performance of the car. You were urged to buy a particular model because it 'widetracks' or because it makes 'you feel and look better.' Although the dealer will gladly tell you how many seconds it takes to go from zero to sixty miles an hour, he could not tell you about comparative braking, acceleration, and tire performance," says Nader. The government, as a result of the auto safety campaigns, however, now requires that each of the automakers provide this information to the prospective buyer. If he wishes, the buyer can then make a comparison at least on these three points.

The auto industry has available—through its own tests—all of the information the buyer could possibly want to have about the car. But the industry is not willing to provide the customer with it. Says Nader:

"In recent decades we are witness to an intense development of styling, packaging, brand name emphasis, and the provocative association of product-glamor with personality or emotional whims. Such marketing themes are not frivolous; they are designed in the tradition of applied social science for the serious purpose of diverting scrutiny from the product to no-product characteristics or imagery. Auto companies have found it much easier to have motorists cultivate an expectation over grille patterns than nonfade, nonlocking brakes, or decent vehicle handling. There is little pressure for engineering innovations under such diversions. Conditioning a response is an easier way to sell than meeting an ever more critical customer scrutiny.

"As more information about a product—what it is and what it can be—filters out to the public, a prime prerequisite is a sufficient proportion of alert consumers and consumer groups who look behind the package, the slogans, and the musical ditty and ask that quality and innovation be shown them. There is as little justification for secrecy in the marketplace as there is for secrecy in government. In both places, secrecy insulates from sight the blunders, the stagnation, the waste, and the incompetence. Yes, and the venal as well.

242

Efficient, clear information flows, brought about by consumer demand, government disclosure statutes, and enlightened business leadership, is much of what is meant by 'consumer democracy.' "

13

DEAR MR. NADER

Dear Ralph,

Excuse the familiar writing style, but I feel that I almost know you personally since you are a friend of the little people of which I am part . . .

—An excerpt from a letter written to Ralph Nader

To find out who the people of the United States think Ralph Nader is, you have to read his mail.

As if he were a miracle worker, the letters are filled with entreaties. "Do something, Mr. Nader." "Help us." "Protect us." "We appeal to your honesty, integrity, and fair play to help us right the wrong done against us." "May God bless you, Mr. Nader." There are even a few "May God damn you, Mr. Nader" letters.

Nader gets more mail (ninety thousand pieces in 1971) than Virginia Knauer, President Nixon's consumer advisor, or the National Highway Traffic Safety Administration. The mail is stuffed into cardboard boxes at the Center for Study of Responsive Law. It is neatly filed, and carefully indexed at the Center for Auto Safety. It is jammed in Nader's pockets. It is piled in heaps in his lairs around Washington. It is stacked on the table in the hall of his rooming house, and dumped on the porch of his family home in Winsted, Connecticut, where it is sorted by Nader's elderly mother who likes to write comments like "Read this!" on the envelopes of interesting complaints before she forwards the mail.

Letter writers also search out the addresses of his brother and his sisters, and urge them to forward mail to Nader, who neither publicizes his address nor lists his phone. Congressmen and senators forward it, and so do newspapers and radio and television stations.

The Post Office has long since become accustomed to delivering mail addressed simply to: "Ralph Nader, Washington, D.C." Others write to "Ralph Nader, the White House." Nader notes wryly that the letters forwarded from the White House are stamped: "Addressee Not Known Here." One letter writer simply pasted a newspaper photograph of Nader on an envelope and the Post Office delivered it.

If Nader's backers are short on addresses, they are long on titles, however. Letters are delivered addressed to "Ralph Nader, A Well-Known Washington Lawyer," "Senator Ralph Nader," "Ralph Nader, The Little Man's Representative," "Ralph Nader, Everyman's Lawyer," and "Ralph Nader, Consumer Champion." Many of his fans give him government-type titles like these: "Commissioner of Consumer Affairs," "Chairman of the Consumer Rights Committee," and "Head of the National Office of Special Projects." One writer summed up the general tone of most of the mail—his letter was addressed simply to "Ralph Nader, the Greatest."

Nader spends long hours scanning the mail, and insists his staff do likewise. Any of them who don't see *vox populi* in the letters or show less than the right amount of reverence or sympathy for the letter writers get a quick lecture on arrogance, delivered with snarls from Nader. One staff member termed the mail "Nader's umbilical cord to the consumer."

The letters come from consumers in every strata of society. An executive of the Quaker Oats company wrote "your methods may be called liberal, but I personally believe, and hope, that your goals are basically conservative in the best sense of the word and are directed toward conserving what is best in our system." Not quite so erudite, but no less sincere, was a postcard addressed simply to "Mr. Ralph Nader, Washington, D.C." On the reverse side were these two words: "Right On!"

Nader fans use the mail to send him bits and pieces of their problems. A woman sent a pair of shoes "that gave her a rash" and urged Nader to investigate the manufacturer. One man sent a loaf of bread he said looked bad. "It looked worse when it got here," said Nader who is very chary of opening packages that come in the mail. The letters are stuffed with small bills, coins, and checks—enough to make up ten percent of the funds Nader collects to pay the bills for the Center for Study of Responsive Law. A doctor in West Deal, New Jersey, sent a $10 contribution in memory of a friend who was killed in a head-on collision while riding in a Volkswagen. "She was," he said, "only 21." A man who read the center's study on air pollution sent a $500 check to finance more research. In one letter, Nader found a $5,000 check with a note enclosed which said that the donor would "try to make it an annual donation." Another man sent securities valued at $10,000. One batch of contributions was triggered by one of Nader's raiders who got married. The girl asked guests at her wedding to send contributions to Nader rather than spend the money on a wedding present.

Children are some of Nader's biggest fans. There are batches of letters from grade-school children who write along the lines of an eight-year-old from Topeka, Kansas, who wrote:

> Dear Mr. Nader,
> I want to do something about pollution.
> The pollution is bad.
> The people do not care.
> I want to be a raider.
>> Your friend,
>> Ellen

A grade-school girl named Judy in Chicago wrote Nader that on the beaches of Lake Michigan there are "lots of dead fish, and the lake is polluted." No one is doing anything, she said, and "I am disappointed in the world."

Then there was a letter requesting a popsicle crusade from a young man who wrote:

"One day we walked into a little food mart and got a popsicle and my friend Tom said his tasted funny. So I said lets get your money back. So we went back and said we wished to get our money back or we would write to Ralph Nader. So he said go ahead. So we are writing you.

Mike.

P.S. I never new before what your address was. This is no lie."

Some of the youngsters are more specific. A school in Buffalo, New York, singled out a toy called Moon Rocks, Ka-Bongers, or Klick-Klacks which consists of two solid plastic balls on a string that are knocked together like colliding pendulums. Indignantly pointing out that one of the students "got her tooth knocked out" by the toys, the students pleaded with Nader "to take them off the market."

Many of the children even think Nader can stop the war in Vietnam. Said one boy:

"Dear Mr. Nader:

I want a Nader Raider to stop the war. The war does the most polluting. They bloe up places. They cach houses on fire. They make me sick. Why do they do it? Don't they care?

You truly
Martin."

Nader holds a position in the esteem of the younger pollution fighters that is so high that he was featured in *My Weekly Reader,* the grade-school equivalent of *Time* and *Newsweek*. But even Nader doesn't win all the time. What was supposed to be a picture of Nader in *My Weekly Reader* was actually a photograph of John Banzahf, another consumer advocate in Washington.

Then there was a letter from a high-school girl in Odessa,

DEAR MR. NADER

Texas, who for some unexplained reason had Nader mixed up with Howard Hughes. After a letter filled with praise for Nader she said: "I had been down on you before because I thought you were a rich man living in Las Vegas who was sixty years old and married just about as many times."

Another group of thirteen high-school students in Connecticut, however, knew exactly what Nader's movement was all about. They weren't allowed to attend graduation ceremonies because they did not have the required gowns. The youngsters sent Nader the money they planned to spend on the gowns.

Like any public figure, Nader gets his share of hate mail, but it is small, about one letter in a thousand. Usually the writer thinks Nader a busybody, or "meddler." Most of this type of mail comes from automobile owners like the man who wrote:

"Dear Mr. Nader:

You stupid son of a bitch. Why don't you try to educate the stupid drivers. Machines don't kill people, it's the dumb sons of bitches behind them. You should have learned this before now. But may be you are as stupid as they are.

Signed
A driver of 61 years."

Another writer blamed Nader's attacks on business for causing a recession, and wanted him "kept in a cage until the recession ends."

The value of the mail to Nader is that he feels it is an infallible way to spot trends. If the letters repeatedly tell a similar story of a safety defect or a health hazard, Nader investigates. This is the way he spotted tire defects, for example. It also was the mail that led to the investigation into defective camper truck wheel rims and the resultant recall order by GM. And it is the mail that brings Nader what he calls his "insider information"—tips from employees. So important is the mail to Nader that he plans to feed auto

249

safety and appliance defect information from the letters into computers in hopes of spotting trends earlier.

The most impressive thing about Nader's mail is the span of topics it covers. There apparently is nothing his backers think he can't handle. In one pile of about five hundred letters, an aide had sorted out the complaints into bundles marked with some of the following headings: automobiles, veterans, appliances, lawyers, government, banks, pollution, boating, magazine salesmen, Sears, RCA, contests, flammable fabrics, frauds, mobile homes, REA Express, food, pesticides, funerals, tax shelters, air conditioners, utilities, probate court, television repairs, cosmetics, household movers, and insurance.

So omnipotent has Nader become in the public's mind that a woman in Conshohocken, Pennsylvania, wanted Nader to help her 23-year-old son get his corporal stripes back. Another woman in Kansas City went even further. She thought Nader should help Lieutenant William Calley in his My Lai atrocity trial "because you are a man who gets things done." Still another woman in Los Angeles wanted Nader to try to keep Lawrence Welk's television program going. "I hope you will use your influence, not just for me, but for the many people that cannot get out to shows and dances," she wrote.

At the other end of the spectrum was a letter from Savannah, Georgia. "Do you think it would be possible to include in your crusade a study of homosexuals. I believe, since I am a homosexual, that we are wasted as human resources because of cruel and archaic laws," the writer said.

A man in Hamlet, Nebraska, frustrated by the bureaucracy, made a plea for help to save the mustang herds. "I am not a crank. My occupation is county agricultural agent, but I feel it is fruitless to go through the Bureau of Land Management for help," he wrote Nader.

Nader's own profession, the law—the one he hopes will be able to do the most in changing the system—comes in for some of the sharpest cuts from consumers.

A man in Mankuto, Kansas, wrote about lawyers this way: "We need protection from lawyer pollution. They create dissension among the people and encourage law suits. Why doesn't someone investigate the law profession."

Another man in Snohomish, Washington, was even more pointed in his opinion of lawyers. He told Nader: "You are the first attorney that I have seen who uses the legal profession as it is meant to be used." The complaints about lawyers center on the areas where consumers are most often exposed to them—real estate dealings, probate court, divorces, and fees. One man wrote from Palm Desert, California, and enclosed a check for $100. He asked only that Nader "fill the newspapers with sensational material about the criminal behaviour of lawyers and judges."

Many of Nader's fans flood him with suggestions for his next crusade. A man in Lancaster, Pennsylvania, wanted Nader to campaign for a warning label on alcoholic beverages that would read: "Alcohol is an addictive substance, and chronic use can lead to an incurable disease."

Then there are those who can tell their story in one sentence:

"Dear Mr. Nader:
When are you going to investigate computer dating firms.
Signed
Gypped."

Another writer from Huntington, New York, with an apparent vested interest wanted Nader to start a crusade "to make sure prostitutes have weekly physical checkups."

A landlord in Milwaukee claimed the toilets in his apartment were being clogged by tampons. "It states on the box that they are to be disposed of by throwing them down the toilet, but they plug the toilet. This kind of advertising is a misrepresentation and should be stopped immediately," he told Nader.

Others see a chance to make a profit from Nader's attacks on their competitors' product. When Nader criticized ingredients put in baby food simply to make it taste good to adults,

251

a writer sent him a sample of the baby food that he manufactured which lacked the monosodium glutamate criticized by Nader. The writer suggested it might be a good idea for Nader to promote his baby food, and then, for good measure, threw in the line that like Nader, he too, was Lebanese.

Others are convinced that nothing is free in this world, not even advice from a consumer advocate. A banker from Altenburg, Missouri, wrote Nader a letter describing his problems with a defective Bell and Howell movie projector. After he asked for Nader's advice, he closed with this line: "What is your charge, Mr. Nader?"

There is no paycheck segregation among Nader's backers. There are soiled one-dollar bills in some of the letters which are written on cheap, lined paper. Then there are letters that begin like this one from the president of a chemical corporation in Worcester, Massachusetts. "I've bought 16 Cadillacs in the last 16 years." Then he went on to lament that he could not get his dealer to fix his latest Cadillac.

Some of the professional people like to add a touch of philosophy with their contributions. A certified public accountant from Toms River, New Jersey, described his feelings about Nader's work this way:

"I can't help but think of your efforts as being comparable to those of a repairman working diligently to repair cracks in the plaster of a building to make it more habitable while at the same time the wrecking crew is outside demolishing the building." A life insurance executive in New England sent Nader a contribution to help support a crusade to protect the American Indian. "I am sickened by the spectacle of my government's representatives harassing the Indians," he said.

A lawyer in Houston, Texas, sent Nader a copy of a letter he sent to Ed Cole, GM's president, when a promised Chevrolet still had not been delivered two months after the date set by the dealer. He said: "I am paying $5,200 for this vehicle, and I do not appreciate being treated like some illiterate and ignorant person that has not even a high-school education. I am a professional man, and you are a professional man. If you expect to be so treated by our Congress, and our Courts, then I deserve the same treatment from your corporation. I not only see why more and more people believe Ralph Nader but I am beginning to believe him myself. It seems that I have no other choice; General Motors has made the decision for me . . ."

One congressman put more faith in Nader than he did in his fellow lawmakers or himself to remedy a consumer complaint. A constituent wrote a letter to Congressman Stewart B. McKinney of Connecticut describing how a sixteen-ounce bottle of Pepsi-Cola exploded in his home and showered a room with glass. He urged the congressman to "take a stand in support of the consumer" and help devise tougher safety standards for bottles.

What did McKinney do? He sent the letter to Nader. According to the congressman, he couldn't find anyone else who might help the consumer.

"I called the Committee on Consumer Protection, the Product Safety Division of the Food and Drug Administration, and the Interstate and Foreign Commerce Committee, and found that none of these organizations were doing anything about the problem," McKinney wrote.

Then he confessed to Nader that he had promised his constituent that "I would refer his letter to someone who could do something about the problem, and so I decided to send it to you. I hope you will be able to give the problem some consideration."

A member of the Australian parliament from New South Wales wanted Nader to help him with an investigation of corporate corruption in his district.

"My secretary suggested you could be the person to approach for help. She is forever holding you up as an example to me—her usual goad being 'If Ralph Nader can do it, why can't you?' "

The connecting thread in all of Nader's letters is frustration. The writers constantly exclaim that they started off in good faith. The company which manufactured the product would stand behind it, they thought. After all they had a warranty, or perhaps they owned stock in the corporation, or had been dealing at the same store for twenty-five years. But then they find that no one will help them. They are shuffled back and forth between a seemingly endless series of petty company officials or are turned away with blatant lies. Often their complaints are simple, but the consumer gets treated like a woman in Denison, Texas, who wrote Nader a long letter about how her new air conditioning unit broke down. Asked to fix it, the retail outlet and its service department did not have the parts to do the job. Go to the distributor, she was told. But the distributor said he could not handle the complaint either. The woman was told to return the air conditioner to the manufacturer. When she wrote the manufacturer, she was told her warranty had expired the day before. This kind of treatment, she told Nader, "is a bunch of bullshit." The lady's language was earthy, but her feelings are commonplace. The consumers are indignant; outraged. For most of them, the final explosion is the result not only of the complaint they send to Nader, but of all the indignities they, as consumers, suffered in the past.

Nader's files are replete with consumer horror stories, but the tale told to Nader by a woman in Sunnyvale, California, is the kind that fits a middle ground in its similarity to thousands of others. Its slow-building frustration brings tears of anger to the housewife, and makes her an easy recruit for Nader's army.

The woman bought a common household appliance—an oven. She bought a reputable brand name, an oven manufactured by the Tappan Range Company, a long-time, and well-known, ovenmaker.

Right from the beginning the oven failed to work properly. The upper oven left the food uncooked, but the food in the bottom oven burned when the upper oven was turned on. A call to the dealer produced the following result. A serviceman spent three hours working on the oven, and left claiming the oven was now useable. That night the woman turned on the oven to start dinner, and "the oven threw sparks all over the kitchen which is 18 feet long." She told Nader: "Believe me when I say we were frightened."

But the woman was still confident that the oven was repairable. Another call produced a serviceman who again worked "hours" on the oven. Finally, he left pronouncing the oven ready for use.

That night the woman began cooking dinner. "This time the oven not only burned the roast on the bottom in the top oven but burned the cake on the top in the bottom oven."

More telephone calls to the dealer. But, alas, the situation was crumpling. When the serviceman left this time, the woman found the oven temperature varied as much as 100 degrees. More calls to the serviceman. Then a new problem. "Twice I had to have the Pacific Gas & Electric Company come to the house to look for gas leakage," the woman wrote. Back came the serviceman. Again there are long hours of "adjustment" work done on the oven. The result: The woman told Nader that the oven now baked faster on the right side than it did on the left side. But the final blow that sent the woman begging to Nader for help was this: "The intense heat coming out of the oven" had warped her kitchen cabinets. "Mr. Nader," she pleaded, "can you help me."

Some of the writers want nothing more than someone to commiserate with them. One consumer entreated Nader to answer his letter with "your usual encouragement for the downtrodden and the exploited." For the faith Nader puts in his mail, it would be natural to assume that every letter writer gets a personal answer. They don't. "I don't have the staff to answer all the letters. I may write to the ones that offer leads or documents, but I can't reply to the others." But an aide says Nader is faithful in his letter reading. "You can find him on Sunday afternoon, or on a holiday reading letters. It's like he gets some kind of strength from them." One of Nader's secretaries at the Center for Study of Responsive Law likes to send a picture of Nader to some of the children who write, but that is the extent of Nader's communion with his backers.

But it doesn't seem to make any difference. If anything,

the power ascribed to Nader grows as his inaccessibility grows. One letter writer even wanted Nader to join in the feud over "Lucy, the Margate [N.J.] elephant." The famous six-story-high wood and tin landmark at the beach resort was saved from the wrecker's ball by a $61,750 grant from the Housing and Urban Development Department on the grounds it was a historic site. Not all the taxpayers agreed. In a letter asking Nader to stop the grant, the writer said, "It doesn't make any sense to spend our tax money on an old dilapidated structure when the people need food and housing."

Some of the letter writers make it a point to tell Nader that he can do no wrong even if he doesn't answer their letter. A woman in Raleigh opened her letter this way:

"Here is another letter from a very dissatisfied consumer wanting desperately some advice on how to compete with a large company, but first, let me say that no matter what you do about this letter, I think you are the greatest thing that ever happened to this country. . . ." Then the writer went on to complain about the state's power company not giving "any consideration to the natural beauty of the land" when it cuts swaths across the countryside for power lines.

Pet owners are another group which thinks it has a special claim on Nader. Their complaints revolve not around cruelty to animals in the accepted sense, but in the quality of the cat and dog food put on the market. Since Nader has investigated the quality of food for humans, the letter writers can't see why he shouldn't look into dog food "that is mostly fat," or so low in quality that "my dog broke out in sores," according to one letter writer.

One pet owner opened her letter to Nader with this attention-getting paragraph, "I am the owner of 45 cats and four dogs." Again, the complaint was about the quality of pet food.

There is no doubt that the influence of television shows through in Nader's mail. After an appearance on a late night program like the *Dick Cavett Show*, or a panel show like *Meet the Press*, Nader's mail jumps. Typical is the farmer in Greeley, Nebraska, who tells Nader "I am sitting

256

here watching you on T.V." and then goes on to tell Nader the problem that bothers him most. In the case of the farmer, it was the price of hogs. "I am selling my hogs in the morning for 14 cents a pound, and you watch what you pay for pork," he tells Nader, and adds, "Maybe the farmer can't win, but don't stop what you're doing, Ralphy."

A mother in Philadelphia thought Nader could do something about the sizing of baby clothes. According to the woman, no matter what the size said, the clothes seldom fitted the baby. "This has been going on for a long time, Mr. Nader, and I am getting tired of it," she said.

Many of the complaints from today's consumers have been voiced by other generations. For example, one recurring complaint is about the landlord who takes an extra month's rent as security, but doesn't give the tenant the interest on his own money. Razor blades that don't give as many shaves as they once did is a common complaint. Next to the old standbys are the newest ones which come to Nader from the environmentalists. "Come work with us. Help us save the kelp beds off Oregon," is the plea in one letter. Another entreats Nader to do something about the cosmetic industry's use of turtles to make an oil that is sold as a beauty aide.

To Nader, the letter writers are not kooks or cranks. "These are people with legitimate grievances. They must be heard. Some way must be found for them to communicate. The old way doesn't work, if it ever did, or they wouldn't write to me," Nader says. But Nader does see a change in the consumer attitude. "In the beginning the letters were filled with frustration and despair, but now people are beginning to get a sharpened sense of injustice, and a greater sense of determination to get satisfaction. I see in the letters a growing fighting spirit. People are even beginning to tell me about their victories," says Nader.

To Nader, the reason change has come so slow is that institutions do not understand the importance of these pleas; they prefer to ignore the feelings of the people. This is a cardinal sin in Nader's catechism and one he continually cautions his students against. Here is what he told one group of raiders:

"It's very important to constantly keep your eye on the overall general objectives without forgetting that you're dealing with very concrete problems affecting people. And if they're affecting people, they're going to be what many of us may consider mundane or trivial or superficial or wasteful, but they have to be developed. They have to be given consideration because they're real; because people are concerned about them. And anything that's going to endure is going to have relatively deep roots among the average citizens otherwise it is going to be toppled very easily . . .

"It is very important to keep asking the question: What really bugs the average citizen? What really concerns him? Is it chemical-biological warfare? Or is it the conditions on his block or in the plant where he works? Or the feeling that the people who run the society don't care about him, don't want to consult him?

"Everybody who wants to change the country for the better of course does it in the name of the people, but it's amazing the lack of interest in communicating, the lack of interest in understanding, and empathizing with the so-called people." To Nader, no one should be left out, everyone should be heard, and that includes a man from Tulsa, Oklahoma, who wrote Nader asking him "to put a stop to the perfuming of toilet tissue. I can't see where it helps one bit," he said.

14

NADER FOR PRESIDENT?

There's nothing wrong with my land; it's the best . . .
But I've taken it for granted like the rest . . .
So as a good intentioned resident
Who up to now has been hesitant
I say it's time we had the best man under the sun for President . . .
Nader's the one!

—The chorus of a campaign song written
for Ralph Nader

Nader was angry. He paced the room and chopped the air
with an outstretched hand. "Jesus Christ! The idea is absurd," he said. "No one can be elected who says what he
thinks—politics is a total straightjacket game." Now his voice
was an octave higher and his face was flushed. "Just think
how many of my programs would go down the drain. The
whole movement would be set back!" What was it that made
Nader so angry? Someone had asked him if he would run for
President.

Talking politics with Nader is difficult. He avoids the issue
whenever he can. He doesn't think of himself as a political
animal—if anything, he is afraid of politics. He sees as its base
that very thing he dislikes most: compromise. To him the
politician is a mentally caged man, restricted in what he can
say and do; and that would destroy Nader. But whether he

likes it or not, Nader may have to face the possibility that his movement can arrive at a point in time when the political road will be the best one to take.

Even while Nader was angrily declaiming that "you don't need to be elected to be effective," two blocks away in Suite 232A of the Du Pont Circle Building on Connecticut Avenue, volunteer workers for the New Party were sorting boxes filled with Nader-for-President stickers. The New Party, formed in the aftermath of the 1968 Democratic Convention in Chicago "to provide an alternative for those who were no longer willing to compromise their views or vote for the 'lesser of evils' candidates," was the first political entity to reach out for Nader. Dr. Benjamin M. Spock and author Gore Vidal were the honorary chairmen, but the rest of the party consisted only of a handful of young political activists. Its platform included planks endorsing everything from the Gay Liberation movement to a call for "a thirty-hour workweek at forty-hour pay," and abolition of the CIA. Vidal was actually the publicity man for the New Party and the man behind its drive to prod Nader into politics. Without so much as a phone call to Nader, Vidal offered him as a presidential candidate during an interview in 1971 on a nationwide television show. He followed that up with an article in *Esquire* magazine titled "The Best Man/'72" in which he touted Nader as "a figure around whom those disgusted with traditional politics can rally, a point of hope, a new beginning in our tangled affairs." The result of the article? One angry man: Nader. In a letter laden with sarcasm, Nader wrote to *Esquire* accusing the editors of printing "political fantasies" concocted by an author "I have never seen or spoken to, or have been called by at any time."

But the article and the television show brought in a flood of mail to New Party headquarters with comments ranging from "Maybe Ralph Nader is not the answer to our problems, but by God he's the closest thing the people have to believe in and trust," to a comment from a high-school coach in Oxford, Mississippi, who said simply that "anything might be better than what we have now."

NADER FOR PRESIDENT?

Ask the average voter-in-the-street about Nader as a presidential candidate, and you get a puzzled look followed by an expression that seems to say, "Why not?" Talk to the professional politician, however, and you get scorn. Nader, they say, has no money, no party affiliation, and he would be a one-issue candidate. And worse than a divorced man, he is a bachelor.

As if that were not enough, he is an Arab who was baptized in the Greek Orthodox Church—a combination not very well designed to win the confidence of any sizable ethnic bloc in the United States. Added to these handicaps, he has alienated nearly every corporation chief in the nation, some to the point where they would gladly spend millions to defeat his political ambitions. The politicians claim that even Madison Avenue's slickest hucksters would be thwarted trying to sell Nader—how would they package a candidate who, when he is recognized on the street by a delighted consumer shouting "Hey, aren't you Ralph Nader?," will reply, "No, what makes you think that?" and hurry by. Or what kind of charisma could the voters find in a man who asks restaurant waiters to take the ice out of his tomato juice because it cheats the customer who paid for a full glass of juice? Finally, the politicians ask, do you think a man could get elected who castigates the public for the hours it wastes seated in front of the television set or for playing bridge when that time could be spent practicing citizenship? If he is not doing that, he is prodding one of society's most sacred cows—the college student—whom he has accused of everything from "intellectual diletantism" to short-lived idealism. According to Nader, this latter criticism was exemplified by the Harvard Law School students who, the minute the recession constricted the job market, stopped sending out resumés which included questions asking what prospective employers were doing to clean up the environment and instead "went out and bought vests" to show those same employers that "they really wanted to be part of the establishment." There is much talk about the "new politics," and politicians agree there is a flux in politics today to a degree never before seen.

261

However, the "pols" argue that any candidate who wants to get elected President of the United States still must play the game all the way from the chicken-and-peas fund-raising dinners to the shopping center handshaking tours. But Nader does only those things he thinks he should do, and advocates blowing the whistle on anyone who tries to pressure him into a different course. Again the politicians ask, how long would he last in the political arena with a *modus operandi* like that?

As if any further proof were needed, they cite political history and single out Upton Sinclair, Nader's earlier-in-the-century muckraking counterpart. Sinclair's book, *The Jungle*, exposed conditions in Chicago's slaughterhouses, and brought him fame which he tried to convert into political currency, failing miserably. Sinclair ran and lost in New Jersey as the Socialist party candidate for Congress in 1906. In 1920 he ran for a congressional seat from California and lost. In 1922 he ran for the Senate. In 1926 and 1930 he was the Socialist candidate for governor, and lost again. He even switched in 1934 to the Democratic ticket as a gubernatorial candidate but the result was the same. "Muckrakers are the public's sweethearts when they are on the attack, but that doesn't mean the public wants them to run things," a long-time Washington politician said. Theodore Roosevelt, whose swipes at big business with his trust-busting campaigns won him votes, put it another way: "The men with the muck-rakes are often indispensable to the well-being of society; but only if they know when to stop raking the muck."

Nader shows no signs of turning in his muckrake. If anything, he swings it with more gusto now than he ever did. But of all the groups touched by Nader, the politician has shown the least understanding of what his movement is all about. To some senators and congressmen, Nader is a publicity-generator for their committee hearings. Of the many games played on Capitol Hill, one of the most common is devising a list of witnesses for a hearing which will "bring out the press." In effect, any committee counsel who is worth his $25,000-a-year paycheck is not only a good lawyer but also a good publicity man. Nothing brings smiles quicker to a committee chairman's face than to see the press tables in his hearing room filled, and the television camera lights bathing the room in a glow so sharp he must conduct the hearings wearing sunglasses, an indignity he gladly abides in hopes his constituents will see him toiling in their behalf when they switch on the evening news. Nader's name on a witness list usually guarantees a full press quota, or, if it is some forum outside the committee room, sharing the platform with Nader is a cheap way to reap publicity without making any commitment. As for Nader's theories on corporate reform, they are much too radical for most of the lawmakers. For example, the thought of passing legislation, as Nader has asked, to make corporate chiefs liable for criminal penalties is considered a drastic step by Congress, but only a natural one by Nader. Put another way, there is a limit to which many lawmakers will go in calling for corporate accountability in fear of losing industry's campaign contributions. It is true that a handful of the more independent-minded senators have endorsed concepts like Campaign GM and its reform program for giving the public and GM stockholders a bigger voice in the company's policy-making decisions, but no lawmaker has made an issue out of corporate accountability, nor is one likely to.

For the most part, there is a fragile relationship between Nader and even the senators and congressmen with whom he is most friendly. For example, it was Connecticut Senator Abraham Ribicoff's committee that gave Nader the platform he needed to bring the auto safety issue to the public. So distant was the relationship between the two men in those early days that Ribicoff could truthfully say "the first time I had ever seen Mr. Nader was when he walked into the committee room" and began his testimony on auto safety. Once the issue of auto safety took hold, the two men worked together closely and Nader became almost an extension of Ribicoff's committee staff—but inevitably, there was a split. Nader insisted on criminal penalties for violations of the National Traffic and Motor Vehicle Safety Act, and Ribicoff backed away from the idea. Unwilling to compromise, Nader went down to defeat. More recently, Nader cooled the relationship further by insisting that Ribicoff reopen the 1966 auto safety hearings to investigate Nader's charge that GM lied to the committee on the safety of the Corvair. Nader even publicly attacked Ribicoff's committee staff for foot-dragging on the hearings, a move that has created a perhaps unbridgeable rift between Nader and Ribicoff.

But Nader is philosophical about his relationship with the lawmakers. "I don't really see that much of them. If I have something important, I'll call, but I don't invest time in jollying them along. Whether they like me or not, they'll usually talk to me, but I find that there are a lot of senators who will 'listen' to you, but they don't hear you."

Of all the senators, Nader has the closest rapport with Senator Gaylord Nelson of Wisconsin, who Nader regards as being in the old populist tradition, which is as close as Nader himself comes to a political label.

Senator Edmund Muskie is a lawmaker who keeps Nader in a public embrace, but privately is standoffish. Since Muskie started running for President, "I never see him," says Nader with a grin that shows there is a lot more to Muskie's disappearance than his run for the Presidency, something that would make Nader a pariah for him when he went in search of campaign funds in corporate board rooms. The break between the two men actually came in a battle over air-pollution standards. Muskie built his national reputation on his work as chairman of the Senate Subcommittee on Air and Water Pollution. But Nader publicly accused Muskie of gutting the Air Quality Act to pander to the demands of industry. In the Nader Task Force Report on air pollution—*The Vanishing Air*—Muskie is painted as a villain, not in the "Mr. Clean" role he prefers. According to the task force, Muskie was a conciliator who gave the public only "politically expedient platitudes" about tough air-pollution standards when he should have been leading a hard-nosed fight to pass stronger antipollution legislation. "Senator Muskie has failed the nation in the field of air-pollution-control legislation," the report said. To Muskie, whose temper is legendary, that was the kind of rhetoric that would cool any love affair.

As presidential timber, Nader sees Muskie as "the Democrats' Nixon." "He will bend to every pressure group, and will say what they want him to say. If he is elected, the country will be no different than it is under the Nixon Administration. Muskie is not the type of man who could make the changes needed," says Nader.

But Nader does get strong support from a small band of lawmakers, most of whom are mavericks like Nader. But Nader's main problem is that the lawmakers who do support him have little or no power. Senator Philip Hart, the Michigan Democrat, is an example. As chairman of the Senate Antitrust and Monopoly Subcommittee, Hart has held a series of hearings on consumer-oriented legislation and has been vocal in his criticism of corporations, particularly the auto industry. But Hart is stymied when it comes to turning out legislation since he lacks support from his committee, and those bills that do come out of his committee must still get approval from the parent Judiciary Committee which is run by Mississippi conservative James Eastland, who evinces no interest in correcting corporate abuses.

According to Nader, the only bills that are allowed through to the floor for a vote "are those that weaken existing antitrust laws rather than strengthen them." But even if the chairman of the committee is consumer-oriented, the corporations through their lobbyists have found a way to bring pressure to block legislation. Congressman Wright Patman of the House Banking and Currency Committee is an example of a should-be powerful committee chairman who finds himself strapped. The banking lobbyists exercise their control through members of the committee who are so pro-bankers that they hold stock in banks. This, tied to the banks' ample supply of campaign funds for cooperative committee members, gives the industry "a working majority of the committee members" who can restrict reporting out of the committee any unfavorable banking legislation backed by the chairman.

Senators who have been most effective in Nader's crusades have actually made end runs around the encrusted congressional establishment. Senator Nelson of Wisconsin was not a member of the Senate Commerce Committee which had jurisdiction over tire-safety legislation, but Nelson was able to whip up a storm of publicity using what Nader termed "detailed complaints" sent to his office by consumers and whistle-blowers inside the tire industry. The result was tremendous pressure on the Commerce Committee to report out a tire-safety bill. Congressman Philip Burton, a California Democrat, tried to sue the Bureau of Mines for not enforcing the Coal Mine Safety Law. The court refused to accept the congressman's standing to sue, but the threat was not lost on the Bureau of Mines which realizes that it can be a target for legal action for lax enforcement of the law. Representative John Moss, another California Democrat, was more successful in court with an ongoing Nader battle—lower air fares. He and thirty-one other congressmen filed suit against the Civil Aeronautics Board alleging that the agency violated requirements of the Federal Aviation Act when it granted the airlines a fare hike. The court upheld the congressmen, and ordered the CAB to obey the law.

Another of what Nader terms "new reaches" available for the lawmakers is the simple procedure of hurdling committees which refuse to take up key issues that fall into their jurisdiction. Nader is always looking for lawmakers like former congressman Leonard Farbstein who along with several other New York congressmen staged ad-hoc hearings in New York City on air pollution. Congressman David Pryor held his own public hearings on nursing homes as part of a campaign to set up a special committee on aging, which was being blocked by senior members of the House Rules Committee. Nader is incessantly preaching to politicians who claim they are trapped by the system that there are ways to be effective. Just as he was shut out and had to fight to be heard, the lawmakers can develop new roles and a new power basis inside Congress that will benefit them and their constituents.

There is a list of lawmakers who Nader feels have won

medals of dishonor as far as the consumer movement is concerned. One of the most callous is Senator Russell Long of Louisiana who mouths the populist theories of his father, Huey Long, but in fact ignores the little people of Louisiana to cultivate the state's big business interests, particularly the oil barons. Senator Jacob K. Javits, the New York Republican, is another poseur. Nader says Javits outwardly cultivates the image of a fighting liberal, but, in practice, he has not been too reluctant to use his influence to thwart the public interest to the benefit of big business.

Nader's first critic in the Senate—Republican Carl Curtis of Nebraska—gets equally low marks. He and his fellow Republican senator from Nebraska—Roman L. Hruska—are mouthpieces for special interest lobbyists, according to Nader. In Nader's senatorial rating book, however, one of the all-time great enemies of consumer legislation was the late Republican leader Everett M. Dirksen whom Nader once described as an "errand boy" for the auto industry, the drug industry, the atomic-power industry, the oil industry, and the pipeline industry.

Nader has tried to avoid being labeled as the property of one party over the other. But there is no doubt that he has found more support in the Democratic ranks than the Republican. Traditionally more aligned with business, the Republicans have not made as much use of Nader as have the Democrats. Part of the reason for reluctance on the part of the Republicans is that Nader shows no more deference to the White House than he does to any other power bloc. Time and time again he has accused the Nixon Administration of watering down legislation and kowtowing to industry at the expense of the consumer. His most common target in the White House is Presidential Assistant Peter J. Flanigan who is Nixon's man on key consumer issues. To Nader, Flanigan is a hatchetman whose job is to block or emasculate consumer-oriented legislation by rallying Republican congressional opposition on the slightest cue from big business. But the Administration's prize Neanderthal is Commerce Secretary Maurice H. Stans, the investment banker, big-game hunter, and the creator of memorable quotes. It was Stans who worried to a group of trade association officials and lobbyists that there might be a danger in letting "the wave of consumerism move too far," and at a meeting of the Business Council in Hot Springs, Virginia, in 1971 contended that:

"Business is more than 99.44 percent pure. That is the percentage of transactions that bring full satisfaction to the buyer." Nader's solution to the "Stans problem"—he should be fired.

"Stans is not a public official by any sense of the term, and should resign immediately," says Nader, who claims Stans "unabashedly represents a special, narrow, business-interest viewpoint."

With undisguised sarcasm, Nader gave a "cursory review" of Stans' consumer-oriented career in the Administration. He has, said Nader, opposed:

"The Clean Air Act of 1970; the relaxation of oil import controls; the regulation of phosphate and detergents; the ban on DDT; the regulation of auto mechanics; the Transportation Department's plan to back no-fault insurance; class action lawsuits; the Federal Trade Commission's plan to impose restrictions and penalties on false advertising; the barring of federal contracts to companies convicted of pollution offenses; mandatory state inspection of motor vehicles for pollution control."

Then in the biting manner that raises the hackles of many politicians, Nader added: "This is not to say that Stans has always been negative; he has been positive. He has supported the Alaska pipeline; he has supported the Supersonic Transport; he has supported tax relief programs for corporations; and he has advocated the dismantling of the Flammable Fabrics Act."

Rather than work for the government, where he is supposed to represent the people, Nader says Stans is more qualified by his views to be a Washington lobbyist for some business. Even Vice President Agnew, who considers himself something of a critic, has been cut by Nader's tongue. In a typical approach, Nader has accused Agnew of violating the law by being a "political pitchman" for the Nixon Administration. Agnew, one of the Administration's most forceful salesmen of the law-and-order theme, is himself violating the law, Nader says. "Federal law states that no government employee will be used to influence or affect a political campaign, but yet Agnew is constantly on the campaign trail raising funds for the Republican party. I don't think he should do that at taxpayers' expense . . . and I don't think a Vice President should go around talking law and order when he is performing an illegal act." Nixon himself did not do anything to defuse Nader's outrage at the Republican party when he even botched an attempt at small talk with Nader on the receiving line at his daughter Tricia's wedding. Nixon animatedly told Nader about a gift his new son-in-law Edward Cox had gotten—a miniature statue of the blindfolded woman who symbolizes justice. "Now, wasn't that an appropriate gift for a Raider's Nader?" said Nixon happily jumbling the Nader's Raider label. Said Nader: "I thought about saying 'Thank you, Richard's Nixon!' "

Of all the people around Richard Nixon, there was only one with whom Nader had any rapport, and that was Robert Finch, the one-time Health, Education, and Welfare secretary, and now presidential assistant. "At least I could talk to Finch and he would listen," says Nader, who would like to see an evaluation system set up for cabinet officers and top-ranked government appointees. He argues that a way must be found to allow citizens to give officials a performance rating which would indicate to the voters how the individual is performing his job in relation to the needs of the people.

But if Nader takes his politicians with a heavy dose of disdain, he still votes regularly. "I am registered in Connecticut as an independent, and I have voted in every presidential election since I turned twenty-one," says Nader in what is for him a long-winded statement on politics. But Nader has not been able to limit his direct involvement in politics to quietly casting his secret ballot. The reason is this: The politicians may doubt his ability to get elected President at any time soon, but his running for senator or congressman is another kettle of votes.

In Connecticut, Nader has long been standing political timber to independents and regular party dissidents. Why not? For a state like Connecticut, he is close to the perfect candidate. His intellectualism and activism appeal to the well-paid professionals who commute to New York City, his humanism and consumer programs could woo the state's sizable industrial workers vote, and he is, in an age of jaded city sophisticates, a booster of the virtues of small-town living. With this combination working for him, it is not surprising to hear Nader say that he has gotten "at least a half-dozen feelers" to run for Connecticut Senate and House seats. The late Connecticut Senator Thomas Dodd was one of the reasons for the bids. Dodd, once considered Vice Presidential material by President Lyndon Johnson, got embroiled in the late 1960s in a scandal over campaign-fund spending which was triggered by revelations of his aide, James Boyd. Dodd's case climaxed in 1967 with the Senate censuring the one-time FBI agent and Nuremberg war crimes trial prosecutor—the first senator to be censured for financial misconduct. Dodd ended his political career by trying to run for a third term as an independent, a venture that ended in predictable defeat. But the years of feuding and mud-slinging badly split the state Democratic party and the climate was ideal for a man like Nader. "There was never any formal bid from the party," Nader said. "The people who came to me tried to sound me out; get a commitment from me, but I turned them all away. I gave them all the same message: I just wasn't interested."

But politicians and the politically-minded don't give up easily. The feelers kept coming and Nader kept turning them away. "I kept sending out the message loud and clear that they were wasting their time," he said. Why isn't he interested? Nader explains his stand this way: "I am already more effective than many politicians. I would lose rather than gain if I was elected to office. Look at the good politicians today. They are strapped. The institutions they are trying to deal with are so obsolete or cumbersome, or beholden to special interests groups, that a senator or a congressman can hardly make a dent.

"There is no room in a system like that for a person like I am. To my mind, politics is too full of compromises that should not be made. No matter how independent a politician wants to be, he still is dependent on campaign contributors just to enter the election campaign.

"Then there are pressures outside of money that close in on you. For example, you might like what a labor union is doing in the worker-safety area, but you don't like the way it fails to protect workers' pensions. But if you are a politician, you have to go one way or the other.

"Take another example. Suppose I became a senator. Do you think I could run my student task forces out of my office? If I tried, how long do you think it would be before the constituency got boiled up because the students were going after their banks, or their unions? Before you know it, I would be thrown out of office. This is the type of intricate web that I just refuse to participate in.

"But obviously you've got to reform the American political system. The question is do you try to do it with all kinds of straps around you inside the system, or do you do it from outside the system. I think there is more leverage from outside.

"But I don't think you can have a new type of politics unless you have a new type of citizenship," Nader says. To him, "a new type of citizenship" means a society that puts the emphasis on man and man's needs. But what has happened in the past, he says, is that the individual has been submerged and subordinated to abstractions like the state, political theory, religion, and the corporation. What needs to be done, Nader says, is to refurbish the concept of citizenship; strip it of its dull textbook definitions and give citizens the skills they need to bring pressures on institutions for change.

"We have forty thousand persons in the United States whose job it is to fix other persons' hair and fingernails. Why

271

can't we have forty thousand full-time citizens, some of whom could reform the political system," he says.

The tools to reform the system are the things he is developing. His public interest law firm is an example of a tool that can be used in the practice of the new citizenship. It is the vehicle that can champion on a local level the interests of all segments of society—the consumer, the voters, the home-owners, the senior citizens. "In Washington, for example, there is no one outside the system working on the problem of election campaign spending or developing legislation to reform it. Can you imagine what could be done, if only five public interest lawyers were assigned to an area like this?" Nader asks. But he is well aware of the mammoth job he faces. "Citizenship action in the United States is about as developed now as physics was in Archimedes's time because we haven't put full-time talent to work on it. But look what happens when full-time citizenship is applied. I am an example of that. What I am trying to do is show that professional citizenship can be a full-time career for some. When I am successful against corporations like GM or Union Carbide, then I feel others might take heart; that is, people in local communities with problems can imitate what we've done and go to work using the same approach on their local problems."

In Washington alone, Nader claims there is a need for five thousand public interest lawyers. That would give the citizens "at least a one-to-two ratio compared to the number of lawyers working on the government in behalf of private interest."

If the citizenship concept catches on, reform of the political structure would quickly follow. "What would happen," says Nader, "is that there would be a change in the kind of people who go into politics, the kind of people who get elected, and the kind of people who get appointed. If you change the quality of citizenship, a lot of people will go into politics because they will know that something can be done. A lot of people stay out of politics now because they know it is a dirty business, or they can't get anything done. But reforming the political system is terribly important. Without

272

changes in politics, my movement will never really break through. As a start, we have got to look on citizenship as a professional career capable of increasing skill levels like a quarterback on a football team, or a lawyer, or a scientist. Once the new techniques are developed, we can get slow institutional reform or dismantling of ineffective institutions."

The biggest obstacle to Nader's citizenship movement is apathy. "There is an enormous 'you can't fight City Hall' syndrome in this country; enormous despair; people just don't dare, they despair instead. The people of this nation have got to begin looking at citizenship as an obligation if they expect to make changes," he says.

There are some persons who already are at work trying to make political changes. They are members of a very elite profession: President-making. In this profession, men usually shun publicity, and even when discovered at work, their names mean little to the newspaper-reading public. If there is any recognition at all, it is because these men are usually wealthy, or scions of famous families, or both. On July 22, 1971, one of these groups met at the posh St. Regis Hotel in New York City, and the presidential prospect being dissected was Eugene McCarthy, the one-time senator, congressman, teacher, and the man who sought the Democratic presidential nomination in 1968 under an anti-war banner.

McCarthy was being sounded out on his plans for the 1972 campaign. Was he willing to run again? If he did run, what kind of campaign would he conduct? What primaries would he enter? Most important, what would the campaign cost? For six hours, the group mulled over McCarthy's prospects for another race. At the time, McCarthy gave no firm answer to any of the questions. In fact, McCarthy stayed only two hours and left for a trip to Europe. But the group stayed on to discuss the politics of the future; the need for a man with a fresh point of view to rally the massive bloc of dissatisfied voters in the nation. One of the heady strategies discussed revolved around the possibility of winning in 1972 with a fourth-party candidate. The group pictured an election where eighty million persons voted in a campaign which pitted Nixon against a Democratic "me-too" candidate. With Alabama's Governor George Wallace running on a third-party ticket, about twelve million votes would be drained away from the two major parties. That would leave Nixon, the Democratic contender, and their fourth-party candidate to divide up the remaining sixty-eight million votes. This would mean that a fourth-party candidate could win with only twenty-five million or so votes if he got the right electoral votes combination. Taking off from this premise, the group argued that the fourth-party candidate could be the man to tap the newly-enfranchised eighteen-year-old vote. There are twenty-five million young persons eligible to vote for the first time in 1972. If only fifteen million of them vote, a fourth-party candidate with "youth appeal" could conceivably pick up ten million votes. All the fourth-party candidate would then need would be to get another fifteen million votes from the older voters to put together the twenty-five-million-vote total needed to win.

Political daydreams? Yes. But these were the same people who took the vacillating McCarthy from an obscure senator with a deep feeling about the war in Vietnam and little else in the way of assets, and for a brief period in the primary elections of the 1968 presidential campaign they kept his star blazing—bright enough to attract hordes of dissident youths, intellectuals, and some of the middle-class Americans who were so disenchanted with the war that they were willing to follow any leader who promised to let their voices be heard. These also were the people who raised $11 million for McCarthy's primary campaigns, more than was spent by Hubert Humphrey ($4 million), Governor Nelson Rockefeller ($8 million), and almost as much as was spent by President Nixon ($12 million). The group also was influential enough to woo at least five contributors who gave McCarthy over $100,000. These were, in fact, the people who would put together the beginnings of what could be a new face in politics, one whose main themes were reform and change.

Two of the persons in the hotel room were of particular

interest to anyone conjecturing on the political future of Ralph Nader. One of the men was Howard M. Stein, president of the Dreyfus Fund, a man who played a major role in raising McCarthy's campaign funds. The other was Dr. Martin Peretz, a political-science professor at Harvard, whose wife is an heir to the Singer sewing machine forture.

According to the official records of the 1968 presidential campaign, Peretz gave McCarthy at least $100,000. Jack Dreyfus, who was chairman of the huge Dreyfus Fund, contributed at least another $100,000. A check of Nader's financial records showed the two made individual contributions totaling over $25,000 to Nader's movement. Still another heavy contributor to the liberal wing of the Democratic party, though not a member of the McCarthy fund-raising group, was Samuel Rubin, a retired executive of Fabergé, Inc., who put $75,000 into the Democratic war chest. Through the Rubin Foundation, Rubin funneled $10,000 into Nader's Center for Study of Responsive Law. The Dreyfus Fund's interest in Nader's movement goes even farther than simple financial support. Under Howard Stein's leadership, the Dreyfus Fund was one of the first to accept Campaign GM's bid to poll its mutual fund members as to whether the Dreyfus Fund should vote its shares of GM stock in support of the corporate reform proposals backed by the Nader-supported Campaign GM.

However, the fact that Nader's movement has gotten some of its funds from political-minded philanthropists does not mean that Nader is only waiting in the shadows until the time is right for him to unveil himself as a political candidate. But it does show that he is already familiar with the type of persons who are interested in the new politics; who are searching for candidates and who do have the money, the experience, and the drive to market a presidential candidate to the voters.

Nader, however, sees no possibility that his contributors will come looking for a payback in the form of a Nader candidacy.

"Peretz? He is a minor contributor to the Center for Study

of Responsive Law. I've seen him once, and he has never discussed politics with me." As for Howard Stein, Nader admits that he and Stein have met "three or four times."

"We talked about public events; where the country is going. Most of the discussions were about corporate responsibility. He thinks that one of the big problems in the country is lack of accountability by people in power. Stein is very eloquent on that, but we have never discussed a possible political candidacy for me.

"These people are not looking for someone like me; they are not that change-oriented. McCarthy is about as far as they would go in terms of a political candidate. And McCarthy is really very conservative in many ways, particularly in dealing with corporate reform. His backers are not ready to go the distance needed to bring about the kind of reform I am talking about.

"There is no one on the political scene who really is willing to address the issues of corporate power. Just look at the candidates—McGovern and Muskie! None of these men are going to attack corporations.

"If you ask me who would I choose, I would say McGovern seems to be the most candid and humanely oriented. At least he is fairly good on foreign affairs, including the problems of disarmament."

But a good proportion of the population does not seem to think that Nader's reform campaign is either subversive, anti-business, or radical in any way. Pollster Louis Harris ran a survey of 1,620 families in March, 1971, asking a nationwide cross-section this question:

"Do you feel that in his attacks on American industry consumer-advocate Ralph Nader has done more good than harm, or more harm than good?"

The result: a lopsided fifty-three percent to nine percent agreed that Nader was doing more good than harm. Thirty-eight percent said they were not familiar enough with Nader's programs to pass judgment. The poll also showed that by a sixty-nine to three percent margin most persons feel "it's good to have critics such as Nader to keep industry on its toes." By a fifty-nine to five percent margin, the public rejected the idea that "Nader is a troublemaker who is against the free-enterprise system." Harris said the survey showed that, basically, the efforts of Nader "have been extremely well received by the American public." A poll by George Gallup taken in the same month showed that out of 1,571 persons sampled Nader was known to fifty percent of the American men and thirty-seven percent of the women. That would be a recognition factor at the time higher than most of the announced presidential candidates, particularly Senators George McGovern of South Dakota and Oklahoma's Fred Harris. Harris, whose campaign for the nomination lasted only a month, admitted "Ralph Nader is talking about what's on people's minds and the rest of the candidates are not."

Obviously Nader is going nowhere politically in 1972 no matter what his standing in public-opinion polls, or regardless of how many "Draft Nader in 1972" bumper stickers the New Party is able to afford. Even Jimmy the Greek, the famous Las Vegas oddsmaker, rated Nader in September, 1971, as a 500-to-1 shot. More importantly, Nader's protestations that he is more interested in who will be the next president of GM than he is in who will sit in the White House are true.

Without an ego to nourish, without a desire for political power, and without debts to any vested interest, Nader is sincere when he says in a Shermanesque statement that he is "absolutely not interested" in a political office. But whether he can hold to this position in the future is debatable. Nader, after all, has become a rallying point for a mass of Americans who see in him and his values the hope of the future. He calls continually for corporate reform and a society that emphasizes the dignity of the individual. To bring about these changes will require a forceful movement, and movements of force need leaders, and not simply moral leaders but political leaders as well.

If the time should ever come when he does enter politics, it probably would be through the medium of a third party, or a fourth party. In an article written for the Harvard Law

Record in 1958 Nader described the third political party at the very least as sort of "a steam-valve mechanism" that will allow citizens to express views they feel are not being served by the majority parties. And, in what could describe the very reason Nader should be in politics, he wrote: "At a minimum, minor parties have many times in our history deeply stirred opinion and illuminated the murky atmosphere of politics with a flash of idealism."

15

CONCLUSION

Perhaps, someday, the captains of the legal profession, the captains of industry, the representatives of special interests, will erect a statue of Ralph Nader to be put in the lobby of the General Motors building with an inscription that says: "He saved us from ourselves."

—Closing remarks made by a student
moderator at the University of
Southern California in thanking
Ralph Nader for making an appearance
at a school seminar

In the end, Ralph Nader's real value may be in the example he is setting. Where once his brand of moral outrage was considered freakish, it has now become contagious—politicians are adopting it as their own and corporate executives can risk the ire of stockholders if they ignore it. It was only six years ago that Nader came back to his rooming house after his Senate confrontation with GM's James Roche to have his landlady ask incredulously if that was "really you I saw on television." But today, Nader's folk-hero image has so penetrated society that high-school students taking the New York State Regents examination in social studies are quizzed on his work. Even President Nixon cracked "Where's Ralph Nader?" when a music box given to Mrs. Dwight Eisenhower at a 75th birthday celebration in 1971 failed to play.

The notoriety, the admiration, and the imitation doesn't mean, however, that the James Roches and the Henry Fords of the corporate world will shortly see issues as Nader does, or that Nader will become a universally-loved figure. Nader is much too dogmatic in his views and too spartan in his life-style to become everybody's hero, but he has stirred in many Americans a fervor to transform the American government and industry into truer expressions of the public interest. Under Nader, this fervor could bring widespread "renewal" to the marketplace of the 1970s. The renewal will not be the result of a religious-like conversion, but will be a recognition by industry that it must be more responsive, or risk still tighter regulation. It will be a recognition, too, that the consumer movement, though still puny, now has a fighting-cock spirit which is a direct result of Nader's success. But as important as this infusion of spirit has been, it is not Nader's only contribution. If it were, he would be nothing more than a temporary phenomenon like his earlier muckraking counterparts. As they did, he would wind up as a chapter in the social history of the United States. But the one thing that makes Nader different from them is his drive to establish a concerned, ongoing constituency equipped with the means to force institutions such as government and industry to respond to its needs. In a sense, Nader is changing the consumer movement from an ofttimes hobbyhorse for faddists into a lean and hard pressure group.

One of the first results of Nader's battle has been a broader definition of consumer rights. It is now clear that the consumer must not only be protected from the dangers of "voluntary use" of a product—such as flammable material—but also from "involuntary" consumption of industrial by-products such as air and water pollution, excessive pesticides on vegetables, and antibiotics in meat. At the same time this "broader definition" of consumer rights is evolving, the consumer movement is finding that the reform of corporate abuses and the restriction of corporate power are closely connected. In fact, what Nader has shown to the public is

280

that the marketplace is really a high crime area in need of law and order.

Nader has been the first public figure to fully understand this and to offer a program that would give the consumer weapons with which he can fight back. To Nader, one of the best of these weapons is the consumer class action suit. In an era when products are mass-produced, fraud is too, and the remedy must be the ability to face the mulcter with the threat that one of his victims may go to court and ask for damages on behalf of all of his victims. In the past, it was relatively safe for a chain store or a mammoth department store to cheat customers out of pennies, dimes, and quarters with, for example, inaccurately computed billings, and turn a tidy profit on the volume. And it was easier still for large corporations to rig prices. When a customer realized what was happening, the amount involved in his case may have been too small to warrant taking legal action, but with a class action filed on behalf of all the mulcted customers, the recoverable damages would be more than enough to justify the annoyance and expense of a court suit.

Product recall is another of the weapons in Nader's consumer-protection arsenal. He gave the concept a tremendous shove forward when the auto safety crusade resulted in the acceptance by the automakers of massive recalls as a part of the price that must be paid for faulty quality control. Just as important, but still lagging, is the concept of refunds. Up to now, the usual practice of agencies like the Federal Trade Commission has been simply to slap the wrists of a manufacturer once it uncovered a fraud. But there is no requirement that the cheated consumer be repaid. Consequently, what has happened is that marketplace swindlers simply operate until told to stop by the FTC, an action that in some cases has taken longer than a decade to make its way through the bureaucratic mill. In the meantime, the offending corporation is turning a profit on its fraud.

If there is a keystone in Nader's wall of consumer protection, it is the need for the government to set safety standards.

To him it was an indication of the pitiful strength of the consumer and the power of the auto industry that as late as 1966 there were no comprehensive federal safety standards for automobiles, despite the fact that tens of thousands of persons died every year, and millions of others were injured. But since Nader forced the auto industry into line, the battle for better meat, fish, pipeline, and job safety standards was made somewhat easier in the sense that Nader had come out of his auto safety crusade with a strategy that could be used in any field.

Tied directly to the safety standards is another deterrent to shoddy merchandise: the ability of the government to do its own testing and not be forced to rely on industry for its information. Because of Nader and the auto safety crusade, the government now is building an auto test center. But without the ability to do the same thing for other industrial products, the government is hampered in insuring that its legislation is being carried out by the manufacturers. Large-scale testing facilities would also produce still another spur to quality in the marketplace. It would allow the government to develop prototypes of safer products and use the prototypes to pressure industry into duplicating them for sale in the marketplace, Nader feels. Equally as important, says Nader, is the need to inform the public about the damage done to it by price-fixing. "People must begin to understand that the prices they pay for items like drugs and bread, and houses can often be directly related to price-fixing either through conspiracy or by mutually understood cues."

Writing in *The Closed Enterprise System: A Report on Antitrust Enforcement* which was produced by his raiders, Nader said the government now is not only slipshod in its antitrust enforcement but at times actually aids and abets antitrust violators through its inaction. To put life into its antitrust prosecution, Nader has urged a series of reforms including the growth of a professional antitrust constituency outside the federal government. This would include state attorneys general, city corporation counsels, and public interest lawyers. He also has urged that wide publicity be given to

CONCLUSION

the "contempt" many large corporations have for competitive capitalism, and that the public be made aware of the weak and politically-controlled antitrust program now conducted by the Justice Department and the Federal Trade Commission. Nader says it is a charade to contend there really is an antitrust enforcement program when the combined antitrust budgets of the two agencies does not exceed $20 million while the nation's economy which they must police has passed the trillion dollar mark.

One consumer weapon—a federal consumer protection agency (CPA)—has been an obsession with Nader since the start of his crusade. He put more time and effort into lobbying for the agency than he did for any of the other consumer bills credited to him. The concept of an activist consumer agency that could intervene in formal and informal hearings before other agencies, and be allowed to cross examine witnesses, present arguments and evidence on behalf of the consumer, and even appeal in the courts if necessary, was the ideal way to end bureaucratic secrecy, delay, and collusion with the vested interests. In his words, the bill to set up the Consumer Protection Agency was "the most important piece of consumer legislation ever to come before Congress." But the fight over the agency illustrated graphically Nader's strengths and weaknesses on Capitol Hill. His antagonist in the fight was Democratic Representative Chet Holifield of California, the chairman of the Government Operations Committee which handled the bill. Heading the Nader forces on the committee was Congressman Benjamin Rosenthal (D-N.Y.), a long-time consumer-advocate in Congress who worked well in tandem with Nader.

In 1970, the bill died in the House Rules Committee, but in 1971 it had gained more supporters even though the concept was opposed by the White House. Nader lobbied furiously for a strong bill, but he broke his lance on the portly frame of Holifield who gutted the bill, partly out of spite for Nader.

Holifield, encrusted with seniority, was a petty tyrant of a committee chairman. He also was a master at playing the

283

game of middleman between the vested interests. To Holifield, he was doing his job by taking from one lobby group and giving to another until he had a compromise acceptable to all, but satisfactory to none. Nader didn't play the game that way. He wanted a consumer protection agency that would have the power to slash through the bureaucracy with a bright sword and the special interest be damned. But what finally came out of Holifield's committee was to Nader "a sham" of a bill.

Under the bill, the agency could represent the consumer's interest in formal rule-making hearings before federal agencies. It also was given power to collect, investigate, and publicize consumer complaints. But the CPA got no power to act on behalf of the consumer in any case where a government agency seeks primarily to impose a fine, penalty, or forfeiture for an alleged violation of law or an agency rule. This would include antitrust actions, and crackdowns on violations of food, health, and toy safety laws, all key consumer areas.

When Holifield first began to whittle away at the bill, Nader screamed. He called press conferences to attack Holifield and he spent endless hours lobbying the other committee members, nor was he afraid to attack the lion in his den.

"I was personally lobbied by this man—both through phone calls at home and office visits—more than I've been lobbied by anyone on anything for ten years," said Holifield.

The congressman had his own opinion of Nader's mode of operation, and it was none too kind, and even less factual. Said Holifield:

"Nader's method of opposition is to continuously make derogatory charges against any person of prominence that comes within his rifle sights. A new charge every day gives him a new headline.

"This is a time-proven method of obtaining publicity, practiced at one time by Senator Joe McCarthy. Mr. Nader's cry of 'wolf, wolf' against anyone who disagrees with him will soon cease to cause alarm or attention."

Nader didn't think his lobbying was out of order. Far from

it, he feels the lack of citizen lobbies is one of the reasons consumer interests have never carried any priority with Congress. As far as Holifield personally was concerned, Nader had a view of his own. Noting Holifield's long-time membership on the Joint House-Senate Atomic Energy Committee, Nader asked "why doesn't Holifield tell the people how much General Electric and Westinghouse have wined and dined him to curry his favor on atomic energy projects?"

The Holifield-Nader feud was a deeply personal thing for Holifield. Nader irritated him; Nader was arrogant, and worse, Nader, in Holifield's eyes, did not have the proper credentials to be in the arena with the recognized lobbyists for business and labor. Nader, after all, was a man without a formal constituency; who is he to tell the chairman of a congressional committee what he wants and what he doesn't want? Holifield's anger went deeper than the showdown fight over a consumer protection agency. Earlier in 1971, Holifield had abolished a Government Operations Committee consumer panel headed by Congressman Rosenthal. Nader went to his typewriter and hammered out one of his famous angry letters in which he accused Holifield of "consciously proposing to abandon the committee's responsibility for the problems of the American consumer." Reconsider the decision, Nader urged. Snapped Holifield: "Ralph Nader is not going to run the House Government Operations Committee. Let him run his own damn affairs." Nader replied by having militant consumers picket Holifield's congressional district office in Los Angeles.

The difference between the approaches of the two men to the needs of the consumer dramatically emphasize how far Nader still must go, and how hard the road will be. Holifield represents the old, established way of doing business. He saw Nader's proposed strong Consumer Protection Agency as a disruptive gadfly among government agencies, not an efficient way to prod the agencies into action on behalf of the consumer. He simply wanted to add another agency, and not allow it to revolutionize the old way of business. His own words show the different approaches. Any consumer protection agency should not be allowed "to become a super agency which would direct the course of another agency's investigations." Nor, he said, should it be allowed to sit in on every private conference an agency might have with business representatives. As far as giving the Consumer Protection Agency direct power of subpoena, it would only allow it to go on "fishing expeditions," said Holifield.

To Nader, "interference on behalf of the consumer" was what a consumer protection agency was all about. To be effective it must have power to be a party to the informal hearings between government and business offenders. This is where most of the decisions are made. It can't be called "disruptive" if it is trying to correct wrongs the record shows exist under the old system. Probably it was Presidential Consumer Advisor Virginia Knauer who best described those who wanted a weak consumer protection agency. This bill, she said "is compatible with the way government functions and will permit government to continue to operate as efficiently as possible." That "efficient operation" of government is what Nader was trying to change. Who was it operating efficiently for? Certainly not the consumer, whose very victimization resulted from the old way of operation between government regulators and business operators.

Where were Nader's supporters in this fight? The other consumer organizations? They were not really exerting any pressure. In fact, the consumer lobby in Congress still is poorly organized. One of the strongest of the consumer groups is the Consumer Federation of America, which has close ties with the AFL-CIO, but Nader got little help from it, and for the same reasons Holifield battled him. In theory the union should back any legislation which is designed to help its members, but it doesn't. The labor union plays by the old rules, not Nader's rules, and Holifield to the AFL-CIO chieftains is a powerful committee chairman who can act on issues of great concern to the leaders of the union, and as such should not be challenged where the stakes—a bill for powerless consumers—are not high enough. According to Nader, the AFL-CIO's legislative representative, Andrew J.

Biemiller, a personal friend of Holifield's, lead the campaign to give nothing but lukewarm support to Nader's campaign. This buddy-buddy approach is typical of what is wrong with lobbying structure in the Congress. The relationship between the lawmaker and the congressman is equally as important as the validity of the issue before the Congress. In the case of the strong Consumer Protection Agency bill, "twenty million workers were sold down the river purely and solely because of the long-time friendship between Andy Biemiller and Chet Holifield," Nader said.

But the bitter fight over the bill points up a flaw in Nader's manner of operation. He may reject the idea of cultivating contacts in Congress, but he still has not been able to translate his growing mandate from the consumer into an effective pressure bloc inside Congress. The committee system, the power of the vested interests, and the system of tradeoffs used by the lawmakers among themselves, has slowed Nader in winning support for his legislative program. But typical of him, he is planning a Nader Raider investigation of Congress in hopes of triggering a campaign to reform the archaic institution.

But if Nader is finding Congress hard to crack, the Nixon White House is even more impregnable. It refuses to even admit that Nader is a representative of a large and growing body of consumers, no less listen to him. Nothing could dramatize its stance more than a routine White House news briefing held on September 20, 1971—six years after most of the nation, both friends and enemies, recognized Nader as one, if not the leading consumer advocate. At the briefing, White House Press Secretary Ronald L. Ziegler was asked why Nader was not invited to a consumer meeting scheduled by Nixon for the next day with twenty consumer representatives who would give President Nixon their views on his wage-price freeze and recommend what action should be taken when the freeze ended.

Ziegler, obviously embarrassed, fumbled for an answer to the reporter's question, and finally gave the lame explanation that Nader was not a member of any "official" organized consumer group. Then followed this exchange between Ziegler and the White House reporter:

Ziegler: Those who have been invited to the session tomorrow are those who head membership organizations representing consumers. Mr. Nader, of course, is an outspoken advocate on the part of the consumer, but he doesn't fall into that category.

Reporter: Does the White House know of any other group which has been as effective as Mr. Nader's?

Ziegler: Yes.

Reporter: What groups are they?

Ziegler: I won't go through the list.

Reporter: Was this a presidential level decision not to invite Mr. Nader?

Ziegler: The recommendation was made as it is posted. You have the list of those who have been invited, and the President agrees with the list.

The White House argument would have been laughable if it did not so tragically show the influence of the corporate community on the White House. Nixon did not invite Nader for two reasons: One, Nader criticized Nixon's anti-inflation program as benefiting business at the expense of the consumer, and two, recognition of Nader might alienate corporate fat cats whose campaign funds were counted on in an upcoming election year. But on the same day Nader was being shut out, Nixon found time for another well-publicized personality. He met with the newly-elected Miss America, Laura Lea Schaefer.

Nader, however, managed to get in the last word. "I think Nixon's decision to keep me out was unfortunate because there should be a place in this country for an individual standing on his own two feet," he said. There is little doubt that, like GM's gaff, the crude brush-off given Nader by the White House won him even more supporters.

Nader's ability to take setbacks is something he has perfected over a lifetime as a professional underdog. "I have a very stable set of purposes and convictions. I know it is going to be a rocky road so I am not ruffled very easily. I am sort of programmed to anticipate all these things, and I try to do what I can to prepare myself. For example, I don't get all clutched up or nervous if things go wrong. I have an inner consistency that carries me through," Nader says.

The White House slight may have been another obvious indicator of how far the consumer movement has to go. But Nader sees no reason to despair. His answer to the Jeremiahs who lament his impossible mission is this:

"It is true that the interests of the consumer take a low priority on the list of election issues and that the government's expenses to correct consumer problems is negligible.

"Some would argue that this situation will inevitably prevail in view of the overwhelming power of American corporations—in and out of government. But as I have tried to show, new approaches to judging and influencing corporate behavior have begun to emerge in the last few years. These new approaches can illuminate the enormity of consumer deprivation by corporations and this in turn can trigger a rush of anger from the public which will speed reform." But Nader is not expecting any instant fulfillment of his predictions. "Society has not yet recognized fully that the mere delegation of citizen power to so-called representative institutions—be they in government or industry—is a course for disaster unless that power is continually pulled back, challenged, monitored, and probed." This challenging, monitoring, and probing is what Naderism is all about.

This is what is being done by his Center for Study of Responsive Law and the Public Interest Research Group in Washington, and those spreading across the nation's campuses. The consumer protection agency represents a tool for this kind of action. So does Nader's fund-raising group, the Public Citizen, which is simply an attempt to bring into the fight those who can, or will only, contribute money. The Clearinghouse for Professional Responsibility is another way of monitoring institutional power. The Aviation Consumer Action Project is obviously a check on the airline industry and its government regulators. The establishment of Campaign GM follows this strategy as does the Center for Auto Safety and the smaller spinoff groups like the Center for Concerned Engineering and the Professionals for Auto Safety. What is Nader's Fishermen's Clean Water Action Project but a challenge to those who pollute the nation's streams and offshore waters? The same can be said of the Corporate Accountability Research Group whose job it is to monitor corporate crime such as antitrust violations. This doesn't mean that Nader's goal is to organize 200 million Americans into social-concern clubs. But he does feel it is necessary to develop a larger coterie of trained dedicated citizen advocates like himself who will make a lifetime career out of watchdogging the institutions of society. His personal role is two-fold: To show it can be done, and to create some of the vehicles with which to do it. This new citizen Nader talks of must provide the dedication, and most important the consistency.

"Institutions tend not to control power democratically, but concentrate it, and to serve special interest groups at the expense of voiceless citizens. Almost all the organized legal representation in our country is working to protect private interest and private wealth. Who represents the citizen? Who can? Only ourselves.

"We have seen how a few dedicated and determined citizens can overcome overwhelming odds to better their communities. If more valiant and concerned people were able to work similarly, continuously and on a broader scale, think how much more could be accomplished," Nader wrote in a plea for funds to support his crusade.

Stripped of its mysticism, its hyperbole, Naderism simply is a plea to Americans not to adjust. Part of the problem with society is that the abnormal is being accepted as the normal. Americans, for example, are adjusting to air pollution, filthy rivers and lakes, doctored food, slums, and cars that kill. They are doing this even though the financial and technological means exist to solve all of these problems. Unless this passivity is reversed, the deprivation will get worse since the institutions of society have nothing to fear from their victims.

CONCLUSION

Most certainly Nader is a moralist; he may qualify as the most moral man on the public scene today, but that doesn't mean he is without sin. When he is convinced his cause is right, he will manipulate situations and use people. His estimation of his enemies' abilities can be touched with arrogance, and he has a disdain for those who give up the good fight just because of a defeat. But he has unlimited compassion, too. He is basically a gentle, sensitive man. He feels deeply and openly about people. When the wife of one of his raiders was attacked on a Washington street, Nader was beside himself with anguish. When New York State Representative and fellow auto safety critic Edward Speno died, Nader talked incessantly about the man for days. And it was typical of Nader to quietly memorialize his first raider, Michael Wollan, who died in a Volkswagen accident in 1968 while on his honeymoon in Nova Scotia. In Wollan's name, Nader set up a memorial essay fund with $1,000 in prizes for the law student who submits the best paper on the corporation. Again in remembrance, Nader's report on the hazards of the Volkswagen (*The Volkswagen—An Assessment of Distinctive Hazards*, Center for Auto Safety, Washington, D.C., 1971) was dedicated to Wollan.

This compassion and loyalty given by Nader is returned in a full measure by his staffers, and by his amazingly wide circle of friends who are seeded in every level of society. These people are often Nader's "brains." They are lawyers, engineers, tax experts, university professors, think-tank intellectuals, yes, and even corporate executives. They either must, or prefer to, remain anonymous, but when Nader calls they produce. This is the group, for example, that can evaluate information turned in by whistleblowers, or provide him with up-to-date briefings on problems that may be ripe for a Nader attack. But with all his seemingly strange modes of operation, Nader is on the scene to stay. He rose to prominence on an appealing idea—one man can make a difference—and the concept is no less appealing now than it was when he brought the idea to Washington. Industry can prattle all it wishes about radicalism and antibusiness bias, and the cynics can sit and wait for the "one catastrophic error" to be committed by one of Nader's young staffers, but Nader is going on. As it is now, government and industry must deal with the "Nader factor" in their decision-making process, and the public knows it. The public also knows that Nader almost singlehandedly created public policy in areas like auto safety where there was no public policy and it knows that what Nader argues for is not only for his benefit, but theirs.

By virtue of his drive, his candor, and his endless supply of outrage, Nader has made himself a folk hero, an American original. To literally millions, he is the man who ended the age of the organization man, and put life back into the concept that the individual has worth and an opinion of value. In a society plagued by a dearth of any other examples of this feat, Nader has gathered the support of those pools of angry, frustrated persons who had no champion on the public stage. They show no signs of leaving him, now or in the future, nor has Nader any plans to retire from the field. Those who predict that he will end up teaching on a college campus (he's had offers to be the dean of several large law schools), or claim he may finally succumb to the all-American urge to make money and open a law firm of the more conventional kind, are mistaken. So are those who predict his rag-tag band will eventually become melded into some kind of more recognizable Washington lobby group. "Nader at thirty-seven will be Nader at sixty-seven," he says, and there is no reason to doubt he means it. Nader knows his real value is to show the way, to prove again and again that one man can make changes and redress wrongs. Former Attorney General Ramsey Clark went right to the heart of the Nader phenomenon when he wrote in a copy of his book *Crime in America* this personal inscription: "For Ralph Nader, whose passion after justice has given faith to millions that we can find it."

292

NADERISMS

Ralph Nader can use words with precision. He has a highly developed ability to slice through the murk of corporate economics or governmentese and outline in a few sentences the real problem. His critics argue that he tailors his language for the benefit of newspaper headline writers, but in fact the ability to express himself through words was one of his very first skills acquired through years of practice starting as far back as his editorship of the Harvard Law School *Record* and culminating in his book *Unsafe At Any Speed.* Here are some examples of Naderisms:

On society: A society is like a fish—it rots from the head down. And unless there's really an exemplary performance by the people who've got the power, and the privilege and the status—you can't expect a similar restraint on the part of people who have less.

On Americans: Americans have often set up models which do not exist, which never existed, and which they may never permit to exist, yet they pacify our frontieristic, democratic spirit. Equal justice, economic opportunity, racial freedom, a peace-loving nation—our list of unachieved hyperboles is long. Among them must be included our faith in "the free-enterprise system" and in the anti-trust laws which maintain it. This phrase, and these laws, are of such vintage, and have been so repeated into catechism, that they are accepted on faith as part of the great American tradition. Yet like many of our democratic models, the reality is more apparent than the actual.

On giant corporations: The megacorporations are basically anti-free market and thus actually anti-ethical to capitalism, where I am all in favor of fostering genuine free enterprise and putting the people back into people's capitalism.

On consumerism: We will see consumer demonstrations someday that will make civil rights demonstrations look small by comparison.

On lawyers: The best lawyers should be spending their time on the great problems—on water and air pollution, on racial justice, on poverty and juvenile deliquency, on the joke that ordinary rights have become—but they are not. They are spending their time defending Geritol, Rice Krispies, and the oil-import quota.

On law schools: Possibly the greatest failure of the law schools—a failure of the faculty—was not to articulate a theory and practice of a just deployment of legal manpower. Lawyers labored for polluters, not anti-polluters, for sellers, not consumers, for corporations, not citizens, for labor leaders, not rank and file, for, not against rate increases, for highway builders, not displaced residents . . . None of this and much more seemed to trouble the law schools.

On capitalism: I have little faith in the automatic power of government to right all wrongs. In any area of government control, there is always the danger of inaction, overbureaucratization, under imagination, and surrender to special interests. Some form of socialism may very well be a solution for poverty-ridden countries of the "third world," but in America the answer is not to scrap the free-enterprise system, but to reform it—by correcting the abuses committed in its name and ensuring that it operates responsibly and effectively.

NADERISMS

On corporate responsibility: I am responsible for my actions, but who is responsible for those of General Motors? An individual's capital is basically his integrity. He can lose only once. A corporation can lose many times, and not be affected. This unequal contest between the individual and any complex organization, whether it is a corporation, a union, government, or other group, is something which bears the closest scrutiny in order to try to protect the individual from such invasions.

On corporate crime: Individual embezzlement, theft of industrial secrets, stealing a horse, or negligent homicide on the highway can and do bring jail terms up to several decades duration. Large corporations, on the other hand, have deliberately kept secret reports on the effects of drugs, refused to notify owners of defective vehicles, deliberately bilked the government out of millions of public funds in inflated contract costs, without, in many cases, resulting in sanctions and almost never in criminal penalties.

On the power of the corporation: The problem of corporate power comes in three expressions—misfeasance (the improper use of proper power), malfeasance (the use of improper power), and non-feasance (the non-use of proper power).

On advertising: Madison Avenue is engaged in an epidemic campaign of marketing fraud. It has done more to subvert and destroy the market system in this country than ten Kremlins ever dreamed of.

On Washington lobbyists: The gentlemen who run these lobby operations are eminent specialists in cutting down consumer programs in their incipiency or undermining them if they mature. They are masters of the ex parte contact, the private deals and tradeoffs, the greasing of the corporate wheels and the softening of the bureaucrats' will.

On the Nixon Administration: I don't think it's prepared to commit the funds, to engage the enforcement resources to ask for the sanctions, or to promote the disclosure of unsavory facts about the marketplace and various industries that's necessary.

On social ills: Our common problems are inflation, war racism, decaying cities, hunger, consumer abuses, nonresponsive agencies. I ask you—can any of these problems be blamed on "yippies, hippies, discontents, and malcontents"?

On patriotism: If it is unpatriotic to tear down the flag (which is a symbol of the country), why isn't it more unpatriotic to desecrate the country itself—to pollute, despoil, and ravage the air, land, and water? Such environmental degradation makes the "pursuit of happiness" ragged indeed. Why isn't it unpatriotic to engage in the colossal waste that characterizes so many defense contracts? Why isn't it unpatriotic to draw our country into a mistaken war and then keep extending the involvement, with untold casualties to soldiers and innocents, while not telling Americans the truth? Why isn't the systematic contravention of the U.S. Constitution and the Declaration of Independence in our treatment of minority groups, the poor, the young, the old, and other disadvantaged or helpless crassly unpatriotic?

On work: I've got to set a very high standard. If I ever have to ask someone to work on New Year's Eve, I want them to be sure that I have already done 17 times more work on the project than I am asking them to do.

On labor unions: There is quite clearly a great deal wrong with the labor movement—it is ageing; it is bureaucratic, and it is being debilitated by internal politics. Finally, it is incredibly susceptible to being manipulated by corporate management.

On management: I've always thought it was a good idea for every head of an organization to spend two weeks on the line—for the president of the copper company to spend two weeks in the smelter; for the president of a coal mine to spend two weeks in the mines working next to the rank and file. People at the top must find out what is really going on rather than relying on a sanitized memo from a public relations man. If people learn by experience, there is hope of toning down some of the insensitivities of society.

NADER AND CONGRESS

Ralph Nader testifies before Congress with regularity. In many of his appearances, he delivers detailed testimony, and provides much material for the record. The congressional reports on these hearings provide the bulk of the existing material on Nader's philosophy. Here is a list of Nader's appearances before congressional committees.

Senate Committee on Government Operations Subcommittee on Executive Reorganization. Nader testified February 10, 1966, on federal role in traffic safety. He attacked model changes and auto advertising.

Senate Committee on Government Operations Subcommittee on Executive Reorganization. Nader testified March 22, 1966, on federal role in traffic safety. General Motors President James Roche apologized to Nader for using private detectives to spy on him.

Senate Committee on Public Works. Nader testified on April 14, 1966, on the safety of the Volkswagen. He termed the Volkswagen "pound for pound one of the world's most expensive cars," and told the committee "it is hard to find a more dangerous car than the Volkswagen."

Senate Committee on Public Works Subcommittee on Public Roads. Nader testified April 14, 1966, on the Highway Safety Act of 1966. He cited secrecy on accident data, tire failures, and general inability to get information from auto industry.

Senate Commerce Committee Hearing on Implementation of National Traffic and Motor Vehicle Safety Act of 1966. Nader appeared March 21, 1967. He testified on strength of safety standards, discussed effectiveness of recall campaign, and urged criminal penalities be added to the act.

Senate Committee on Government Operations Subcommittee on Executive Reorganization. Nader testified February 2, 1968, on price of motor vehicle safety equipment. He attacked industry for its nondisclosure of price breakdown on safety devices and outlined ways to achieve disclosure of what he said was the actual cost of the equipment.

Subcommittees of the Senate Select Committee on Small Business. Nader testified July 10, 1968, on planning, regulation, and competition in the auto industry. He urged that General Motors be split up to improve competition in the industry.

Senate Committee on Government Operations Subcommittee on Executive Reorganization. Nader testified March 20, 1969, on bill to establish a Department of Consumer Affairs. He cited the need for the department by outlining examples of consumer frauds.

Senate Commerce Committee Subcommittee on Consumer Affairs. Nader testified on July 2, 1969, on legislation to insure the wholesomeness of fish. Nader urged continuous inspection of fish plants.

Senate Judiciary Committee Subcommittee on Improvement in Judicial Machinery. Nader testified on July 29, 1969, in support of allowing consumer class action suits based on violations of state consumer protection laws to be brought in federal courts regardless of the domicile of the parties or the amount involved in the controversy.

300

House Government Operations Subcommittee on Executive and Legislative Reorganization. Nader testified on September 18, 1969, in favor of a bill to establish a Department of Consumer Affairs and transfer to it all the government's existing consumer affairs programs. Nader also condemned the government's failure to stop consumer abuses.

Senate Committee on Government Operations. Nader testified on September 18, 1969, on a proposed Department of Consumer Affairs.

House-Senate Joint Subcommittee on Economy in Government. Nader testified on October 6, 1969, on the inadequacies of the government's sanctions and compliance policies in regulatory activities. Nader argued for more congressional staff members to oversee the public interest in the regulatory agency field.

Senate Commerce Committee Subcommittee on Surface Transportation. Nader testified on October 29, 1969, on the Federal Railroad Safety and the absence of federal regulation. He also discussed the possibility of criminal penalties.

Senate Labor and Public Welfare Subcommittee on Labor. Nader testified before the committee on December 15, 1969, on the Occupational Safety and Health Act. Nader criticized the inadequacies of state and federal officials in dealing with health and safety programs. He also called for an overhaul in workman's compensation.

Senate Government Operations Subcommittee on Executive Reorganization. Nader testified January 21, 1970, on a bill to establish a consumer affairs office in government. Nader said the proposed legislation was inadequate to do the job.

Senate Commerce Committee Subcommittee on Surface Transportation. Nader appeared before the committee on March 16, 1970, along with a raider team to report on the team's investigation of the Interstate Commerce Commission.

House Banking and Currency Committee Subcommittee on Consumer Affairs. Nader testified before the committee March 24, 1970, on the Fair Credit Reporting Act. Nader argued for the right of a citizen to be given access to his credit records.

Senate Judiciary Committee Subcommittee on Administrative Practice and Procedure. Nader testified July 21, 1970, on a bill to set up a Public Counsel Corporation. Nader pointed out the inadequacies of the existing legal system to handle public interest legal cases.

House Government Operations Committee Subcommittee on Conservation and Natural Resources. Nader testified July 28, 1970, at a hearing to evaluate railroad waste disposal practices. He urged that the railroads be barred from dropping human wastes on roadbeds.

Senate Commerce Committee Subcommittee on Energy, Natural Resources and the Environment. Nader testified on July 29, 1970, on the problem of the use of mercury in industry and agriculture. Nader outlined the scope of the problem, and urged action to cut back on mercury pollution.

Senate Labor and Public Welfare Committee Subcommittee on Labor. Nader testified on August 6, 1970, and alleged improper action by the Bureau of Mines in administering the Federal Coal Mine, Health, and Safety Act.

Senate Commerce Committee Subcommittee on Consumer Affairs. Committee held hearings to amend the Federal Trade Commission Act to provide increased protection for consumers. Nader testified on August 31, 1970, on the need for consumer class action lawsuits to provide effective access to courts for small consumer claims.

Government Operations Subcommittee on Conservation and Natural Resources. Nader testified on September 17, 1970, criticizing the failure of the executive branch of government to enforce the provisions of the Refuse Act of 1899 against industrial polluters.

House Banking and Currency Committee Subcommittee on Intergovernmental Relations. Nader testified on October 8, 1970, and criticized the administration of the Federal Reports Act, recommending its repeal. The act sets up boards to advise the government on specific industries. But Nader charged the boards were dominated by industry representatives to the exclusion of the public.

Special Senate Committee on Aging. Nader testified on December 17, 1970, on conditions in nursing homes along with a raider team which studied nursing homes and produced a report, *Old Age: The Last Segregation.*

Senate Public Works Committee Subcommittee on Air and Water Pollution. Nader appeared before the committee on May 17, 1971, to criticize the lack of governmental action against water polluters.

The House-Senate Joint Economic Committee Subcommittee on Priorities and Economy in Government. Nader testified on June 4, 1971, on how the nation could more efficiently and justly make use of its wealth. He termed the heart of the problem as a misallocation of resources, and said the consumer was constantly being mulcted in the marketplace.

House Select Committee on Small Business Subcommittee on Activities of Regulatory Agencies. Nader appeared before the committee on June 25, 1971, along with Aileen Adams Cowan, one of his raiders. Nader testified to the need for more control of deceptive television advertising.

Senate Commerce Committee. Nader testified on July 29, 1971. He urged Congress to include in a proposed product safety bill sanctions that can be taken against individual bureaucrats who don't do their jobs. He cited as an example the Agriculture Department officials who admitted that millions of chickens had been fed on contaminated fish meal, but said they issued no public warning on the incident.

House-Senate Joint Economic Committee. Nader testified on August 8, 1971. He charged that General Motors apparently

303

had advance knowledge of President Nixon's wage-price freeze and tried to evade it by telling its dealers to start selling 1972 models earlier than the normally scheduled date.

House Ways and Means Committee. Nader testified on September 14, 1971. He urged Congress to reject the tax reduction package in President Nixon's economic program and instead pass a $4 billion temporary tax refund for all consumers. The refund would amount to $50, he said, and would be more equitable than what amounted to a $9.3 billion tax cut for business.

Senate Commerce Subcommittee on Environment. Nader testified on September 27, 1971. He said Congress should give citizens the right to sue public officials for not enforcing antipollution laws. Nader said citizens should have this right when the government failed to act.

Senate Select Committee on Equal Educational Opportunity. Nader testified on September 30, 1971. He said many of the nation's richest corporations are not assessed properly, cutting their share of taxes which should be used to provide services to communities, particularly public schools, where the main source of financing is the property tax. Nader said states and cities create the problem of under-assessed corporations in an effort to create a "favorable tax climate" to lure businesses to a community.

Senate Subcommittee on Alcoholism and Narcotics. Nader testified on October 1, 1971. He told Congress that the nation's long-haul truck drivers are subject to pressures which force them to resort to drugs. He said the drivers are forced by companies to remain at the wheel for periods exceeding federal regulations, and are encouraged to speed to complete runs in the shortest possible time.

Senate Subcommittee on Intergovernmental Relations of the Government Operations Committee. Nader testified on October 10, 1971. He said President Nixon was violating the constitution by delegating wage-price control authority to

NADER AND CONGRESS

independent boards. Nixon used the "vague authority" in the Economic Stabilization Act to make an unconstitutional assumption of power, Nader said.

House Banking Committee. Nader testified November 2, 1971. He told the committee that a Nixon-administration proposed bill to extend the wage-price controls on the economy delegated too much power to President Nixon. He urged the committee to scrap the bill and write its own, narrower measure to include more review procedures.

Senate Subcommittee on Executive Reorganization. Nader testified on November 4, 1971. He accused the administration of trying to keep consumer affairs from becoming a full-blown issue in the 1972 presidential election year by pushing a consumer bill that appeared strong, but actually gave the consumer little protection. He urged the committee to reject the bill.

Senate Subcommittee on Antitrust and Monopoly. Nader testified before the subcommittee on November 9, 1971. He said large corporations used the claim of "trade secrets" to hide from the government information about illegal or anticompetitive practices. He said some of the data withheld from the public was costing consumers hundreds of millions of dollars in excessive prices.

NADER BIBLIOGRAPHY

Ralph Nader is a prolific magazine article writer. Here is a list of the major articles produced since his Harvard Law School days.

The Commonwealth Status of Puerto Rico	Harvard Law School *Record*	December 13, 1956
Legislative Neglect Keeps Migrant Workers Mired in Asiatic-type Poverty	Harvard Law School *Record*	April 10, 1958
Do Third Parties Have a Chance?	Harvard Law School *Record*	October 9, 1958
The American Automobile—Designed for Death?	Harvard Law School *Record*	December 11, 1958
The Safe Car You Can't Buy	*Nation*	April 11, 1959
Business is Deserting America	*American Mercury*	March 1960
Grand Old Man of the Law	*Reader's Digest*	February 1961
Blue-Law Blues	*Nation*	June 10, 1961
An Answer to Administrative Abuse	Harvard Law School *Record*	December 20, 1962
An Ombudsman for the U.S.?	*Christian Science Monitor*	April 1, 1963

307

Fashion or Safety: Detroit Makes Your Choice	*Nation*	October 12, 1963
Patent Laws Prime Sources to Secure Safety; Auto Design to Reduce Highway Deaths	*Trial*	January 1965
Profits vs. Engineering: The Corvair Story— excerpts from *Unsafe At Any Speed*	*Nation*	November 1, 1965
Coming Struggle for Auto Safety—ex- cerpts from *Unsafe At Any Speed*	*Consumer Report*	February 1966
Safer Cars: Time for Decision	*Consumer Report*	April 1966
Seven Safety Features Cars Need Most	*Science Digest*	August 1966
Business Crime	*New Republic*	September 9, 1967
Automobile Design and Judicial Process	*California Law Review*	Vol. 55: 645, 1967
Inventions and Their Uses	*New Republic*	July 22, 1967
Watch That Hamburger	*New Republic*	August 19, 1967
We're Still in the Jungle	*New Republic*	July 15, 1967
X-ray Exposures	*New Republic*	September 2, 1967
Something Fishy	*New Republic*	January 6, 1968
Infernal, Eternal, Inter- nal Combustion En- gine	*New Republic*	April 27, 1968
Lo, the Poor Indian	*New Republic*	March 30, 1968
Protecting the Con- sumer; Toward a Just Economy	*Current*	December 1968
Consumer Protection and Corporate Dis- closure	*Business Today*	Autumn, 1968
The Hidden Executives	*Business Today*	Winter, 1968
The Distorted Priorities	*Business Today*	Spring, 1969
Corporate Crime	*Business Today*	Summer, 1969
Who Runs the GSA?	*Business Today*	Autumn, 1969

The Corporate Colleges	*Business Today*	Summer, 1970
Micro-Tyrannies	*Business Today*	Autumn, 1970
Ombudsmen for State Governments	*The Ombudsman; Citizen Defender* edited by Donald C. Rowat, London, Allen & Unwin	1968
They're Still Breathing	*New Republic*	February 3, 1968
Wake Up America, Unsafe X Rays	*Ladies' Home Journal*	May 1968
Safety on the Job	*New Republic*	June 15, 1968
Danger in Toyland	*Ladies' Home Journal*	November 1969
Law Schools and Law Firms	*New Republic*	October 11, 1969
Swiss Cheese	*New Republic*	November 22, 1969
Violence of Omission	*Nation*	February 10, 1969
Yes, It Is Safe to Fly, But Is It Safe to Crash	*Holiday*	July 1969
Yablonski's Unfinished Business	*Nation*	January 26, 1970
Why They Should Tell You the Octane Rating of the Gasoline You Buy	*Popular Science*	April 1970
The Profits in Pollution	*Progressive*	April 1970
Baby Foods: Can You (and Your Baby) Afford Them?	*McCall's*	November 1970
Freedom from Information: The Act and the Agencies	Harvard Civil Rights –Civil Liberties Law Review	January 1970
The Professional Responsibilities of a Professional Society	*American Institute of Planners Newsletter*	November 1970
Cotton Mill Killer	*Nation*	March 15, 1971
Excerpt from testimony April 17, 1970	*Congressional Digest*	February 1971
Ralph Nader's Most Shocking Exposé	*Ladies' Home Journal*	March 1971
Dossier Invades the Home	*Saturday Review*	April 17, 1971

The Professional Responsibility of Executives	The *Newsletter* of the Association of Master of Business Administration Executives	May 1971
We Need a New Kind of Patriotism	*Life*	July 9, 1971
Making Congress Work	*New Republic*	August 20, 1971
How to Think About the American Economy	*The New York Review of Books*	September 2, 1971
Deceptive Package— Nixon's Economic Sales Pitch	*New Republic*	September 4, 1971